This is the story of a quiet, kind, determined ` Falklands War of 1982, became the only Comma War II to have directed British forces to victor enemy. But that was only one success in a achievements straddling the Cold War.

John Fieldhouse went to sea in 1945, seeing active service in Indonesia in the troubled period of post-war decolonisation. He volunteered for submarines and, after an adventurous time in conventional boats, became one of the first officers to be selected for nuclear training. He was captain of HMS *Dreadnought* and later commanded the Royal Navy's new squadron of Polaris submarines. He saw distinguished service in surface ships and, as a young Rear Admiral, led a group of warships on a working voyage around the world.

He then commanded the Submarine Service before becoming Controller of the Navy - the member of the Admiralty Board responsible for ship, equipment and weapon system procurement. Thereafter, as Fleet Commander, he became tri-service Commander-in-Chief in the Falklands War. He held high office for six further years, both as First Sea Lord and as Chief of Defence Staff. As an Admiral of the Fleet, he became the most senior-ever submarine officer. A major illness caused his premature retirement from public service in 1988, just before the collapse of communism in Eastern Europe led to the end of the Cold War.

Although serious heart surgery left him weakened, he continued to contribute to public life in many ways; taking his seat in the House of Lords in 1990. He died in 1992, aged 64. This book is not just an account of a highly distinguished naval career: it is an intensely moving story of a much loved and respected human being; of a happy family life; of a perfect blend of duty, loyalty and laughter. Prime Minister Margaret Thatcher wrote of his 'warm humanity and sureness of touch' and called him 'a great commander'. United States President Ronald Reagan wrote of his selfless dedication and contribution to world peace.'

This book not only provides a new perspective of the post-World War 11 Royal Navy, its Submarine Service and the Cold and Falklands Wars; it also shows how a modest and frankly unexceptional young man grew to be one of the nation's greatest military leaders of recent times.

Also a product of the Royal Naval College Dartmouth, Basil Watson went to sea in 1948. He, too, joined the submarine service and became one of the earlier officers in the nuclear programme. He served twice under John Fieldhouse and retired as a Captain in 1982, having held six sea-going commands. Since then, in his own words, he has become something of 'a jack of all trades and a master of none'. He has turned his hand to administration, fundraising and hospice management. This is his first serious attempt at writing.

with best wishes

Basil Watson

Commander-in-Chief

A celebration of the life of

Admiral of the Fleet
The Lord Fieldhouse of Gosport
GCB GBE

by

Basil Watson

Sponsored by The White Ensign Association
and
Published by The Royal Navy Submarine Museum

First published in the United Kingdom in 2005 by the Royal Navy Submarine Museum, Gosport, Hampshire

ISBN 0 9526696 2 5

Published by the Royal Navy Submarine Museum, Gosport, Hampshire
Printed in Great Britain in association with Enigma, Huddersfield, Yorkshire

This book is for

Midge
of the 'indestructible partnership'

for Mark, Amanda and Sarah

and for Ruby, Tom, Jonathan (JJ), Bethany and Rebecca
all of whom are too young to have met their illustrious grandfather

John David Elliott Fieldhouse
1928 - 1992

He has achieved success who has lived well, laughed often and loved much, who has gained the respect of intelligent men and the love of little children; who has filled his niche and accomplished his task; who has left the world better than he found it, who has never lacked appreciation of earth's beauty or failed to express it; who has always looked for the best in others and given the best he had, whose life was an inspiration, whose memory a benediction.

These words from the life and works of Ralph Comba Jackson appeared on the service sheet at the Service of Thanksgiving at Westminster Abbey on 27th May 1992

Contents

Foreword

Acknowledgements

Introduction

1	Childhood: 1928 – 1941	1
2	Officer Under Training: 1941 – 1948	8
3	Submariner: 1948 – 1955	25
4	Early Commands: 1955 – 1962	37
5	Rising Star: 1962 – 1967	49
6	Career Lift Off: 1967 – 1968	58
7	Polaris Squadron: 1968 – 1970	67
8	More Sea Time: 1970 – 1973	75
9	Introduction to Whitehall: 1973 – 1974	87
10	The Second Flotilla: 1974 – 1975	92
11	Around the World: 1975 – 1976	102
12	Submarine Admiral: 1976 – 1979	116
13	Controller: 1979 – 1981	124
14	Fleet Commander: 1981 – 1982	132
15	Tri-Service Commander-in-Chief: 1982	147
16	Forward to Victory: 1982	161

17 First Sea Lord: 1982 – 1985 179

18 Defence Supremo: 1985 – 1988 193

19 Twilight Years: 1988 – 1992 207

A Dates, Ranks, Honours and Awards: 1928 – 1992

B Milestones of Period in High Office: 1982 – 1988

C Maiden Speech in the House of Lords: 1991

D Address in Westminster Abbey: 1992

List of Abbreviations

Index

Foreword

by

The Rt Hon The Baroness Thatcher LG OM FRS

Margaret Thatcher

The most difficult decision any Prime Minister has to take is to order the men and women of our armed forces into battle. Other decisions taken in Government might alter people's lives – war can cost people's lives.

The months which followed the Argentinian invasion of the Falkland Islands at the beginning of April 1982 were the longest of my life. Though surrounded by the constant bustle and activity of Number Ten, being Prime Minister never seemed so lonely, nor such a heavy burden. But in one thing I was remarkably fortunate – the quality and professionalism of the military advice I received during those long weeks. And at the centre of all our preparations and all our planning was John Fieldhouse.

From our first meeting at his headquarters at Northwood I was impressed by his unshakable confidence and the authority with which he commanded the situation. That evening I returned to Downing Street certain that the overall control of our operations in the South Atlantic could not be in better hands.

John Fieldhouse knew we would succeed because he knew his men. He never doubted the determination and professionalism of our armed forces and he knew that they would prevail. He was an inspiring leader. His unruffled and easy manner at times of greatest crisis calmed and steadied all those around him, and his unwavering belief in victory lifted our spirits even in the blackest hours.

Through all of this, and through much more, he had the support and love of Midge. Her encouragement and cheerfulness were to prove invaluable to him, and indeed to us all. They formed an "indestructible partnership".

After the Falklands War, I continued to watch John's career with admiration as he progressed from Fleet command to be First Sea Lord, and from there to be Chief of Defence Staff. Tragically, his last illness denied him the opportunity, which would almost certainly have been his, to serve NATO as Chairman of its Military Committee.

John Fieldhouse's death deprived us of his wisdom, his experience and his friendship. But the record of his life and career will remain as a glowing example of all that is best.

Margaret Thatcher

Acknowledgements

I am deeply grateful to Baroness Thatcher for writing the Foreword.

* * * * * * * *

The following people have very kindly given me the opportunity to talk to them face to face, some of them on several occasions. Not all of their names appear in the script; but, in larger or smaller ways, they have all helped me to paint my picture.

Vice Admiral Sir Edward Anson, Captain and Mrs Charles Baker, Admiral Sir Jonathon Band, Admiral of the Fleet Sir Benjamin Bathurst, Vice Admiral Sir Lancelot Bell Davies, Dr David Black, Admiral Sir Jeremy Black, the late General Sir Jeremy Blacker, Captain Andy Buchanan, Rear Admiral John Burgess, Surgeon Captain James Campbell, Admiral Sir Simon Cassels, Captain Mike Clapp, Mr and Mrs Greg Courtier, Commander Gordon Crosbie, Vice Admiral Sir John Coward, Vice Admiral Sir John and Lady Cox, Dr Dermot Crean, Captain Garth de Courcy-Ireland, General Sir Peter and Lady de la Billiere, Brigadier Christopher Dunphie, Sir Robert Easton, Rear Admiral David Eckersley-Maslin, Air Vice Marshal and Mrs David Emmerson, Hon Mark Fieldhouse, Lady (Midge) Fieldhouse, Mr and Mrs Richard Fieldhouse, Hon Amanda Fieldhouse-Chalmers, Captain Jake Francis-Jones, Commander Ken Frewer, Lieutenant Commander 'Jock' Gardner, Captain Bob Garson, Sir Donald Gosling, Rear Admiral 'Spam' Hammersley, Captain and Mrs George Hayhoe, Rear Admiral Dick Heaslip, Captain Robin Heath, Captain Mike Henry, Captain Roger Heptinstall, Admiral Sir Peter and Lady Herbert, Rear Admiral John Hervey, Rear Admiral Richard Hill, Major General Malcolm Hunt, Captain Dick Husk, Captain Brian Hutchings, Captain John Jacobsen, Commander and Mrs Al Kennedy, Captain and Mrs Peter Kimm, Air Chief Marshal Sir Michael and Lady Knight, Admiral of the Fleet Sir Henry Leach, Captain Bob Leathes, Hon Mrs Sarah le Maitre, Captain and Mrs Tom le Marchand, Rear Admiral Guy Liardet, Miss June Light, Rear Admiral John Mackenzie, Commander Howard Mann, Rear Admiral Peter Marsden, Commander Ken Mills, Major General Sir Jeremy Moore, Warrant Officer Communications Yeoman David Morris, Commander and Mrs Ian Morrison, Commodore Adrian Munns, Captain and Mrs David Oddie, Admiral of the Fleet Sir Julian Oswald, Chief Petty Officer Cook Michael Palmer, Captain Christopher Page, Captain Blake Parker, Commander Rex Phillips, Mr Stephen Prince, Captain Tony Provest, Vice Admiral Sir Iwan Raikes, Admiral Sir Derek Reffell, Captain John Roberts, Commander Chris Russell, Lieutenant Commander Dick Sharp, Lieutenant Commander 'Olly' Sharp, Captain Richard Sharpe, Captain John Shillingford, Admiral Sir Jock Slater, Vice

Admiral 'Tubby' Squires, Commander Jeff Tall, Major General Julian Thompson, Captain Terry Thompson, General Sir Richard Trant, Dr Peter Usher, Field Marshal Lord Vincent, Lieutenant Commander 'Kipper' Walker, Captain and Mrs Barry Wallace, Vice Admiral Sir John Webster, Rear Admiral Anthony Wheatley, Rear Admiral and Mrs Tony Whetstone and Admiral Sir John 'Sandy' Woodward.

* * * * * * * *

Additionally, I have spoken to by telephone, corresponded with or received contributions or assistance from several others, including:

Admiral Sir Peter Abbott, Lady (Margaret) Allen, Rear Admiral Derek Anthony, Admiral Lord Boyce, Field Marshal Lord Bramall, Captain David Brown, Mr Paul Buckland, Lord Butler of Brockwell, Air Vice Marshal George Chesworth, Captain Nick Clack, Staff Sergeant Ken Crouch, Air Marshal Sir John Curtiss, Mrs Sharon Davies, Brigadier Tim Donkin, Captain Toby Elliot, Chief Petty Officer Steward Adrian Hill, Rear Admiral Jeremy Larken, Mr Jeff Mays, Captain Graham Meredith, William H Mills Jr, Captain Don Mitchell, Professor Tony Naylor, Mr Charlie Newby, Mr Joe Rooney, Mr George Standen, Captain John Trinder, Sir Clive Whitmore, Rear Admiral Sir Robert Woodard, Chief Petty Officer Steward John Woodley, and relatives of the late Tom Yarrow.

* * * * * * * *

In the course of my research, I have quoted or drawn information from the following books, publications and private memoirs:

Aft Through The Hawsepipe by Bryan Smalley, *Amphibious Assault Falklands* by Michael Clapp and Ewen Southby-Tailyour, *The Battle and the Breeze* by Admiral of the Fleet Sir Edward Ashmore, *The Battle for the Falklands* by Max Hastings and Simon Jenkins, *British Command and Control in the Falklands Campaign* by Stephen Prince, *The Chiefs* by Bill Jackson and Dwin Bramall, *Dear Joe* by Peter Kimm, *The Downing Street Years* by Margaret Thatcher, *Endure No Makeshifts* by Henry Leach, *The Falklands War* by the Sunday Times Insight Team, *Here Today Gone Tomorrow* by John Knott, *How to Become a Naval Officer* by Messrs Gieves Ltd, *The Hundred Days* by Patrick O'Brian, *The Impact of Polaris* edited by Captain JE Moore RN, *Lewin of Greenwich* by Richard Hill, *Looking for Trouble* by General Sir Peter de la Billiere, *Mountbatten* by Philip Kiegler, *The Nassau Connection* by Peter Nailor, *No Picnic* by Julian Thompson, *One Hundred Days* by Admiral Sandy Woodward with Patrick Robinson, *Operation Corporate* by Martin Middlebrook, *Profile in the Sunday Times of 1st September 1985* by James Adams, *The Royal Naval College Dartmouth* by E A Hughes, *The Royal Navy and the Falklands War* by David Brown, *The Secret War for the Falklands* by Nigel West, *Submariner* by John Coote, *Supplement to the London Gazette of*

8th October 1982 Honours and Awards for operations in the South Atlantic, Supplement to the London Gazette of 13th December 1982. Despatch by Admiral Sir John Fieldhouse, GCB, GBE, Commander of the Task Force Operations in the South Atlantic: April to June 1982, *The Sword of Damocles* by Vice Admiral Sir Rufus Mackenzie, *We Come Unseen* by Jim Ring, notes for *When the Music Stopped* by John Coote, *Yarrow and Company Limited 1977: Yarrow Shipbuilders 1990* by Alastair Borthwick and others.

* * * * * * * *

Many of the photographs are from the family collection. I must also thank the *Navy News* and The RN Submarine Museum for putting their archives at my disposal. A large number have been taken by Service photographers and are thus Crown Copyright. I am very grateful to be able to produce them free of charge as all proceeds from the sale of this book will go to the RN Submarine Museum, a charitable trust promoting Service interests. A few of the photographs have already appeared in other publications. I apologise for not being able to acknowledge the source of all those that I have used.

* * * * * * * *

There are a few people to whom I am especially indebted for their work in putting this book together. Chris Page and his team at The RN Historical Branch were most helpful while I was researching. My old submarine shipmate Mike Forder carried out the indexing and proof reading. Colin Way, JJ Molloy and Debbie Corner and others unnamed on the staff of the RN Submarine Museum all made significant contributions.

* * * * * * * *

Finally, I must apologise whole-heartedly for my mistakes. Though I have listened carefully to those I have spoken to, I appreciate that there may have been some instances of misrepresentation. I am only too well aware that memories can play strange tricks, and that one person's recollections may vary substantially from another's. Where possible, I have tried to substantiate what I have written from more than one source. Nevertheless, I take full responsibility for any inaccuracies. No offence to anyone has been intended.

Introduction

23rd April 1982

A man and a woman stood on the terrace of a rather grand suburban home fifteen miles northwest of central London. He wore Naval uniform and was slightly overweight; but was relaxed, assured and avuncular. She stood tall and confident with an aura of great authority. Grassy slopes fell away to a ring of trees at the bottom of a pleasant garden enhanced by clumps of daffodils in full bloom. Spring and bird song were in the air. Vapour trails criss-crossed the bright blue sky. Though their eyes took in this peaceful scene, their thoughts were on harsher horizons thousands of miles away.

The lady had accepted an invitation to lunch at Admiralty House following a briefing arranged for her at the nearby headquarters charged with the conduct of the Falklands War. It was she who broke the silence.

> 'Now that it seems likely that we shall have to fight, do you think we are going to win?'
> 'I feel sure we will, Prime Minister; and if we don't, I'll be looking for a new job.'
> 'If we don't, the nation will want a new PM', was the blunt rejoinder.

This brief exchange established a bond of mutual trust that was to serve the country well in the troubled times that lay ahead.

* * * * * * * *

> 29th June 1982
>
> *Dear Admiral Fieldhouse,*
> As one of your ship's company in 1961, I feel absolutely compelled to write and congratulate you and your staff on the magnificent execution and conclusion of the Falkland Islands campaign. I only hope the politicians complete the job as well as the services did.
> As your Electrical Artificer in *Walrus* I spent many an hour alongside you in the attack team and since then have followed your career with great interest. Although a little belatedly perhaps, my congratulations on your knighthood and being made Admiral. I'm looking forward to your next promotion as Admiral of the Fleet!! In conclusion I would like to add that *Walrus* was a great submarine.
> The best of health, luck and complete success in all you do.
> *Yours very sincerely Tom Yarrow*

2nd July 1982

Dear Tom,
How very kind of you to write on the successful conclusion of our operations in the South Atlantic. I much appreciate your generous remarks. The Task Force performed magnificently and I am proud of their achievements.
It is always nice to hear from old shipmates and I enjoyed your reminiscences of *Walrus* days.
With best wishes and renewed thanks.
Yours aye John Fieldhouse

* * * * * * * *

The 1982 Falklands War ensured a place for John Fieldhouse in the annals of British military history. Since World War II he has been the only Commander-in-Chief to have directed British forces to unilateral victory against a well-equipped enemy. The extreme unlikelihood that this unique set of circumstances will ever repeat itself has inspired the choice of title for this book.

But it was an entirely different sort of conflict, the Cold War, which embraced most of the second half of the twentieth century. When it started John was a young officer on the threshold of a naval career that showed no immediate promise of spectacular success. By the time it had been put to rest through the collapse of the Soviet Union he had become one of the principal players on its global stage. Meanwhile, more than any other single person, he epitomised the new breed of officer who pioneered for the Royal Navy the era of the nuclear submarine. After rising to the office of First Sea Lord, he became the first submariner to reach the apex of the nation's military structure as Chief of the Defence Staff. His overall career achievements, so sadly cut short by severe illness and early death, mark him as one of the nation's most significant and successful military leaders of recent times.

The cliché that this couldn't have happened to a nicer man continues to resonate loud and clear. He did not reach the top by clambering over or elbowing aside his fellow men. Once he had been singled out amongst his peers, he made an entirely predictable and natural progression through the higher ranks; fuelled by his outstanding professional skills and by the respect in which he was held by all who knew him. Above all he was a people's person; still widely remembered with pride and affection up and down the land. Like all great men he made one feel bigger and better for having met him, however humble one's station, unimportant one's business or heinous one's crime. He was a man totally without side; to whom an exchange of letters with an old shipmate meant just as much as the receipt of honours and awards.

* * * * * * * *

For some years I have thought it odd that nobody had yet come forward to write specifically about his remarkable life. I now know that two accomplished authors came close to getting an official biography under way. Sadly, neither of these initiatives bore fruit and the best moment for such a tribute has passed. However there are still scores of people around who knew John well; who, when asked, have been only too willing to contribute towards honouring his memory in any way they can. Thirteen years after his death, his name has been perpetuated by the 'John Fieldhouse Building' at the Royal Navy Submarine Museum at Gosport. This seemed to be a good moment to do something about putting the matter right.

Having no track record as a writer, historian or student of military affairs, I have felt ill-equipped to grapple with the challenges of an 'official' biography, preferring to regard this as 'a celebration of John's life'. Perhaps this is more in line with what John himself would have wanted; because had he lived into the normal, spacious retirement he so richly deserved, he did not intend to write his memoirs; preferring, as he put it, 'to keep all my friends.' Throughout his life, John was equally admired by both men and women. Service colleagues, mostly men, will be able to cope with the jargon and acronyms that litter these pages. Social admirers, many of whom were women, will find this side of things rather boring. For their benefit I have included a list of abbreviations in the hope of achieving a sensible balance that may be acceptable to all. My own shallow passage through John's life has been a humbling yet delightfully rewarding experience. Although each generation throws up a handful of leaders of the highest stature, I know of no one who was so universally respected.

Any enjoyment for the reader will be entirely due to the many people I have been in touch with, and their names appear separately. These include professional colleagues, shipmates, close friends and of course the family. The production of the book has been due to the generous sponsorship of The White Ensign Association and the professional support of The RN Submarine Museum. Its contents have been inspired by the people who knew John best and loved him most. Without exception they have all been very kind to me and it has been a privilege and joy to have spent some time with them.

Of overriding importance have been the three staunch partners who have guided me along my often-uncertain way. John's Dartmouth term-mate Peter Kimm has held my hand – and slapped it when necessary – as I have sought advice chapter by chapter over a period of many months. Publisher and Museum Director Jeff Tall has also entered fully into the spirit of things – not least with his unparalleled knowledge of all matters 'submarine'. Finally, nothing at all would have happened without the wholehearted encouragement and support of John's devoted wife Midge.

Basil Watson – Bishops Waltham, Hampshire – June 2005

CHAPTER ONE

Childhood

1928 – 1941

THIS STORY OF THE LIFE of a famous Admiral begins in the unlikely city of Leeds. Now a vibrant multi-racial society of 700,000 inhabitants, it owes it eminence to the Industrial Revolution. At the time of the Doomsday Book it was a hamlet of less than 100 souls. In the 12th century Cistercian monks from Chartres built over 100 monasteries up and down the country, eight of them in the Yorkshire Dales. The great abbey of Kirkstall, now a suburb of Leeds, was built of locally quarried stone in 1160. In clearings amongst the forests the monks grazed sheep, from which derived the world's leading wool industry. The Anglo-Saxon word for a clearing in the woods is 'leah'; hence the suffix of many local place names such as Armley, Bramley, Morley and Headingley of Yorkshire cricket fame.

The town developed slowly. A poll of 1379 listed its population at 300, whereas York with its great Minster had 10,000. In 1626, when Charles I granted its first charter of incorporation as a city, its coat of arms featured Yorkshire lambs that had been the source of its staple industry since Tudor times. In 1982, when John Fieldhouse was granted Arms, lambs from the city of his roots gambolled with dolphins, emblematic of the Submarine Service that had been the central core of his career.

In the 17th and 18th centuries, cloth continued to be woven on narrow hand looms from yarn spun on distaffs in hundreds of cottages in the countryside all around. In common with other Yorkshire cities, Leeds, with its many street markets, developed into an important centre for its distribution and sales. An Act of Parliament of 1678 gave the industry a further boost. All dead bodies were required to be wrapped in woollen shrouds before being boxed up. Failure to register that a body had been 'buryed in woollen' empowered churchwardens to collect a fine of £5, a princely sum at today's prices. In 1775 the population had risen to 17,000 and by 1900 it was over 50,000. This reflected the growth of the woollen and textile industry, now driven by steam power in eight large mills of the dark, satanic variety; where even small children were put to work throughout daylight hours. Sundays and feast days provided the only respite to a rugged working life. It is not surprising that the great majority of the populace was given a hard time by the local 'barons'; or that it turned for a degree of comfort to the church.

Communications had always been a problem. The stagecoach to London took twenty bone-shaking hours. Situated equidistant sixty miles between east and west coasts, Leeds' main outlet to the sea was by canals constructed in the nineteenth century. The Leeds to Liverpool canal opened in 1816. At its eastern end it linked with the Aire – Wharfedale Navigation, a waterway that reached Goole at the head of the Humber estuary. These canals were essential to the economy of the region until long past the end of the Industrial Revolution. The last working vessels to be seen in Leeds were the coal-carrying tubs known as 'Tom Puddings'; used to supply power stations until the 1990s. One of Leeds' most eminent citizens was civil engineer John Smeeton who rebuilt the Eddystone Lighthouse in 1759 and was involved in the construction of many harbours. Other distinguished sons include Reformation playwright William Congreve, historian Ralph Thoresby and 17th century philanthropist John Harrison; whose statue in the City Square commemorates his building and endowment of churches, schools and alms houses. After the Reform Act of 1832, Leeds returned a number of interesting members to Westminster. Gladstone was elected in 1880 without his consent; whilst simultaneously having been chosen to represent Midlothian; his son taking the local vacancy. In the early 20th century Prime Minister Herbert Asquith had a home in the suburb of Morley. Until Fieldhouse, there is no record of any distinguished sailor in the city archives. The great 18th century navigator James Cook was born in Marston in the North Riding of Yorkshire; but this was a considerable distance away. Rather closer, in Bradford Cathedral, is a plaque in memory of Leading Seaman JJ Magennis, who in midget submarines won the last Victoria Cross of World War II at about the same time as John himself first went to sea.

* * * * * * * *

Harold Fieldhouse was born in Leeds in 1892; the son of Frank, a mill foreman, and his wife Ellen. At West Leeds High School he was bright and ambitious, setting his sights on becoming a solicitor. However the family could not afford the cost of him becoming an articled clerk, so he left school at fifteen and took a job as an office boy with the Leeds Board of Guardians. In these humble circumstances he started on a distinguished career that was in many ways as remarkable as that of his elder son. One of his daily tasks was to go out and buy sandwich lunches for his eight colleagues. When he took a note of their orders in writing, he was reprimanded: 'Learn to carry it all in your head, my boy. It's good training for you.'

At the outbreak of the First World War he was aged twenty-two. Much to his dismay his call up was delayed because of his importance to his office superiors. Eventually he was allowed to join the colours, arriving in France in 1916, just in time to be present at the carnage of the First Battle of the Somme. As an artillery lance bombardier he was spared the infantryman's trenches, but endured what must have been an equally terrifying experience. Successful bombardment depended on efficient forward observation. The task of his unit was to keep communication links open along the inter-connecting wire telephone system. When a line went dead for any reason, someone was required to crawl forward along the wire until the break could be found and repaired. Returning alone from one of these hazardous assignments, Harold could find only an enormous crater where his unit had been. All his colleagues had been either wiped out or had disappeared. He was in a deeply shocked and worrying situation. As he wandered around in the confusion of the battlefield, nobody really wanted to know about him; treating him rather as if he had been a deserter. A longer-term affect was that the papers recommending him for a commission had been lost and it took some time for them to be regenerated. When the war ended in 1918 he was at Folkestone undergoing an essential prerequisite for officer training. With no little difficulty he was learning to ride a horse!

Harold returned to Leeds and resumed his work for the Board of Guardians. It seems that he was a highly motivated young man with a strong sense of social justice. He was quick to realise that the only recipe for success in the harsh post war world in which he had found himself was application and hard work. These words appeared in the 'Diary of a Yorkshireman' in the *Yorkshire Evening Post*:

> When I called on James Ford, the Clerk to the Board of Governors, he rang for a young man called Fieldhouse; a quiet, pleasant and enormously capable young chap who seemed to have every detail of Poor Law administration ready for instant quotation. A certain knotty point having been settled, I remarked on his quiet efficiency. 'Mark him; he will go far' said my host.

After some years as assistant clerk and twenty-one years service in all, Harold succeeded James Ford in the new title of Public Assistance Officer in 1930. By then he had acquired a new domestic status that has much relevance to this tale.

In 1922 Harold married Mabel Elaine, the daughter of George Elliott of Conisborough near Doncaster. He was aged thirty and she was twenty-one. It is not known what brought them together, but they were both athletic and enjoyed a common interest in sport. Their first son John David Elliott was born on 12th February 1928. Five years later James Richard arrived – always known as Richard – who later became a successful Harley Street orthodontist. Throughout this time the family lived in a typical middle-management semi-detached home, part stone, part pebbledash, in suburban Armley Grange Road.

Richard has suggested that their Yorkshire antecedents may have been over-emphasised, observing that the family moved to Harrow when John was six and he was one year old. The upheaval was entirely due to Harold's promotion to the head office of national Poor Law Administration in London and there is little doubt that without this career move the family would have stayed in Leeds. In either event Harold was content that both his sons were qualified by birth to play cricket for Yorkshire. In later years John rarely mentioned his home county, and certainly he was totally uninterested in cricket. The city of his birth lists thirty Fieldhouses in its telephone directory, three times more than Greater London. In recent years another John Fieldhouse became a Rugby League international, but John showed even less interest in him than he did in the antics of Geoffrey Boycott.

Yet there was clear evidence of his origins in his personality, and even in his speech. His character was enriched by many of the traits of Yorkshiremen. He had dogged, quiet determination, echoed by the motto he later chose for his coat of arms. This was '*perficio quod incipio*', meaning 'I shall finish that which I start.' He was undemonstrative, hated fuss or self-aggrandisement of any kind, made friends cautiously and remained fiercely loyal to them in all circumstances. Nothing escaped his observant eye, but he kept most of his opinions to himself unless called for, when he expressed them with great conviction and clarity. He was to retain a few small reminders of the Yorkshire way of speaking. The figure one he pronounced as 'won' and collectively we were 'uz'. Trusted subordinates often found themselves being called 'lad'.

As for the city of Leeds itself, there seems to have been little evidence of pride in the only great sailor ever to emerge from it. His appointment as Commander-in-Chief in 1981 made three brief paragraphs in the *Yorkshire Post* under the heading of 'Admirable Admiral', making no reference to his distinguished father and incorrectly stating that he had joined Dartmouth from West Leeds High School which he never attended. A last sentence 'He now lives in Hampshire' is probably why he never received any civil recognition for the Falklands victory or when he later went on to become Chief of the Defence Staff. Some might have found these omissions surprising, but to John they mattered not at all.

Harold moved the family south in 1934 having been awarded the OBE for his services in Leeds. He was appointed to the National Assistance Board in London, moving steadily up the ranks to become Permanent Secretary in 1946. He was made a Companion of the Order of the Bath (CB) in 1947, receiving a Knighthood (KBE) two years later. He retired in 1959, much honoured and widely respected, having been one of the principal architects of what is now known as the Welfare State. Considering that he had left school at the age of fifteen, his career had been one of most remarkable achievement.

* * * * * * * *

On arrival in London, the family home was established in a detached corner house in Kenton, near Harrow. From there it was an easy cycle ride to Quainton Hall, an Anglican preparatory school for 120 day boys up to the age of fourteen, now under the trusteeship of the Guardians of the Shrine of Walsingham. At that time, however, the headmaster, the Reverend Montague Eyden, privately owned it. 'Mont' was evidently a dedicated schoolmaster who attracted and kept staff of the highest calibre. His belief in the scouting movement was such that he was said to run a scout troop with a school attached. Fieldhouse profited by its process of character building, being put into a wolf-cub uniform on his arrival at the school at the age of eight. Games were not his forte, although he is said to have been a strong swimmer and captain of his house team. If this was a disappointment to his father, it was compensated for by Richard's subsequent development into a fine all round athlete. Much later in life Harold and Richard did conspicuously well in an elitist father-and-son golf tournament. With a fairly large age difference of five years there was limited contact between the two boys. Yet Richard considered John to be a kind and supportive elder brother, despite 'having two left feet and being useless at team games'. There were certain similarities in the brothers' appearance, but Richard grew to be taller and slimmer.

John's first thoughts about a career at sea originated from regular family holidays on the Yorkshire coast at Bridlington. It was at the age of five that he returned from a trip in a local fishing boat to announce that he intended to become a sailor. Later, when his ambitions persisted, his father came up with some crucial advice. 'If you're determined to go to sea, you'd best make it the proper navy'. At his preparatory school the idea began to take on a more distinct shape and 'Mont' started to coach him for the Dartmouth entry examination. It had added meaning with the outbreak of World War II when John was in the middle school.

It is unfortunate that John kept very few papers from his later life, especially anything he wrote himself. It is interesting, therefore, to have no less than two offerings from the school magazine when he was aged thirteen and in his last term. The first one is called:

The Six Things That Irritate Me Most

A knife being ground against metal
A bird being put in a small cage
Being put in a single bed with another person
Flies crawling on a window trying to get out
Spiders and other such animals crawling over me
Butterflies being caught and pinned to a board

The second one, which is entitled *Through the Open Door*, is rather longer:

> Through the open door a soft breeze was blowing. The sun was shining into the room and making shadows on the floor and walls. Outside the snowdrops and a crocus or two had sprung up to welcome the sun back to England. The grass was green and fresh and the green tips of the bulbs were peeping out. Up in the blue sky there were one or two clouds scattered about the scornful sun looking down on a foolish world, a world full of hate and selfishness. The birds chattering and building their nests between the green buds on the trees made one forget the rest of the world, and only remember the small world of one's surroundings. An aeroplane rushed over, and one's mind was brought with a rush back to the happenings in the outer world and all the wicked things that disturb one's happy dreams.

For a boy of his age, John seems to have had an unusual caring interest for the softer things of life. The joys of birds, butterflies, bulbs, buds and spring flowers are seen in contrast to his fleeting mention of the war that then dominated everyone's lives. The source of his reference to sharing a single bed is unknown, but a friend who also became an admiral will reveal later how his worst fears were realised in the submarine HMS *Tiptoe*.

Entry to Dartmouth at the age of thirteen was highly competitive, although it was not a severe test academically. The standard of scholarship required was based on the Common Entrance examination needed for entry into any public school; but success depended upon achieving extremely high marks across the full range of subjects. John's only potential stumbling block was Latin. He told his form master: 'Fair enough, Sir, to have to take Maths, English, History, Geography and even French; but what use will Latin be to me when I am in the Navy?'

Unconvinced by the reply that basic Latin was essential to the development of an orderly mind, John accepted the need for extra tuition on Saturdays and worked hard to make up this deficiency. When Harold asked him to think of an alternative career in case he should fail the examination, he received the blunt reply: 'Dad, I am going to Dartmouth and that's that!'

Out of the several hundreds who sat the examination, about one hundred would be called forward for interview and medical examination, half of whom would be rewarded with cadetships.

* * * * * * * *

By a stroke of great good fortune a valuable source document exists to cover much of what happened to John over the next several years. After he himself had retired from the navy as a captain, term mate and close friend Peter Kimm wrote a very detailed private memoir. Entitled *Dear Joe* and addressed to his grandson, it is a fascinating catalogue of the life and times of John's exact contemporary. These two grew up together and did virtually all the same things between 1941 and 1948 when John entered the Submarine Service. Peter has generously made the relevant chapters of his *magnum opus* available and much of the rest of this chapter is the result of his astute observations. Who could have possibly forecast that one of these young boys was destined to deliver an address in Westminster Abbey in thanksgiving for the life of the other?

The worst day of the Blitz had been 10th May 1941. On that day all but one of the main line railway stations had been put out of action and the Chamber of the House of Commons destroyed. For that reason the interview board and medical examination were held a few weeks later at Worcester College, Oxford, well away from London. The first person to greet candidates was Mr Allen of Messrs Gieves Ltd, the naval outfitters. He measured everyone for their uniforms, whether they were going to ever wear one or not. Each boy was then handed a small book called *How to Become a Naval Officer* and told in a condescending way that an account had already been opened in his name at the London branch.

While waiting, boys were required to write an essay on 'Women in Wartime', but whether or not anyone bothered to read it is not revealed. Then the great moment arrived as each small and nervous person, many of whose voices had not yet broken, was ushered into a room to sit at a long table before four elderly, yet kindly, gentleman. The interviewing team consisted of an admiral, a captain, a headmaster and a psychologist. It is not known what passed between them and John, but Peter remembers being asked 'What is the menace in the Mediterranean?' He claims that his inspired reply of 'Admiral Cunningham, Sir?' showed the right degree of offensive spirit to get him past the finishing post! Finally, the medical examination was very thorough, particularly in the matter of eyesight. All successful boys were destined to become seaman officers and only the very highest standards were acceptable.

John passed into Dartmouth without difficulty, about a third of the way down the order list. He was now about to leave home for the first time to take up his chosen career. He had enjoyed a happy early childhood in which his highly successful father had been the dominant influence. But in those early years it was always his mother who had been there to give him her full attention, and both sons loved her dearly. Mabel was to be a wonderfully supportive homemaker while the boys still needed her, but when they left home she found the resulting void very difficult to fill. This undoubtedly caused problems for Harold as he grew older, but he himself may not have been the easiest person to live with through his long retirement. Nevertheless it was to be a predominantly successful and happy marriage lasting altogether sixty-nine years. Both parents lived to enjoy their sons' achievements. Harold was to die the year before John, aged 98, and Mabel the year after, also in her nineties.

CHAPTER TWO

Officer Under Training

1941 – 1948

ON 18th SEPTEMBER 1941 forty-seven new cadets assembled at Paddington station. The Luftwaffe's bombing of London had eased off, but the atmosphere of war was still very evident; with men and women scurrying around in uniform amongst the sand bags and signs indicating the nearest air raid shelters. At thirteen years of age, they must have felt incongruous in their new uniforms and smart officers' caps; as they loaded their identical green suitcases and tin trunks into compartments especially reserved for them. After hurried family farewells a massive steam engine of the Great Western Railway bore them away towards their destination.

An early excitement came soon after Exeter where the main line runs along the foreshore with expansive views of the English Channel. Not long afterwards the train pulled through a cutting onto the eastern bank of the River Dart, gradually slowing down as it approached Kingswear station. Across the water was a first glimpse of the imposing college buildings in their dominant setting on a hill above Dartmouth town. The Gieves booklet had contained the memorable statement that 'On first seeing the Royal Naval College, one recognizes instinctively that it is neither a prison, a lunatic asylum nor the house of a profiteer'. Minutes later the awestruck group embarked in the ferry *Mew* to cross the harbour. This had been one of the small ships that had sailed to Dunkirk just over a year earlier to help bring the British Expeditionary Force back to England at the lowest ebb of the war. Under the charge of cadet captains, the equivalent of school prefects, they were marched up the hill to start settling in; grateful for a short respite in which to find their way around as the remaining cadets were not due to return until the following day.

The basic education at the Dartmouth College of those days was similar to that available at any normal fee paying public school. A Headmaster led a full complement of civilian lecturers and each cadet had one of these as a supervisory tutor. But once outside the classroom everything had a wholly nautical flavour. Under the Captain of the College, who was in overall command, this aspect of training was the responsibility of uniformed naval officers known as House Officers. After two terms in the new entry Drake House, cadets moved on to one of five senior houses for their remaining nine terms. These were known as Blake, Exmouth, Grenville, Hawke and St

Vincent. John was to become a Grenville. Every spare moment was used to steep cadets in an atmosphere of naval hierarchy, tradition and jargon. Second termers were allocated as 'sea daddies' to help teach newcomers the ropes. Officers and masters had to be saluted at all times. The main assembly area was known as the quarterdeck. The clock in the clock tower struck the time every half hour in bells as on board ship. Carved and emblazoned in stone high up along the front of the college was this inscription taken from the preamble to the Naval Discipline Act:

IT:IS:UPON:THE:NAVY:UNDER:THE:GOOD:PROVIDENCE:OF:
GOD:THAT:OUR:WEALTH:PROSPERITY:AND:PEACE:DEPEND

On an average of once every three years, one of the small boys looking up at this message for the first time would be destined to become the professional head of the Royal Navy some forty five years later. Thoughts of that sort must have been very far from John's mind as he rushed around trying to get the hang of everything, particularly as he had arrived in a boarding school for the first time. At least there was one thing that worked to his advantage. Although clearly games were important, cadets were permitted to take alternative exercise on the river. Moored immediately below the college at Sandquay were large service cutters and whalers, and small blue skiffs; all of which could be sailed or pulled competitively. Once these had been mastered, there was the added enjoyment of the more tender 'Dartmouth One' design sailing dinghies. It was there, rather than on the games fields, that he found his metier in a occupation very much in harmony with his new profession.

John gets a rare mention in the *Britannia Magazine* issued at the end of his first term. He is listed as an alto in the choir, which had apparently been going through a difficult patch due to poor attendance at practices. It is further mentioned that the choir ventured forth on its annual outing. Portlemouth was the destination, and the day's enjoyment seems only to have been enhanced by arguments with army lorries, barbed wire, paths that led to nowhere and kettles that wouldn't boil.

Visitors to the College in John's first term were King Haakon of Norway and his son Crown Prince Olaf. The Nazis had overrun their country the previous year. The family had been hastily evacuated in the cruiser HMS *Devonshire* and, like some of the other crowned heads of Europe, the King had set up a government in exile in London. Two terms later the dynamic Commodore Lord Louis Mountbatten came to give a lecture on his new responsibilities. Less than a year after the spectacular sinking of HMS *Kelly*, he was already one of Churchill's favourites and had become his advisor on Combined Operations.

In the same term, John's third, there had been a moment of great excitement when the whole college was fallen in by divisions on the parade ground in expectation of particularly important visitors. As a bugler sounded the 'alert', the parade was called to attention and a large black car drove slowly up the western ramp, stopping opposite the main entrance to the college. In a secret well kept for security reasons, out stepped the King and Queen. As His Majesty walked forward to the saluting base the guard came to the 'present' and the band played the National Anthem, providing a first occasion for almost all of those present to salute their Monarch face to face. The King carried out his inspection looking grey and drawn. Although it had been Prime Minister Churchill who had rallied the nation at its recent lowest ebb with his pugnacious leadership and stirring words, the King remained the embodiment of the loyalty of the British people. Both Their Majesties had chosen to remain in London throughout the blitz. On their tours of devastated areas they had given hope and comfort to many who had lost their loved ones and their homes.

In the summer of 1942 the war was still going badly. The Japanese had inflicted crushing defeats on British forces at sea, in Hong Kong, Malaya, Singapore and Burma. In North Africa Rommel had gained the upper hand and Tobruk was about to fall. The Battle of the Atlantic was entering a critical phase in the quest to contain the U-boat menace that had threatened the nation's very survival. In the House of Commons Churchill was shortly to face a vote of 'no confidence' in his higher direction of the war. Against this background, it seemed very humbling that Their Majesties had chosen to pay one of their periodic visits to the college. The King was very proud of his own early service in the Royal Navy and almost always wore its uniform. How could John Fieldhouse have possibly imagined that one day he too would become an Admiral of the Fleet?

John's brother Richard remembers a family weekend visit to the college when he was about eight. His parents had been invited to attend Sunday divisions as spectators on the terrace above the parade ground, but strict instructions had been issued that no young children were allowed. He had been left on his own outside the main gate in charge of a dog of dubious parentage, which, in the absence of a proper lead, was tethered by a scruffy length of string. Being intrigued by the sound of the band, he slipped through the entrance and wandered up the hill to see what was going on. His father was far from pleased by the appearance of this apparition at a critical stage of the proceedings!

On the last Sunday of term the whole college gathered as usual in the chapel for a service which culminated in a traditional hearty rendering of the familiar two verses of Blake's 'Jerusalem'. As the special train carried John and his friends away for the holidays, it was to be the last time they would see the college until they chose to return to it in later life. Just before noon on Friday 18th September 1942, a year to the day after they had arrived there, the Luftwaffe attacked Dartmouth; inflicting damage on the shipbuilding yard and on shipping in the harbour. There were two direct hits on the College; one of which partially destroyed the quarterdeck.

It is interesting to speculate on the significance of the precise timing of the war's only raid on the 'cradle' of regular officer training for the Royal Navy. Characteristically, the college terms were all the same length, beginning and ending on highly predictable dates. The Head of the History and English Department, E A 'Daddy' Hughes, explained in his book *The Royal Naval College Dartmouth* (c.1950):

> Since in the ordinary year there are fifty-two weeks and an odd day over, one year in six, allowing for one leap year, they must be given an extra week's leave; otherwise in the course of time the Easter term would start before Christmas.

Thus in 1942 the autumn term started a week later than might have been generally expected. If this had not occurred, cadets would have been gathered together on the quarterdeck at the precise moment of the attack and very heavy casualties might have resulted.

Without further explanation John received a telegram instructing him to 'remain on leave pending further instructions'. Meanwhile cadets of the senior college had returned to Dartmouth to assist with the port defences and continue with their education as best they could. On 29th October, barely seven weeks after the bombing, the juniors were summoned to The Royal Naval College Ashley Down. This had been hastily cobbled together in some of the buildings at Muller Orphanage at Bristol, and would have to serve as a base for a shortened term until more permanent arrangements could be made. This in itself was a remarkable feat of emergency organisation.

The college reopened as an integral unit in January 1943 at Eaton Hall, near Chester. This was the home of the Duke of Westminster who remained in residence in one wing of the property. The main building was a monstrous Victorian edifice; blood brother to St Pancras station which it closely resembled. This contained most of the classrooms and the accommodation for the Drake House juniors. All the other houses, including John's Grenville, were spread around in groups of huts. Two extra large buildings provided a dining hall and an assembly room that could be used for a variety of purposes. The whole development resembled an army camp; which is what it had been before and what it eventually reverted to when the navy had finished with it. There were plenty of wide-open spaces for games, but only very limited sailing facilities on the nearby River Dee.

Term mate Gordon Crosbie remembers John as being a rather quiet member of the Grenville group. He always seemed to be around, but without making any noticeable contribution. The nicknames 'Fieldmouse' and 'Fatty Fieldhouse' started to be bandied about, although neither was destined to stick. It was unfortunate, perhaps, that many of his house contemporaries were very forceful characters. By a stroke of chance, there was a high percentage of Grenvilles in the college teams; with Crosbie himself earning multiple sets of 'colours'. As in all schools, popularity and fame came most easily with prowess at games, and John played no part in this.

Meanwhile his naval education continued in these very adequate surroundings. For a boy whose nature it was to be undemonstrative, he did not shine in any particular way although he was appointed a cadet captain in his final term. Simon Cassels (later Admiral) recalls John standing in for his House Cadet Captain Robert Duncan, who was ill, and doing surprisingly well. Perhaps this was the first glimmer of the leadership qualities that were to develop later? The academic side was not progressing quite so well with John dropping into the bottom half of the term list.

What was of much greater concern, however, was whether or not he and his term mates were going to get to sea before the war ended. They were in their ninth term at the time of the Normandy landings, with still two more terms to go. The tide of conflict was flowing very steadily in the Allies' favour, so it was certainly going to be a matter of touch and go. When John left the college in March 1945, the war in Europe was in its final stages; with uncertain prospects over how long it was going to take to overcome Japan. His term had already been disappointed to learn that they would not be joining the active fleet until they had spent a period of training in the Cadet Training Cruiser. In his passing out examinations he received a disappointing Third Class certificate. His House Officer considered that 'he had come on a lot during his last term. He was not outstanding, but was absolutely trustworthy and honest.'

* * * * * * * *

The Naval Cadet entry of September 1941 joined HMS *Frobisher* at Rosyth on 2nd May 1945. The Germans surrendered unconditionally six days later. By Royal Command a signal went out for the Royal Navy to 'Splice the Mainbrace'. This meant an extra tot of rum for the lower deck and, exceptionally, a single tot for wardroom officers. The seventeen-year-old cadets were under age and not entitled. But their one-week's war service did qualify them to wear medal ribbons and be the proud possessors of the Victory Medal, Atlantic Star and Defence Medal. When John Fieldhouse finally left office as Chief of the Defence Staff he had been the last serviceman in an active appointment to wear medals from the Second World War.

Frobisher was an old cruiser that had been laid down in 1916. Her armament had been greatly reduced for her training role, allowing space for upper deck classrooms and extra ship's boats. She had a reduced complement of seamen because the cadets themselves would now undertake most of the mundane tasks. There were about a hundred in all; with the

'Darts' being joined by a smaller group, ex-public school, inevitably known as 'Pubs'. These were slightly older boys who had completed a normal education before gaining special officer entry at a later stage. They included seaman officers, engineers and paymasters; all of whom would now become part of a wider integral term. In addition to these, they were contingents from the Commonwealth navies of Canada, Australia and New Zealand.

Designed to give the young gentlemen a genuine taste of life on the lower deck, the routine was exhausting and unrelenting. They slung their hammocks in a large mess deck and the day started at 0600 with a shrill boatswain's call and traditional 'wakey-wakey' exhortation over the ship's broadcast system. They were hard at work scrubbing decks in bare feet by 0620, with the chill northern waters being hosed around them. After breakfast at 0700 some cadets went to instruction, while others carried out normal tasks around the ship. They were introduced to the mysteries of the Watch and Quarter Bill which formed the basis of the organisation of any ship's company. Particular stress was placed on seamanship and navigation, the rudiments of which they had already learnt at Dartmouth. There were also regular signal exercises with a view to achieving an acceptable standard in the reading of messages by flashing light, semaphore and flags. Those hours of the day that were not filled by undertaking normal seamen's tasks such as cleaning, polishing and painting were devoted to the loftier goals of officer training. There was only occasional respite for shore leave, for games or to land on the shores of a deserted loch and climb a mountain. All but a handful of dutymen were back in their hammocks by 'pipe down' at 2200.

Frobisher's main operating area was in the Firth of Forth; but she sailed for two short cruises in Scottish waters, visiting such places as Ullapool, Ballachulish, Portree, Stornoway, Scapa Flow and Invergordon. She also visited Stranraer, near where sixty-four surrendered German U-boats lay moored in trots. It is not known when John started to think about the possibility of joining the submarine service and certainly no decision would need to be made on this for three more years. However he is bound to have found this evidence of the very recent conflict very interesting. One of the boats was brought alongside to enable all the cadets to visit it. There was a feeling of some surprise that the German crew members still on board looked and behaved remarkably like our own sailors; giving strength to the axiom that it was differences in the ideology of leaders rather than in the behaviour of the masses that led to war. During the latter part of the conflict the proud U-boat arm had sustained massive losses. Despite the advent of the 'snorkel' mast that allowed battery charging to be undertaken while still submerged, it had been quite unable to cope with the steadily increasing weight and technological advances of surface and air forces that had been deployed against it. Almost 800 boats had been lost and about two thirds of all the men who served in them had perished.

On completion of the second Scottish cruise, *Frobisher* came south to Portsmouth where the cadets sat a round of written and practical examinations. As at Dartmouth, Fieldhouse was awarded another undistinguished Third Class pass. His seamanship qualities were deemed to have been 'Very good', his torpedo and electrical work 'Good', his navigation, pilotage and gunnery 'Fair' and his engineering 'Poor'. The general comments in his report are brief and unrevealing. Above the Captain's signature are the words 'Slightly below average ability'. In later life, John looked back upon *Frobisher* as one of the least enjoyable parts of his service; but he had undoubtedly learnt much from his introduction to life at sea.

* * * * * * * *

Fieldhouse would have been the first to acknowledge that his career had been helped along by a number of instances where fortune had favoured him. These lucky breaks had the effect of creating opportunities and valuable experience, often through being in the right place at the right time. The first of these was his appointment as midshipman to HMS *Nigeria* on the East Indies Station. This started a train of events that enabled him not only to see some active service in the turbulent post-war scene of decolonisation, but also to observe differing cultures in distant places whilst travelling widely over many thousands of miles.

Together with term mates Peter Kimm, Sandie Coats, John Read and Hugh Smyth, he sailed from Southampton in the troopship *Mooltan* on 26th August 1945. This was just twelve days after the unconditional surrender of the Japanese following the dropping of atomic bombs on Hiroshima and Nagasaki. On board this requisitioned P & O liner there was something of a party atmosphere, with only a token amount of work and some attractive female company in the form of nurses and members of the Woman's Royal Naval Service (Wrens) who were also taking passage. On 2nd September, while they were in the Mediterranean, General MacArthur, with our own Admiral Fraser beside him, formally accepted the Japanese surrender on board USS *Missouri* in Tokyo Bay. *Mooltan* passed through the Suez Canal three days later to the taunts of 'You're going the wrong way!' from a group of British soldiers lining its banks. After the usual fuelling stop at Aden the ship arrived at Colombo and the five midshipmen were amongst many who disembarked into a transit camp. John was one of several who had not previously travelled abroad, and the three-week voyage to the mystic East had been an exciting introduction to the many adventures that followed. They amused themselves with visits to the Galle Face Hotel and Colombo Swimming Club, as well as attending an ENSA concert given by the incomparable Gracie Fields. A week or so later they made a slow train journey through the night to the main East Indies naval base of Trincomalee.

This was a superb natural harbour in the northeast corner of Ceylon, although somewhat lacking in the shore facilities associated with a city or large town. There the *Nigeria* draft embarked in two destroyers.

Kimm and Fieldhouse took passage in HMS *Virago*, proud member of the 26th Destroyer Flotilla. On 16th May, just four months earlier, the five ships of this flotilla, under the command of Captain (later Admiral) 'Lofty' Power in HMS *Saumarez*, had sunk the Japanese heavy cruiser *Haguro* at the western entrance to the Malacca Strait. This had been a classic coordinated torpedo attack by night in the finest traditions of the service; the RN's last major surface action of the war. After a boisterous voyage with much seasickness, they steamed into the beautiful bay at Sabang; on the island of Pulo We off the northern tip of Sumatra. There lay *Nigeria*, still in her wartime camouflage paint and at anchor in what had previously been a strategic Japanese outpost which she herself had recently bombarded. As this book goes to press in 2005, Sabang is one of many places to have suffered from the devastation caused by the major Indian Ocean tsunami.

Of recent construction, *Nigeria* was a Colony class cruiser displacing 8,000 tons. She was armed with 9 x 6-inch guns in triple turrets, 8 x 4-inch guns in twin mountings and numerous close-range 'pom-poms'. She carried 6 x 21-inch torpedo tubes and had a top speed of 31.5 knots. Her complement was 980. Although slightly smaller, she was similar to HMS *Belfast*, which has been preserved as a war monument in the Pool of London. Once on board, John and his friends quickly settled into gunroom life in the company of a more senior group of midshipmen. Under the guidance of the ship's Sub Lieutenant, the Gunroom mess became their 'home'. There was just enough space for feeding and for relaxation. They kept their kit in the crowded 'chest flat' outside. They slept on camp beds; if at all possible on deck; if not, in one of the adjacent 'flats' or passages.

Under the supervision of a lieutenant commander, or 'Snotties Nurse', midshipmen were required to undertake a strenuous fifteen month 'on the job' syllabus to cover many aspects of a seaman officer's profession. Not least was to complete a detailed journal or diary to cover their whole period on board. Sadly, the Fieldhouse log has not survived but, again, many of his experiences were entirely similar to those of Kimm, at all times a meticulous record taker. Routine tasks included understudying the roles of Officer of the Watch both at sea and in harbour, where they also took twenty-four shifts in command of ship's boats. There was much activity in practical navigation and signals, with many seamanship drills and evolutions to witness and master. Their lowly status gave them a special relationship with the lower deck that they would have been extremely unwise to ignore. Once they achieved a gold stripe on their shoulder or sleeve they would be expected to get things right and take a lead. But 'Snotties' fell short of full officer status and good sailors took pride in helping them along. It was a time to knuckle down and learn from the old salts while there was still an opportunity.

It was not surprising that *Nigeria* was a happy ship. Her war was run and, ten days after the new midshipmen joined her, she began her long passage home. They called at Trincomalee and Colombo, and retraced *Mooltan*'s track across the Indian Ocean and Red Sea to Suez. Here there was a delightful interlude. The 'Snotties' Nurse' led his charges on an overland adventure to rejoin the ship at Alexandria. They visited the Pyramids at Giza and the treasures of Tutankhamen at the National Museum in Cairo. They lunched at the Ghazira Club, had ice cream at Groppi's and even caught a glimpse of King Farouk as he drove by in a magnificent red and black Rolls Royce, escorted by mounted cavalry.

On arrival at Alexandria, the five younger midshipmen learnt that they would not be returning to the UK in *Nigeria.* Initial feelings of acute disappointment over not being home for Christmas were allayed by their transfer to HMS *Norfolk*, outward bound for service on the East Indies Station that they had just left. They were still in the early stages of their sea training and service abroad was far more professionally rewarding. This was a larger and older County class cruiser, built between the wars. She displaced 12,000 tons and had 6 x 8-inch guns in three turrets that packed a considerable punch. Despite her age, she could still manage 32 knots. *Norfolk* had had a distinguished war record, having taken part in the sinking of both *Bismarck* and *Scharnhorst*, and in support of the North African landings, 'Operation Torch'. These ships had been designed for tropical service in protection of the Empire's far flung trade routes.

The midshipmen found their new quarters palatial by comparison, with a large, airy gunroom on the main deck. They settled in easily on the passage out East, resuming their training syllabus more or less where they had left it. At Colombo John and Peter had saved up enough of their meagre pay to give two Wrens they had met in *Mooltan* a slap up dinner at the Galle Face Hotel. What they got in return for this is not known, but in those days well in advance of the permissive society it is unlikely to have been more than a stolen kiss in the back of a horse drawn gharry! Three weeks later they were back in Trincomalee where a young Fleet Air Arm friend took them both for a first flight in a military aircraft. They noted that the Stinson Reliant had unusual blue and white roundels, and learnt that the colour red had never been used on any allied aircraft in the Pacific theatre to avoid confusion with markings used by the Japanese. Soon after this, *Norfolk* was ordered to Singapore.

* * * * * * * *

As long as the war had lasted, Japanese forces of occupation had maintained order in the Netherlands East Indies by brute force of arms. Now that it was over, a dormant revolutionary movement against Dutch colonisation began again to rear its head. The increasing activities of Dr Soerkano's paramilitaries became a matter of grave concern. First and foremost there was a need to guarantee the safety of the many Repatriated Allied Prisoners of War and Internees (RAPWI) still in the region. The situation was further complicated by the fact that many camps were still under Japanese protection. Any political considerations concerning either Dutch or British commercial interests were clearly subordinate to the more immediate humane objectives. On her arrival at Singapore *Norfolk* was sailed 'with all despatch' to Semarang on the north coast of Java.

After carrying out a crossing-the-line ceremony en route, a naval party at company strength and a Royal Marine detachment were landed on 7th December. This force augmented the army who were already ashore in brigade strength to confront a large concentration of revolutionaries behind the town. While Kimm acted as assistant to the Company Commander, Fieldhouse found himself in charge of a lorry with an Oerlikon gun on the back of it; acting as escort to the RAPWI as they were convoyed from an internment camp in the hinterland to Semarang for onward passage to Singapore. It was the task of the naval party to guard important installations in the town, and members of the technical staff were landed to keep the power station and telephone exchange operating. But the main purpose of *Norfolk's* presence was to provide gunfire support, as her shells whistled over the heads of those serving ashore. An extraordinary aspect of the operation was that the British forces found themselves fighting side by side with the Japanese who had been instructed to continue to protect their prisoners. The situation was further confused by looting and severe tropical storms.

After ten days the critical part of the RAPWI evacuation had been completed, allowing the shore parties to return on board. There had been an unfortunate incident during their absence ashore. During the bombardment a high explosive eight-inch shell fired from 'B' turret struck the right hand gun barrel in the adjacent 'A' turret, blowing its end off. This had caused a considerable mess on the forecastle, but providentially no casualties. The Gunnery Officer's name was brought to wider attention, but it did him no harm, as he was one of two 'Norfolks' of that commission to become First Sea Lord.

Although he was to receive plenty of 'flak' of an entirely different nature from politicians and others in later life, the Semarang landing exposed Fieldhouse to enemy fire for the first and only time. There is no doubt that the brief experience left a lasting impression on him. He had seen something of the ravages of war; the effect on innocent people of disease and famine;

the fear in young children's eyes. All this had been fed into a memory bank that would serve him well in later life. In due course it earned him and his colleagues the award of the Naval General Service Medal with clasp 'SE Asia 1945-46'. To give an idea of the scale of these operations, the King's ships involved in the Indonesian Campaign were the cruisers HMS *Cumberland*, *Sussex*, *Norfolk* and *Jamaica*, the destroyers HMS *Caprice*, *Carron*, *Cambrian*, *Carysfort*, *Cavalier* and *Caesar*, together with various Loch class frigates.

Meanwhile *Norfolk* left for Batavia with the 5th Cruiser Squadron Admiral embarked. Rear Admiral Wilfred Patterson was a warm and friendly man. When the lower deck was cleared for him to speak to the ship's company, he told them that at pre-war dances he always seemed to end up with the least attractive partners. Now, he added, 'I have again been landed with a very ugly and heavy partner called Java; and it seems that we will be waltzing for quite a time!'

A first Christmas abroad was spent in traditional naval style at anchor off Batavia. Shore leave was given, but there was little on which to spend the available mountains of worthless currency other than on wood carvings and other souvenirs Later *Norfolk* returned to the gun-line off Semarang to continue bombarding the rebels with her remaining serviceable guns; but the tension ashore had eased and a shore contingent was no longer required. After the Admiral had transferred his Flag to another ship, she began the long voyage to Bombay on 16th January 1945 to get her damaged gun replaced, calling briefly at Singapore and Colombo. On arrival, she berthed in the Royal Indian Navy's dockyard, which still showed signs of the devastation caused by the explosion of an ammunition ship in the harbour during the war.

After the instability and chaos of what later became Indonesia, they had arrived in yet another highly charged cauldron of humanity. For the Indians, also, Independence was just around the corner; but in the absence of a Japanese occupation, a structured orderliness continued to exist. Even then the young midshipmen had to literally force their way through crowds of beggars as they headed ashore. They also enjoyed the benefits of the other end of the wide social scale created by the British Raj. Kimm records having been taken under the wing of local property developer Sir Hugh Clayton, brother to the Rev 'Tubby' Clayton, founder of the World War I servicemen's club 'Toc H'. They were introduced to the Willingdon Club with its magnificent pool and were taken by the Claytons to the races. There they saw the Governor of Bombay Province, Sir John Colville, arrive in a landau with a cavalry escort in rather more style than The Queen now enjoys at Royal Ascot. On another occasion Fieldhouse and Kimm were present at a magnificent dinner party at Government House. In the usual way of the King's representative, guests were assembled in line around the ballroom, after which Their Excellencies made an entrance to the accompaniment of the National Anthem. As they moved round the circle, each guest either bowed or curtsied on being formally presented. Dinner was served at small tables on an exquisite garden terrace, illuminated by candles and fairy lights, after which there was dancing and charades.

With the gun replaced, *Norfolk* returned to Batavia by way of Colombo, Trincomalee and Singapore. It was there that the Supreme Allied Commander South East Asia, Admiral Mountbatten, visited the ship to speak informally to the ship's company. He was photographed speaking to Midshipman Fieldhouse and although the appointment of Chief of the Defence Staff did not then exist, it produced a delightful record of two holders of the office separated in age by twenty-eight years.

Back in Batavia, affairs were beginning to enter a political phase. Admiral Patterson was re-embarked and, for a time, so was Sir Archibald Clark-Kerr, later to become Lord Inverchapel. As the recently appointed 'Ambassador Extraordinary and Minister Plenipotentiary', he used the ship as a floating embassy, receiving various revolutionary emissaries on board. Laurens van der Post, who had been a prisoner of war and knew the area well, was then a member of the Embassy staff. *Norfolk* visited Padang on the west coast of Sumatra and then Surabaya, the second city of Java, where the ship anchored in a harbour strewn with wartime wrecks. This was the scene of the worst massacres of the revolution. The situation was still turbulent and no shore leave was given; but the next visit would more than make up for that.

Neither the war nor the revolution seemed to have affected Bali, which all agreed was the most enchanting port of call of the whole commission. Kimm recalls having the morning watch as *Norfolk* approached the island, 'as the rising sun coloured the 10,100 foot volcanic Mount Bali a pale pastel pink.' The ship anchored off Benoa shortly afterwards, lying rolling in the heavy swell as outrigger canoes came out, selling paw-paws and other tropical fruit. In total contrast to the dirty and surly people of Java, the Balinese were spotlessly clean and friendly. Traditionally, the women wore sarongs and went bare-breasted; but some of the younger and shapelier girls wore loose stoles to protect their modesty. This was well before the days of air travel and tourism, so the principal habitation of Denpasar had the appearance of a large and totally unspoilt village. *Norfolk* returned briefly to Batavia before leaving Netherlands East Indies waters for the last time on 2nd April.

Back in Singapore the ship visited the old British naval base in the Johore Strait, not yet fully operational but soon to be built up again to its former status. Here the midshipmen boarded the Japanese heavy cruiser *Takao* that had been immobilised in a daring attack by British midget submarines, for which Lieutenant Fraser and Leading Seaman Magennis had received the

Victoria Cross. Kimm recalls a dinner he and Fieldhouse attended in an army mess at Johore Bahru. The regimental mascot, a baby elephant, was brought in after dinner to drink rum and water from a bucket; after which it disappeared into the night squealing happily with a couple of subalterns in hot pursuit.

For a brief period *Norfolk* became the Fleet flagship when the C-in-C East Indies, Vice Admiral Sir Arthur Palliser, embarked with his Staff. Then, freshly painted and shining like a new pin, she sailed for the main base at Trincomalee. At the point of making a full ceremonial entry, a small motor launch chugged out of the bay on the port side and crossed the Flagship's bow so closely that astern power was needed to avoid a collision. 'Report name and rank of commanding officer' went out the imperious signal. The reply came back almost as quickly. 'Lieutenant Snodgrass, Royal Naval Volunteer Reserve. Release Group Two'. Like many others around the globe, Snodgrass was cheerfully awaiting immediate demobilisation!

Further visits as a private ship followed to Colombo, Bombay and Karachi. At Colombo the ship's company received a week's station leave in two watches. Five hundred men at a time were entrained to the services leave camp at Diyatalawa, 4,000 feet up in the cool, clean air of Ceylon's central mountains. For the men of the sea it was a fascinating journey; first through low lying paddy fields; then slowly ascending through tropical rain forest into foothills with spectacular views; culminating in rubber and tea plantations. At the camp there were facilities for organised sport and memorable walks. In addition they enjoyed plenty of fresh food, rest, and dancing in the evenings with Wrens and nurses who were on leave there as well.

This narrative has concentrated more on places visited than on the midshipman's training programme, which continued relentlessly whether in harbour or at sea. During ocean passages they worked hard on their astro-navigation. They also spent time with the engineering department, sweating it out in machinery spaces barely able to support human life in the fierce tropical heat. As they gained in experience, they were encouraged to stand bridge and harbour watches on their own, with a qualified ship's officer on immediate call. They became accomplished hosts at social occasions, remembering to look after the duller, lonelier guests, rather than make a beeline for the nearest attractive girl.

Norfolk returned to Colombo in time for the ceremonial surrounding the King's Birthday. A new captain had assumed command and the C-in-C was back on board. The feathered helmet-topped Governor of Ceylon and other dignitaries came on board for a formal lunch party, to be greeted by a guard of honour and the appropriate musical salutes. One of a midshipman's duties on these occasions was to stand at the bottom of the gangway to help the wives of distinguished guests in and out of the boats. It is hoped that they remembered to avert their eyes from the billowing skirts of the ladies ascending the steep steps above them!

Out of the blue came another instruction to 'proceed with all despatch', this time to the Persian Gulf. There had been riots in the Anglo-Persian oil installation at Abadan, then the largest oil refinery in the world. The ship sailed not knowing quite what to expect, but prepared for any eventuality, including the evacuation of British personnel. Abadan lay on the Shatt al Arab, the confluence of the Tigris and Euphrates rivers. *Norfolk* anchored in the stream in blistering heat opposite the vast array of refinery paraphernalia. The riots had been brought under control but, in a typical example of low-key gunboat diplomacy, the ship was required to withdraw to Bahrain, thus remaining within easy distance. Although the 'Counties' were renowned for their space and comfort, these were times well before the fitting of air conditioning. Being summer, *Norfolk* remained on stand by in one of the hottest places on earth for five whole weeks. The crew could be likened to the ingredients of a casserole slowly cooking away inside an oven. Prickly heat and other discomforts made it the least comfortable period yet of the midshipmen's young lives.

On being relieved by another cruiser, *Norfolk* retired to Bombay. The atmosphere had changed from the uneasy peace of previous visits. There were major riots in the city associated with India's quest for Independence. Following hundreds of deaths, a curfew was in force and no shore leave was possible. In later life, Kimm became very interested in politics. Even at this early age, his journal was full of comment about the troubled local scene. It must be assumed that Fieldhouse also wrote about it, but probably in less detail than his friend.

As they left Bombay for the last time, the group of five had more important things to occupy their attention. In Colombo they sat a dummy Board for their all important seamanship examination. A few days later, in Trincomalee, they faced the Board itself. They were quizzed on damage control, anchor work and rigging; on the Rule of the Road at Sea, for which nothing less than full marks were a prerequisite. There were also questions on signals, radar and ship's organisation. Following the lengthy verbal interrogation they sat two written navigation papers. Finally, one by one, they were called before the President of the Board to receive their results. Kimm was awarded a First Class Pass. Fieldhouse and the rest received Seconds. From that time on it was all downhill sailing.

In mid-October *Norfolk* departed for Mauritius and then for the naval base at Simonstown, where she was due to be taken in hand for a docking and refit. After enjoying a few days of traditional Cape Colony hospitality, the five midshipmen left the ship for the last time as part of a large draft to begin their long voyage home. First they joined a troop train at Cape Town for a fascinating two-day journey to Durban, via Kimberley, the Great

Karroo Desert, Bloemfontein and Pietermaritzburg. There they embarked in the Orient Line liner *Orontes*, which was acting as a troopship. As they left the quay, they were sung on their way by the celebrated 'Lady in White', who had gained fame by singing every troopship out of Durban during the war, and was still doing so. After an entirely relaxing passage, the coast of England appeared out of the mist after an absence of sixteen months. Fieldhouse returned to his family in Harrow to enjoy an extended Christmas leave.

The period abroad as a midshipman had been an essential part of the future admiral's character-building process. Never having been abroad before, he had left England very much a boy; uncertain about what the future might hold in store for him. Although still a teenager, he had returned home as a young man, at ease with himself and with his profession. He had thrived in the 'give and take' atmosphere of comradeship in confined spaces. He had laid the foundations of what was to become a very special empathy with the lower deck. He had experienced the aftermath of war in which millions of restless people were seeking to throw off the burden of colonisation. He had been under fire ashore and had seen evidence of a deeply troubled populace beset with famine, disease and poverty. At first hand, he had learnt something about the new world order that was emerging, having visited over ten countries that would shortly be gaining their independence. Relaxed and undemonstrative; alert and observant; he had hoisted in a great deal of what had been going on around him.

* * * * * * * *

In January 1947 John's term were distributed around the Fleet for a short period of small ship experience in home waters. He spent several weeks in the destroyers HMS *Fame* and *Easton* of the 3rd Escort Flotilla, mainly operating off Portland. He seems to have made a good impression on his last Commanding Officer who wrote:

> Has shown considerable confidence on occasions when he has handled the ship during exercises. A confident and promising youngster. Social manners are excellent. Thinks before he acts and appears well balanced.

In May, the extended term from HMS *Frobisher* days reassembled at the Royal Naval College Greenwich, in which thirty-seven years later the Fieldhouses were to have their final service home. Here they spent two terms in what equated to a university atmosphere. There was a relaxed routine of academic studies, embracing subjects such as naval history, maths and applied mechanics. Of particular interest was a rudimentary staff course, in which young officers were introduced to the art of constructive thought. From this early age they were taught how to 'appreciate the situation' through a logical process designed to assist military planners and staff officers. It was based on the principle of first deciding exactly what one wanted to do, that is identifying the aim in its simplest terms. After that, one was encouraged to consider the factors affecting its attainment, such as resources, time, space, weather etc. Then, in a military context, one listed the courses of action open to the enemy before summarising one's own options. Having done so, one selected the best course of action and made one's plans accordingly. As well as accommodating acting sub lieutenants, Greenwich was the home of the Naval Staff College, a much more serious undertaking designed to prepare more senior officers for the middle ranks.

The college itself was a place of architectural splendour, with Christopher Wren's finely proportioned buildings gracing the southern and outer bank of a gentle curve of the River Thames. They had been constructed in two lots of symmetrical blocks with a gap right through the middle, allowing an unrestricted view of the river from the older Queen's House, built earlier by Inigo Jones in the Royal Park behind. The main feature on the east side was the well proportioned chapel; but opposite this was the magnificent Painted Hall, of its kind one of the nation's greatest treasures. Its main feature was its beautiful painted ceiling and it was there that Nelson's body lay in state before his burial at St Paul's. Officers moved from the wardroom anteroom in the basement of the east side by way of an underground tunnel or 'chalk walk' to take their meals in a setting fit for, and often used by, Kings. They dined there formally once a week, often with a Royal Marine orchestra in attendance.

Although some took full advantage of the college's scholarly facilities, most were more appreciative of its proximity to the delights of London. John Fieldhouse was certainly one of a majority who freewheeled through this part of his training. It was a time for enjoying life to the full; for visits to bars, restaurants and theatres; for girls and for dancing. When his funds ran short, as they often did, there was always a warm welcome for him at the family home not too far distant.

* * * * * * * *

In January 1948 the term started on the last lap of what was to become just over seven years of general training. They were split up into several groups to attend courses at the major professional schools in the Portsmouth area. These consisted of HMS *Excellent* for gunnery, *Vernon* for torpedo and anti-submarine (TAS), *Dryad* for navigation and *Mercury* for signals. These courses lasted from four to eight weeks; preparing junior officers to take charge of any of these departments in a small ship. There were further, shorter courses in damage control, divisional officer's duties and naval aviation. The latter was a blatant attempt at recruiting pilots for the Fleet Air Arm, with all officers being given an opportunity to learn to fly. Fieldhouse actually obtained a First Class Certificate having competed 4 hours 45 minutes solo flying in a 'Tiger Moth' biplane, reaching an 'A' licence standard of proficiency. He was assessed as 'suitable to specialise in aviation.' More to his liking, however, were the practical pilotage training in the Navigation School tender HMS *Redpole* and the day he spent at sea in a submarine as part of his course at *Vernon*. He came through these professional courses with credit and with an equal mixture of First and Second class passes. The results of all these examinations, going back to his days at Dartmouth, would determine his seniority in the rank of Lieutenant.

The completion of courses towards the end of 1948 marked the parting of the ways for his term who, on and off, had spent so many years together. The largest group were appointed Sub Lieutenants in the surface fleet, with Kimm joining HMS *Superb*, a fine modern cruiser. Others left to begin their flying training. Fieldhouse was one of twelve volunteers to join HMS *Dolphin* to commence their preparation for service in submarines. The world had become a more complicated place since he had begun his training. During the latter stages the Second World War, Winston Churchill had been deeply concerned about the post-war balance of power in Europe. On 5th March 1946, while John had been learning his trade out east as a midshipman in HMS *Norfolk*, the ex-Prime Minister made his prophetic speech at Westminster College, Fulton, Missouri. In the course of this he said: 'From Stettin in the Baltic to Trieste in the Adriatic an iron curtain has descended across the continent'.

These words were the precursor of the Cold War that was to dominate international affairs for the next forty-five years. Unknown to John at that time, the submarine service that he had joined was to become very much involved. Through a succession of appointments bearing an ever-increasing degree of responsibility, he himself was destined to play a major part in it.

CHAPTER THREE

Submariner

1948 – 1955

HMS *DOLPHIN* WAS SITUATED in Fort Blockhouse, Gosport, commanding the entrance to Portsmouth harbour on the starboard hand as one proceeded to sea. It was the headquarters of the Flag Officer Submarines (FOSM), a rear admiral responsible for the operating, training and administration of the submarine service; a fully independent 'Type Commander' with direct access to the Board of Admiralty over all aspects of submarine affairs. Also at *Dolphin* were the Fifth Submarine Flotilla and the command training complex. A few years later, all the navy's flotillas became squadrons and groups of squadrons became flotillas. To avoid adding to the confusion already caused, the narrative uses the new nomenclature from this moment on.

It was a perceptibly different John who arrived there in October 1948. He was twenty-one and a half years old, having rather drifted through seven years of general naval training during which he had been given very little responsibility for anything other than himself. His career was about to begin in earnest and he intended to take it very seriously. From the outset he liked everything he saw about the Submarine Command. He found it to be an organisation of challenge and opportunity, very much in accord with his emerging personal philosophy. Totally lacking in the 'bull' and pomposity associated with the big-ship navy, it relied upon a very special relationship and degree of mutual trust across the officer/rating divide. As he settled into a busy period of classroom work, he was very quickly made aware that, for their very safety, the sixty or so souls in a submarine's company were totally dependent upon each other. Seamen officers, such as John, were expected to know everything there was to know about their boat; such as the battery and electrical power distribution, the high and low pressure air, hydraulic, ventilation, oil fuel, fresh water, slop drain and sewage systems. They were also taught about sensors, weapons and the primitive fire control arrangements. They were required to undergo escape training before proceeding to sea.

John came top in his training class in the mid-course examinations, after which the group dispersed for practical continuation training in individual submarines. This period as a supernumerary officer was something of a lottery, with its value being entirely proportional to the trouble that was taken over supervising it. John struck lucky with his Commanding Officer. Ernie Turner was an experienced and highly decorated wartime CO who took great personal interest in John's early development. He returned to *Dolphin* in an enthusiastic frame of mind to find that some of his colleagues had had less rewarding experiences. On completion of the three-month training class he was given first choice of the available sea appointments. It is not surprising that he chose to rejoin Ernie Turner, then in command of HMS *Thule* in the Third Submarine Squadron.

In 1949 the submarine flotilla consisted of about fifty boats, more or less equally divided between the 'S', 'T' and A-classes. The first two were all of World War II construction and had seen service in that conflict. Boats of the A-class, with their higher surface speed and increased diving depth, had been designed and built for the Pacific Ocean, but the war had ended before they had been able to play a part. Except for a few 'S' boats used for training purposes, the whole flotilla had been fitted with hinged 'snort' masts, which made it possible to recharge batteries while submerged. The fitting of reliable radar had made peacetime operating safer; yet there was already an air of increasing antiquity about the boats and their equipment. The larger 'T' and A-classes still sported their casing-mounted 4-inch guns. Dived performance on battery power was strictly limited with conning tower streamlining yet to be introduced. In addition, there were no effective radar search receivers to prevent boats being 'bounced' by maritime patrol aircraft whilst snorting. On the credit side was the hard core of officers and senior ratings with war time experience, even though some of these had become bored with peace time operating and were beginning to get a little frayed around the edges.

Running boats were equally divided into four operational squadrons. The First was based on the depot ship HMS *Forth* in Malta; the Second on HMS *Maidstone* at Portland; the Third on HMS *Montclare* at Rothesay in the Isle of Bute and the Fifth at *Dolphin* as already stated. Later, smaller divisions were established to assist Commonwealth forces with anti-submarine training: the Fourth in Sydney, NSW, and the Sixth in Halifax, Nova Scotia. A Far East squadron was later re-established in Singapore. The way things turned out, Fieldhouse's active career in submarines gravitated towards the Third Squadron and what was often referred to as the 'frozen north'. Most ambitious submariners developed a love/hate relationship with being based in the Clyde area. They loved it because it was where the heat of the 'action' was to be found. They hated it because, except for a very few, it was so decidedly inconvenient domestically. As a submariner, John was to spend very little time in the sunnier or more exotic places.

* * * * * * * *

Fieldhouse settled in well as the 4th Hand and Navigating Officer of HMS *Thule*. But soon after he joined there was an unfortunate incident in which the 3rd Hand (the Torpedo, Correspondence and Casing Officer) inadvertently put his foot in the bight of a rope whilst berthing. He was unceremoniously whipped over the side and fished out of the water with a fractured leg. John's training class colleague, Tony Whetstone, was drafted in from the spare crew as a permanent replacement. As term mates these two knew each other quite well already, but their time together in *Thule* cemented a life long friendship. The CO had less cause to be pleased about the situation, as both his junior seaman officers were now Sub Lieutenants straight out of the egg and without watchkeeping certificates. But under Turner's wing they were quick to absorb and learn the rudiments of their new profession.

Tony recalls that in later life he met a stalwart of the Scottish Branch of the Submarine Old Comrades Association. Joe Rooney, who had been serving in *Thule* at the time, told him that 'We ratings never thought that you two Subbies would ever make Lootenant!' Make lieutenant they most certainly did, eventually becoming two out of the three in their term to become Flag officers. The boat took part in FOSM's 'Summer War', an annual pro-submarine training bash off the Shetland Islands. There was also a period of advanced anti-submarine warfare (ASW) training at Londonderry, and Tony remembers that John had a meticulously prepared navigator's notebook, needed as a vital source document to negotiate the tricky 22 miles of pilotage waters of the Foyle river and estuary.

Under the command of Captain SM3, the depot ship HMS *Montclare* swung to a buoy in Rothesay Bay with her chicks gathered in clutches around her. As well as mothering her own squadron, she served as the workup base for all boats emerging from refits in UK dockyards. Some of the families lived locally and a cheerful social atmosphere abounded. Certainly vast quantities of duty free liquor were consumed in the depot ship and in submarine wardrooms. By way of a change in routine *Thule* made a weekend visit to the port of Glasgow. The officers were entertained in the Director's box at a soccer match in the voluminous Hampden Park Stadium. After the home team had won, the board held an impromptu celebration. Some time later Tony and John left together by the players' entrance, only to be greeted by a wildly delirious crowd of fans, upon whom they generously bestowed illegible autographs!

Later that year Ernie Turner was relieved by John Bromage, another experienced CO who, with his crew, had survived the sinking of HMS *Sahib* in the Mediterranean after depth charging. Soon after that *Thule* developed a serious main battery problem, but not before the 3rd and 4th Hands had been awarded the all-important watchkeeping certificates that paved the way for their promotion to lieutenant. The boat sailed south to Portsmouth Dockyard for an extended period of repairs and both Fieldhouse and Whetstone were reappointed.

1949 was a year for dual family celebration. As John's submarine career was successfully launched, Harold went to Buckingham Palace to be invested with his Knighthood. Fieldhouse Senior was at the height of his distinguished career as a Whitehall mandarin and was still a decade short of final retirement.

* * * * * * * *

At the end of 1949 John joined HMS *Astute* at Rothesay, continuing in his previous role as Navigating Officer of a Third Squadron submarine. Peter Jackson-Sytner, the CO, was urbane and courteous, noted for his considerable personal charm. It was a happy wardroom, with John fitting in well with his fellow officers. Early in 1950 Sub Lieutenants Chris Russell and 'Olly' Sharp joined from training class, providing an extra officer for the forthcoming deployment to the USA and Canada.

Astute sailed at the end of March and quickly ran into the most appalling North Atlantic weather. Committed to making a surfaced passage, the boat ploughed on for days into constant westerly gales and huge breaking seas. On one occasion an enormous wave broke over the conning tower and many tons of seawater deluged into the submarine. In these conditions it was necessary for both officer of the watch and lookout to be strapped into safety harnesses. On being relieved after two hours they were more than pleased to be able to struggle down through the roar of the diesel engine air induction to the foot of the conning tower ladder. There they extricated themselves from the canvas 'elephant's trunk' and 'bird bath', placed there to try and keep the ocean at bay; to emerge more like half drowned rats than human beings.

There was a regrettable incident on arrival at the US Navy submarine base at New London, Connecticut. For his first ever landfall in the New World, Fieldhouse had miscalculated the time zone. It would have mattered less if Rear Admiral James Fife, USN, (Commander, Submarine Force, Atlantic Fleet) had not been pacing up and down the jetty for an hour awaiting *Astute*'s arrival. Happily any initial frostiness soon melted away as Fife was a confirmed anglophile, having made Mediterranean war patrols as a liaison officer in the submarine HMS *Triumph* during the war, and having had overall command of British submarines of the Eighth Flotilla serving with the US Seventh Fleet in Fremantle. This was the first time, but not the last, in which John was to become involved in an embarrassing time zone incident. Meanwhile the US Navy was quick to offer its services and a number of storm damage repairs were taken in hand. In a break that extended over the Easter holiday the crew were made to feel very much at home by their new-found American colleagues.

The main purpose of the deployment was to provide basic anti-submarine training for Canadian maritime forces. Indeed this was the first of several visits that eventually led to the setting up of the RN's Sixth Submarine Squadron with its base in Halifax, Nova Scotia. On arrival there, the ship's company moved into comfortable quarters ashore in HMCS *Stadacona* and were given a week to settle down. The local admiral gave a party at which John became captivated by the charms of a certain unattached lady. At that stage of his life he was beginning to become a little more adventurous in his dealings with the fairer sex; but, on leaving Canada, he wisely decided not to pursue the matter further. There was nothing very demanding about *Astute*'s work programme. This consisted of structured ASW exercises off Halifax during the week; often anchoring overnight in St Margaret's Bay, where it was possible to trade duty free liquor for fresh lobsters caught by local fishermen. On return to harbour on one occasion, John was transferred by jackstay to a Canadian destroyer; a common enough evolution for surface ships, but one very seldom practised by submarines.

Despite the often-foggy weather, the complete change of scene from austere post-war Britain proved to be a welcome tonic for all. A short visit was paid to St John's, New Brunswick, on the north shore of the Bay of Fundy, where an accident of geography provides the world's greatest rise and fall of tides. Whether they were at sea or in harbour, the crew fed magnificently. When the boat finally left Halifax, it was heavily stored with unaccustomed luxuries such as steaks, salmon and turkeys. On return to Rothesay after the deployment, *Astute* reverted to a more mundane training routine.

* * * * * * * *

John's next boat was HMS *Aeneas*, which he joined in July 1951 as Navigating Officer and 3rd Hand. She too was in the Rothesay based Third Squadron. His first CO was highly decorated Ian McIntosh. After a few months Iwan Raikes, who also had wartime command experience, relieved him. Both these fine officers rose to the rank of vice admiral and are mentioned again in later chapters. The First Lieutenant was a forthright character named Thomas Augustus Courtney Clack, and it was with him that there is the first evidence of a personality clash involving Fieldhouse. Although they respected each other's qualities, John's laid back and relaxed style rather irritated Clack, who became more needled through finding it difficult to find fault with him. The problem was solved to everyone's satisfaction when Tom left for his command examination and Iwan Raikes was more than happy to accept John as his replacement.

Although it only lasted for three years or so, the time spent as First Lieutenant was a vital period in the career of a submarine officer. It was a time to become immersed in such things as routine, welfare, discipline and administration. Traditionally a CO spent little time on board in harbour; expecting his second-in-command to ensure that at the appointed time the boat was in all respects ready for sea. 'Jimmy', or 'Number One', additionally served as Electrical Officer in the older submarines and had a special responsibility for the submarine's trim. Raikes was delighted with his new First Lieutenant, finding him 'a very efficient young officer. He had an abundance of common sense and the lower deck was always entirely comfortable with his natural style of leadership.'

While *Aeneas* was employed on the usual fleet tasks, her most important commitment as far as Fieldhouse was concerned was to carry out a period of advanced ASW training at Londonderry. It was there, in May 1952, that he met Third Officer Margaret Cull WRNS at a cocktail party onboard a Dutch warship; afterwards inviting her and her friends for a drink in his submarine. Midge – as she was generally known – was not entirely impressed by the relative squalor of the *Aeneas* wardroom and the significance of this chance encounter might have been lost forever had it not been for John's persistence the following day. After signing the visitor's book, she had accidentally left her silver pen on board and John telephoned her to suggest that he might return it over dinner that evening. At first she was reluctant to accept his invitation, but, on being pressed, decided to change her mind. Later, he told her that if she had refused him then, he would have taken it as a definite negative signal and would not have bothered to contact her again. On such small margins of probability do life's most important decisions depend!

Midge's family came from Northern Ireland, but she had spent most of her childhood in England, where her father worked in the City, and where she gained a music scholarship to Haberdasher's School. Her home during some of the World War II years was near Tunbridge Wells, an exciting but scary experience during Germany's 'Doodle Bug' offensive of 1944. On leaving school she started training as a nurse, but found it to be not exactly her scene and left before completing the course. Looking for an entirely different sort of challenge, she joined the Wrens in 1947. After her basic training at HMS *Dauntless*, Burghfield, Berkshire, she specialised as a radar mechanic, later becoming a Leading Wren and then a Petty Officer. Her enthusiasm and extrovert personality ensured success in what was very much a man's world. Armed with a choice selection of old fashioned naval expressions that she was always to remember, she travelled around the country with the mobile Naval Air Radio Maintenance Group. It was no surprise that she was selected to become an officer and she took naturally to a broader management role. Unlike her future husband, she was very good at games, undergoing a physical training course and returning to Burghfield as a PT instructor. When she met John, she was much enjoying life as one of only four Wren officers at HMS *Sea Eagle* in Londonderry.

From the moment of the return of the silver pen, John and Midge never took a backward glance. About a fortnight later *Aeneas* sailed for Gosport to pay off at the end of the commission. Midge witnessed the departure with a feeling of some trepidation. Before sailing, John had asked her to wash the paying off pennant. The colour of its red St George's Cross had run, causing the long white tail to assume a noticeable shade of pale pink. Happily all went well and on her birthday a few days later she received a beautiful bouquet of flowers. Fate intervened further in their favour. It so happened that the rather crusty Commander of *Sea Eagle* was not exactly a devoted fan of Midge's forthright ways. After appropriate consultation it was decided that it would be in her better interest to be transferred to the naval air station at Lee-on-the-Solent near Gosport. How convenient that proved to be! HMS *Daedalus* was only minutes away from *Dolphin* where John was to be based for the next few months. His old friend Tony Whetstone had already married and he and Betty had set up home locally. With Tony away at sea, John turned up there and informed Betty that she was to arrange to take herself out to the pictures the next evening. With Midge living in the Wren officer's quarters, this provided a much-needed welcome haven for the courting couple to enjoy some privacy. They announced their engagement in August.

* * * * * * * *

Fieldhouse joined HMS *Totem* in Chatham Dockyard in November 1952. Having had a sound grounding as the First Lieutenant of a standard A-class submarine, he was now to be faced with a more demanding challenge. He had learnt much from the five war hardened COs of his first three boats who between them had earned three DSOs and five DSCs. Now he was to work for the flamboyant and hard drinking Johnny Coote, who had made war-patrols as a young officer and had developed into perhaps the most enlightened submariner of the immediate post war years. There were others who had contributed towards a much-needed advance in tactical doctrine, but Coote possessed the sharp brain and sense of showmanship needed to bring these matters to fruition. Following his own early commands, he had developed his ideas further while running the Rothesay Attack Teacher. In one of the 'new' T-conversion class submarines he was to seize the opportunity to put his theories to the test.

The T-conversion was the Navy's first attempt to produce a high performance diesel submarine to match earlier developments in Germany and the USA. Eight standard 'T' boats had been earmarked to be cut in half and lengthened to include a new battery section of 112 cells with an extra main motor on each shaft. This provided the flexibility of diesel-electric drive; but, more importantly, the 480 volts needed to give a maximum burst of 17 knots submerged, or half that speed for a period of 12 hours. There were many other improvements, such as the fitting of stainless steel masts within a streamlined fin. This made possible a vibration free periscope lookout at a best snorting speed of nine knots. This extract is from Coote's book *Submariner*.

> The other officers joined soon after I did, led by the First Lieutenant, a quiet, mild-mannered tubby lad, who announced himself as John Fieldhouse. He was soon known as 'Snorkers', a heavily antonymous soubriquet inspired by the unspeakable Bennett, the Australian First Lieutenant of *Compass Rose* in 'The Cruel Sea' with whom he shared only one characteristic – a love of sausages. He quickly proved himself to be without equal, on personal or professional grounds.

Amongst the others officers were 3rd Hand and Torpedo Officer Robin Heath – who was to serve with Fieldhouse on three later occasions – and Electrical Officer Peter Lucy. Like their CO, the latter was something of a *prima donna*. One of the first of his cloth to serve in submarines, Coote was quick to appreciate Peter's innovative technical ability; and they scurried around the dockyard and research establishments together, managing, through sheer force of personality, to initiate a number of novel and unauthorised equipment modifications which significantly enhanced the boat's operational performance. Fieldhouse's contribution was to provide the bedrock of sound organisation needed for *Totem* to operate effectively. In his own quiet and unassuming way he was the quintessential second-in-command, more than happy to leave the histrionics to others.

Meanwhile John had important personal matters to attend to. He and Midge were married at St Faith's Church, Lee-on-the-Solent on 28th March 1953. With both the bride and groom being serving officers it was very much a naval occasion, well attended by friends on both sides. Richard Fieldhouse was best man. The reception was in the familiar surroundings of the wardroom mess of *Daedalus*. After the wedding, they set forth by ferry for an overnight crossing to Guernsey in one of the worst spring gales of recent memory. Midge was quickly overcome by seasickness and remembers wondering if she had made the right decision in view of the lack of any immediate display of sympathy from John, but he himself was very close to succumbing. Once they got there all was well, and they had a wonderfully happy and enjoyable honeymoon at the Old Government House Hotel. It was all too soon before they were both required to return to work. Although Midge had the freedom to resign her commission on marriage, it had been decided that she should carry on in the Wrens for the time being. This seemed sensible, not only because John was committed to an immediate sea-going future, but also because two salaries, however modest, would certainly be more useful than one. Thus began a remarkable partnership, one that was to create substantial waves on many shores.

After the commissioning ceremony, *Totem* headed north to join the Third Squadron. The rigours of the workup were interrupted by a visit to Oban to coincide with the Queen's Coronation. There were a series of celebratory events to mark the occasion, including a large parade of all-comers under Fieldhouse's command. In June, the whole Fleet assembled in Spithead for the Coronation Review. It was to be the last formal gathering in such large numbers of what for long had been the world's leading maritime power. Assembled in salute to Her Majesty were a battleship, 9 aircraft carriers, 12 cruisers, 32 destroyers, 30 frigates, 28 submarines and scores of other vessels from British, Commonwealth and foreign navies. This was followed by FOSM's 'Summer War' off the Shetland Islands, a first opportunity for *Totem* to be put through her new-found paces.

Meanwhile it had become apparent to Coote and his immediate superiors that the UK now had a submarine of sufficiently high performance to merit putting it to serious use in the prosecution of the Cold War. The Soviets' principal area for the conduct of development trials of new maritime equipment was in the relatively secure waters adjacent to its Northern Fleet bases. Throughout the year the Barents Sea and Kola Inlet were largely ice-free. It was also a declared zone from which western shipping was discouraged from entering because of the rich intelligence pickings to be gained. In the days before sophisticated satellite activity, the only effective way of achieving this was through the covert deployment of submarines. What was not known at that time was exactly how the Russians would react in the event of an intruder being detected and forced to the surface. In addition there were political issues involved because of the need for NATO not to be seen to be escalating international tension. In these circumstances it was decided to delay plans to deploy *Totem* until more could be learnt about her true capabilities in a friendlier environment.

In the autumn of 1953 the boat was sent on temporary attachment to the Mediterranean Fleet. Unknown to all but a handful of staff ashore, she was equipped with an additional radar search receiver, allowing her the range advantage to stop snorting and go deep in the event of 'attack' from the air. Through Coote's tactical flair, no surface ships were able to lay a hand on her and the C-in-C, Admiral Mountbatten, was much impressed with her performance. After a visit to Malta, *Totem* was summoned to the Fleet Regatta in Navarin Bay where the Admiral came on board and addressed the ship's company in the warmest terms. After visits to Taranto and Tunis, where they embarked a plentiful supply of cheap champagne and cognac, they returned to the UK, very much with their tails in the air. On New Year's Eve Coote was promoted to Commander at the unusually early age of 32. Had it not been for *Totem*'s unfinished business, he would undoubtedly have been posted elsewhere.

The spring of 1954 saw the boat undergoing maintenance in Devonport Dockyard. 4th Hand Greg Courtier, then serving in his first submarine, had himself just got married and he and his wife Jane had set up their first temporary home. The name of First Lieutenant John Fieldhouse appears as the initial entry in a visitors' book which unsurprisingly now looks rather tatty fifty years on. In this strange new world of submariners, Jane found John charming and welcoming, and felt comforted that her husband was living in close contact with such a friendly and supportive man when he later went off to sea.

Meanwhile Coote was authorised to carry out the next stage of what he had long been striving for. The British Home and Mediterranean Fleets were due to carry out joint exercises with the USN Sixth Fleet in the area between Malta and Gibraltar. *Totem* was sailed with a cover story of conducting independent trials in the general area of the Azores. In fact, she was given complete freedom to pose as an intruder Soviet submarine. In an extension of the role she had played the previous autumn, she was now fitted with more surveillance equipment and the additional watchkeepers necessary to monitor 'enemy' communications frequencies. After entering the Mediterranean, she homed in on the combined fleets off Sicily and spent some time operating in close company. In the course of this she penetrated the screen of the mighty US aircraft carriers *Forrestal* and *Franklin Delano Roosevelt*, closely observing operating procedures and later withdrawing to a safer distance to obtain a wealth of tactical information by intercepting tactical voice radio nets. The crowning and final insult was to carry out a submerged sweep of Algeciras Bay; carefully recording and photographing the ships already arrived in Gibraltar Harbour. After four weeks at sea, *Totem* returned to the UK without having been detected, bringing all her evidence with her. It was fortunate that Captain 'Baldy' Hezlet (later Vice Admiral Sir Arthur) was then Chief of Staff to FOSM. Himself a distinguished CO from World War II, he had masterminded the shore end of the operation and was now able to lend his weight in severing the last of the red tape in high places. It was now clear that a similar operation against the Soviets would be unlikely to result in an embarrassing international incident. After reference to Prime Minister Churchill, political approval to proceed was obtained.

In the autumn of 1954, *Totem* sailed for the first ever surveillance patrol by a British submarine to the close vicinity of Soviet Northern Fleet bases. Remaining totally submerged for about six weeks, she rounded the North Cape of Norway to enter the Barents Sea and pioneered what was later to become one of the richest of all sources of 'hot' maritime intelligence gathering. In Coote's capable hands, it was to be an entirely covert operation, fully demonstrating the versatility of the quiet diesel-electric submarine in this important role. A veil of total secrecy surrounded the patrol and it was not until years later that Midge and the other wives became fully aware of what their husbands had been up to.

In his book, Coote referred to a particular drama that puts these activities into full perspective. On one occasion the submarine had to be brought to the surface at night to facilitate a repair involving breaking the watertight seal at the top of the search periscope. This was a lengthy process during which the boat was wide open to detection. Peter Lucy carried out this task alone, knowing that at any moment his CO might have found it necessary to dive the boat under him.

His time in *Totem* had had a profound effect on John Fieldhouse. Although he had learnt much from his previous COs, he was to say in later life that he owed most of all to Coote's astute tactical brain and inspirational leadership. *Totem*'s patrols had been the trailblazers for a new form of operating that was to have enormous importance in the conduct of the Cold War. John's contribution as second-in-command had been very considerable. Coote liked to burn the candle at both ends and had little interest in routine trivia. He was fortunate to be have been served by a first class administrator who was fast becoming a significant leader in his own right. When their ways parted on return from the historic northern patrol, John had a glowing report and a recommendation for submarine command.

Towards the end of *Totem*'s commission Midge became pregnant and served notice of her intention to leave the Wrens. This she did at the beginning of 1955 while John was serving for a short period as Ratings' Training Officer in *Dolphin*. They rented a flat on the sea front at Lee-on-the-Solent. Mark weighed in at 10lbs 6ozs on 8th July. After her many years in the Wrens, it was not the easiest thing in the world for Midge to become domesticated. One day on return to the flat with her shopping her landlord asked her 'Where's Mark?' 'Oh gosh!' she replied. 'I must have left him in his pram outside the chemist!'

John started his Commanding Officers' Qualifying Course (COQC) in September. He was twenty-seven and a half years old.

* * * * * * * *

Much has been written about the 'Perisher', as the COQC was widely known. To put it in simplest terms, it was a three-month period of steadily increasing pressure, structured to ensure that students had the confidence and ability to handle a submarine aggressively and safely in a hostile environment. Each course consisted of a group of five or six officers under the charge of an experienced CO of Commander's rank. John's 'Teacher' was Donald Hay, a dapper and somewhat austere bearded bachelor who took early exception to his charges' dirty shoes. The first part of the course was conducted in an ancient attack simulator at *Dolphin*, after which the group moved north to Rothesay. There, after further training in the more sophisticated local attack teacher, the final test came at sea. It was only then that a trainee's aptitude for a rare gift known as 'periscope eye' could be put fully to the test.

As the weeks progressed, an increasing number of surface ships passed backwards and forwards across the waters to the east of the Isle of Arran, providing multiple attacking opportunities. The Perisher under examination used one periscope, while Teacher, who exceptionally had assumed temporary command from the boat's CO, monitored performance on the other. Although the accuracy of dummy attacks was important, of far greater significance to Teacher was that the submarine should be ordered to a safe depth before there was any chance of it being rammed. But to go deep too early in these circumstances was also a black mark. The later the plug was pulled in perfect safety, the earlier the return to periscope depth, vital when evading an escort to line up on the prime target further on. The CO's judgement in this sort of close-quarters situation was critical for the safety of the submarine and to the lives of all those on board. Not only was he seeing things from a height of eye of inches above the water, he also commanded a very narrow arc of vision. If he was looking at a ship on his starboard beam, for instance, he had to be fully aware of the intended movements of an even closer vessel on his port bow, currently well outside his field of view. Additionally, all his observations had to be taken very quickly to avoid excessive periscope exposure and possible detection. Finally, however much he concentrated on the immediate target, a regular 'all round look' was needed to ensure safety from ships as yet unseen or needing to be closely monitored.

After each day at sea the group returned to the relative comfort of a hotel in Rothesay, where they could relax over the weekend with an occasional round of golf. By the fourth week the long, dark winter nights had started to draw in; yet there was enough daylight for a final surge of activity involving four destroyers and a Royal Fleet Auxiliary (RFA) target; all proceeding on random courses at their maximum speeds. On return to harbour on the final Friday evening each Perisher was called individually before Donald Hay to be informed of the result of perhaps the toughest of all practical examinations. On John's course, unusually, there was cause for general celebration. Despite the scruffy shoes and occasional complaints about rowdiness in the hotel, all had passed successfully.

Seaside holidays with parents, grand parents and brother Richard

Naval Cadet

The Royal Naval College Dartmouth

HMS *Nigeria* with war camouflage

JF fourth from left in group of Midshipmen ashore in Egypt

HMS *Norfolk* in Bombay to replace 'A' turret gun barrel
a journal sketch by Peter Kimm

Future Chiefs of Defence Staff meet in Singapore

The happy couple

HMS *Totem* in Oban: JF framed by totem pole

Mountbatten visits HMS *Totem* in Navarin Bay, Greece

Perisher's eye view

Early Commands

HMS *Acheron*

HMS *Tiptoe*

HMS *Walrus*

CHAPTER FOUR

Early Commands

1955 – 1962

AT THE END OF 1955 Fieldhouse was appointed as spare crew commanding officer in HMS *Adamant*, then the depot ship of the Third Submarine Squadron. In his seven years as a submariner, *Thule*, *Astute*, *Aeneas* and *Totem* had all been based in the Clyde. Now he was required to swallow more of the same medicine. If John and Midge had been able to gaze into the crystal ball to see that he was to have no less than six more submarine jobs in those waters, they might then and there have decided to embark upon some entirely different type of employment! Midge travelled north with infant Mark so that the family could be together.

Fieldhouse was appointed in command of HMS *Acheron* in March 1956. The boat had recently returned from a deployment to South Africa where neither CO nor First Lieutenant had conducted himself with credit. George Hayhoe was already installed as the new second-in-command and John lost no time in establishing his own style of quiet and confident leadership. An early opportunity was taken to spend a few days alongside in Douglas, Isle of Man, giving the new team an excellent opportunity to bond effectively.

Bryan Smalley joined as navigator in June and has kindly madc available the relevant extracts of his autobiography. In August, when dived at 300 feet, there were reports of a leak aft. A fine spray persisted throughout the engine room compartment, but at a shallower depth the leak stopped and it was impossible to identify the source of this most unwelcome ingress of seawater. Back at Rothesay, the Squadron Staff was none the wiser and it became necessary to sail *Acheron* to Rosyth Dockyard for a more detailed examination. The latest X-ray equipment and magnetic crack detectors also drew a blank, but the fault was finally found by the age old process of putting an air pressure in the compartment and sloshing soapy water over the hull and noting exactly where the bubbles were emerging. An area around a faulty weld had to be cut out and rewelded, after which the boat resumed its fully operational status.

Smalley tells of sailing in November to carry out cold weather trials of certain equipments in an operating area to the north of Iceland. Well before reaching Arctic waters *Acheron* was ordered back to base to fully prepare for war in the event of being needed in response to the Suez crisis. The only advantage of this episode was that they had been given a large number of pre-cooked frozen meals as a trial on improving the modest standard of submarine catering. Dishes such as 'Chicken Supreme' proved very popular and, on return to harbour after only a few days at sea, the Coxswain was asked to land the unused packages. He was not very popular when he reported that the cupboard was bare and that the whole consignment had been eaten! Smalley recalls that he and his colleagues were aware that their Captain had acquired the nickname of 'Snorkers' in his last submarine, but it died a natural death as nobody dared to even think about using it. In a wardroom consisting of five officers all of the same rank of lieutenant, Fieldhouse was 'Sir' to the others at all times, the undisputed leader of a small and friendly community.

Acheron was due to pay off for refit at the end of the year. After a visit to Kristiansund in Norway and a period of running from Londonderry, she sailed for Gosport on 13th December. She made a final surface passage to Cammell Laird's yard in Birkenhead in January.

* * * * * * * *

Following his first command, Fieldhouse was due for a two-year appointment in general service. Traditionally, these jobs came in two main types. Some COs went off to destroyers or frigates as First Lieutenants, but others were needed to fill billets in shore establishments where submarine expertise was needed. John's appointment came into this latter category, managing to maintain his record of almost continuous service in the UK's higher latitudes. He was appointed as Submarine Staff Officer at the Joint Anti-Submarine Warfare School at Londonderry. The family moved into a married quarter at HMS *Sea Eagle*. This was a pleasant interlude in the familiar surroundings of where John and Midge had first met five years earlier.

Because of John's experience this was something of a routine job, not presenting too much of a challenge. His main tasks were to present the submarine input on the Tactical Floor and to help plan the various ASW exercises. In October, after eight years service as a Lieutenant, he picked up his half stripe on promotion to Lieutenant Commander. This was to be his last automatic elevation in rank. Any further progress would be a matter of catching the selector's eye in direct competition with his contemporaries. Although he was much liked and respected within the narrow confines of the submarine service, there was still no inkling amongst his peer group that he was destined for high places.

Just as he was nearing the completion of his first year in a post that normally lasted for two, Fieldhouse was reappointed. In the face of an overbearing of middle ranked officers, the Navy decided to offer a generous 'golden bowler' package to those wishing to take early retirement. The reaction of the FOSM of the day was immediately to relieve any submarine

CO who ventured to apply for it. At very short notice, in what was known in the navy as a 'Pier Head Jump', John received the call to take over the T-conversion HMS *Tiptoe*, yet again in the Third Submarine Squadron. This career move provided the first serious mention of Midge in her husband's confidential reports, one of many subsequent official records of approbation.

> Domestically he is assisted and supported by a pleasant, intelligent and forceful wife whose departure from Londonderry will be a real loss to the local Service community.

Midge was quick to realise that the wife of a sea-going officer faced a situation akin to 'no contest' in competing for her husband's affections with the 'grey mistress' of the moment. But her contribution was to become increasingly decisive when John served in shore based appointments.

* * * * * * * *

The good fortune of John's unexpected appointment to *Tiptoe* in January 1958 enabled him to take the fullest possible advantage of a golden opportunity. With her sister ship HMS *Turpin*, she was lying alongside *Dolphin* at Gosport, in the final stages of preparation for a deployment to the Caribbean and Western Atlantic with units of the Home Fleet. Stepping into the wardroom for the first time he noticed the boat's talisman hanging from the deck head. This was a tiny pair of ballet shoes used by actress Moira Shearer in a celebrated film *The Red Shoes*; already very tatty and faded to a sort of dirty brownish pink. He was amongst a confident and willing team of officers, but they must have regarded him with a degree of scepticism. With his predecessor they had just brought the boat through its workup programme successfully. Now they were going to have to adapt themselves to unknown new ways. First Lieutenant Brian Trussler was a steady and phlegmatic character with an unusual propensity for eating wine glasses on social occasions. Highly qualified Engineer Officer 'Spam' Hammersley was to become the RN's first nuclear submarine Marine Engineer Officer, later rising to Flag rank. Dynamic Navigating Officer Al Kennedy was to join 'Spam' as navigator in the first commission of HMS *Dreadnought*, later commanding her on the historic voyage to the North Pole before leaving the Royal Navy early to become a captain of industry. Fieldhouse himself was also destined for *Dreadnought*, but did not arrive there until well after the other two. With the rest of the officers, they formed a team of many talents, all of which were going to be needed in the testing months that lay ahead.

The two submarines made an unusually calm surface passage to the Azores, where they joined the Fleet for the first of a series of training exercises. The ships involved were the depot ship HMS *Tyne*, wearing the Flag of the C-in-C; the aircraft carrier *Bulwark*; cruiser *Ceylon*; destroyers *Dainty*, *Daring*, *Delight*, *Barfleur* and *Camperdown*; and two Royal Fleet

Auxiliary tankers (RFAs). From there it was a long flog to the southwest in heavy weather to enter the Caribbean Sea. Being unable to maintain the speed of the main group, the two boats arrived late for the Fleet assembly at Kingston, Jamaica, after three weeks at sea. Here *Turpin* suffered a catastrophic failure of her main engine frames, which eventually led to her having to be towed back to Portsmouth. The effect of this was to leave *Tiptoe* as the only operational submarine available for the main period of the deployment.

On leaving Kingston, the Governor spent a few hours at sea, accompanied by John's mentor, Commander Johnny Coote, now the Fleet Operations Officer. They were programmed to arrive that afternoon at Port Antonio at the eastern end of the island; a tricky approach into a bay followed by a sharp turn to starboard into a small harbour normally used by banana boats. Due to the delay caused through having to return the Governor to Kingston after his dive, *Tiptoe* arrived off the port after the sudden fall of tropical darkness. Fortified by a message received from a local expatriate offering to shine a bright light from her window to act as a leading mark, Fieldhouse pressed on in without hesitation. Guests already gathering for the cocktail party warmly applauded his neat arrival alongside. The combination of an overcrowded control room, insufferable heat and having no ice to keep the drinks cool added to the novelty of the occasion. A local tycoon was so impressed that he invited all the crew not required for duty to move into a nearby luxury hotel for the period of their visit.

As the rest of the fleet fanned out to visit other Caribbean Islands and dependencies, *Tiptoe* prepared to take on a high priority assignment which at that time was so secret that even those on board were not informed of the full significance of their actions. After visits to the US Navy bases at Guantanamo Bay in Cuba and to San Juan, Puerto Rico, they spent much of the next two months at sea off the eastern seaboard of the USA, broken up by the fleet exercise 'Maple Royal' off Halifax, Nova Scotia and short visits to Bermuda and New London, Connecticut. It was a boring but essential task as they steered a series of random but predetermined tracks; always submerged, yet alternating between snorting in diesel-electric or direct-drive modes and proceeding on main motors at above propeller cavitation speed. These propulsion combinations allowed the submarine to be open to detection by the highly sensitive low frequency passive sonar SOSUS (Sound Surveillance System) arrays that were mounted on a heavy cable laid on the seabed and connected through that cable to terminal equipment ashore. The long-term objective was to build up a network of arrays that would enable any Soviet submarines proceeding into the North Atlantic to be detected and tracked continuously. *Tiptoe*'s trial would also provide the Americans with the acoustic signature of a typical British submarine whilst generally checking out the new equipment that was to play a vitally important part in the escalating complexity of the Cold War.

Tiptoe returned to her base in Faslane in May. Having undertaken the best part of the workload of two submarines in demanding circumstances, the crew had spent an unexpectedly long period at sea. Despite this it was a well-contented team that was sent on leave *en masse* while base staff conducted essential maintenance. Any doubts about their new CO had been long dispelled. *Tiptoe* was riding the crest of a wave and all on board would have cheerfully followed John anywhere.

During his leave Fieldhouse learnt that his boat had been chosen to carry out special surveillance operations in the following autumn. But before that could take place, two important commitments were programmed to sharpen up the crew to the highest possible standard of efficiency. A Joint Maritime Course at Londonderry took John back to the scene of his last appointment. By this time Al Kennedy had developed into a thoroughly competent navigator, but he recalls an incident that reminded him that he still had plenty to learn. After surfacing at the end of the final exercise he was in considerable doubt about the boat's position. The estimated position (EP), based on the dead reckoning (DR), was highly questionable and the weather conditions precluded astro-navigation. The only remaining aids were the Loran and Decca systems that provided reasonably accurate position lines from distinctive radio signals. But the lack of a significant angle of 'cut' between bearings obtained by this means left him very little the wiser. Al weighed up all the options, placed a pencil mark on the chart and informed his Captain where he considered the submarine to be. John's low-key response to a trusted subordinate was entirely instructive without in any way seeming to admonish. Taking a cigarette packet out of his trouser pocket, he placed it squarely on the chart, centred on Al's EP. 'I quite agree, Pilot, but you should work on the assumption that we could be *anywhere* underneath my fag packet'.

The second commitment was to act as Perisher boat for the next Commanding Officer's Qualifying Course (COQC). The Teacher was Commander Lance Bell Davies, another submariner in the fast stream, later to become Vice Admiral Sir Lancelot. Lance and John already knew each other well and the high-pressure weeks they spent together served to strengthen their friendship. During the final tactical phase when a few nights were spent at sea in conditions of severe officer overcrowding, the two COs caught up with what sleep they could by bedding down head to tail on the narrow bunk in John's tiny cabin. This fulfilled his childhood dread of 'having to share a single bed with another person.' In the course of several Perishers, Lance had been uniquely placed to judge differing boat's capabilities. He rated *Tiptoe* the best run of those he worked with. 'An air of calmness and quiet efficiency permeated from the command to every corner of the submarine' was his admiring verdict.

In the late summer *Tiptoe* was taken in hand to prepare for the autumn's surveillance operation. Fieldhouse had already been involved in one such patrol as the First Lieutenant to Johnny Coote four years earlier. Things had moved on apace since those pioneering days in *Totem*. To meet the increasing challenges of the Cold War, Soviet maritime activity had grown immeasurably. The Barents Sea, as the main ice-free area in which new weapon systems could be tested within the 'secure' limits of home bases, remained a rich picking ground for NATO intelligence, led by US Navy and Royal Navy submarines. At that time the Russians were introducing into service increasing numbers of new ships, submarines and aircraft, together with a new range of missile, gun, radar, sonar and communications systems. It was vital that as much as possible should be known about all these before they were deployed to areas where they could pose a threat. In those days before sophisticated satellites, submarines were the only vehicles able to provide the missing links urgently sought by Western intelligence agencies. Using a specially developed range of passive sensors and tactics consisting of measured aggression combined with extreme stealth, a well handled submarine could be positioned to witness a missile firing, identify the platform from which it was fired and obtain details of the sensors used to control it.

These patrols placed great strain on commanding officers, particularly during the years when diesel-electric boats only were available. Although they relied implicitly on their well-trained teams, the 'one man band' culture was still very much in evidence. Later, with nuclear powered submarines, command became more of an exercise of leadership through management, there being so many balls in the air that no one man could possibly catch them all simultaneously. The dichotomy that faced Fieldhouse and others in his position was the balance between remaining undetected at all times and the need to bring home the best possible intelligence 'take'. On the one hand too much caution would lead to an unproductive patrol. On the other, the crowning degradation would be to be forced to the surface off a hostile coast.

Tiptoe slid out of Faslane on 26th September 1958 as heavily laden as it was possible to be. Fourteen specialist intelligence staff augmented her crew of sixty-five, necessitating 'hot bunking' for almost all. A false deck of crates containing much of the food further cramped accommodation spaces. Fresh water was strictly rationed to fifty gallons a day for all purposes. The crew remained unshaven and largely unwashed. Every seven days each man was allowed half a small basin full for rinsing down before shifting into clean underwear. During the seven weeks at sea life continued in an atmosphere of extreme discomfort, permeated by the evil smells of diesel oil, dirty bodies and stale food. Short of actually being in a 'shooting' war, these were the most testing conditions imaginable for a CO and for all the team around him. In due course *Tiptoe* returned to her home base undetected and with results that far exceeded expectations. This spectacular highlight from John's early career had taken him for the second time to the front line of the Cold War. Later, as he rose rapidly through the ranks to positions of greater responsibility, the value of these experiences would prove to be priceless when leading others to emulate his achievements.

Fieldhouse would have had the usual mixed feelings about being appointed ashore after only eleven months in command. Certainly he would have found it a great joy to look forward to spending more time with the family. But inevitably there would have been a sadness in having to say goodbye to the grubby ballet shoes and to the exceptionally gifted team with whom he had shared many high points and privations.

Although this narrative hasn't seen the last of either 'Spam' Hammersley or Al Kennedy, this is an appropriate moment to record the latter's thoughts on his Commanding Officer.

> Of the submariners of my acquaintance he was not the most brilliant attacker or ship handler; but he had a fine sense of tactical awareness and the gift of being able to absorb pressure while seeming to remain relaxed. Where he was pre-eminent was in the field of human relations. He had a natural ability to lead people and inspire loyalty. He was an excellent decentraliser who expected everyone to knuckle down and get on with their jobs. All who sailed with him just wanted to do their very best because it seemed unthinkable to let him down. When I left the Navy he had yet to reach Flag rank, but he was certainly the most outstanding all round officer I ever met.

It is known that Al's sentiments were very largely reciprocated. John always upheld him as the most impressive of his young submariner subordinates.

* * * * * * * *

The last few years had been highly significant in the wider context of submarine development. As long ago as 1955, USS *Nautilus* had become the first submarine underway on nuclear power. As the decade progressed, the UK continued work on its own programme, beset with inevitable delays due to financial constraint and technical problems. The appointment of Lord Mountbatten as First Sea Lord in 1955 added new momentum. The dictatorial leader of the American nuclear propulsion programme, Admiral Hyman G Rickover, was a fiercely jealous custodian of his national interests and secrets, his mind set totally against the cooperation the RN so badly needed. Mountbatten's charm and presence unlocked this door, resulting in the release of a ready-made propulsion plant of the variant used in the USN's latest Skipjack class attack nuclear submarine (SSN). This was in the process of being fitted into the back end of *Dreadnought*, then in an advanced stage of construction in Vickers Yard at Barrow-in-Furness, thereby precipitating into service Britain's first nuclear powered submarine.

Hammersley, who had left *Tiptoe* just before the Barents Sea patrol, had been selected as *Dreadnought*'s first Marine Engineer Officer (MEO). Together with the first CO, Commander Peter Samborne, Executive Officer (XO) 'Tubby' Squires, Weapons Electrical Officer (WEO) John Grove, some junior engineer officers and selected senior ratings, he was already in the USA undergoing Rickover's daunting programme of nuclear training. It was now necessary for more people to be fed into this lengthy process; initially to man up *Dreadnought*, but also in anticipation of the first all-British designed HMS *Valiant* and successive submarines. FOSM and his senior staff were busy identifying the most suitable officers to jump onto the nuclear bandwagon as it rapidly gathered speed. It was no surprise, therefore, that Fieldhouse featured early in these plans.

In US nuclear submarines the propulsion plant watch keepers were 'line' officers, subsequently available for selection as XO and CO. The RN insisted on maintaining its proven system of deep specialisation, in which the best engineers were able to climb the promotion ladder to Flag rank without sea command. The hard won *Dreadnought* agreement required all officers to train to the extremely high academic content of the American syllabus. This resulted in the setting up of a year long Nuclear Reactor Course at the Royal Naval College Greenwich in September 1959.

While he was waiting for this, John put his experience to good use in the role of Exercise Plans Officer on the staff of Flag Officer Submarines. At least this allowed the expanding family some valuable time together. Amanda was born in April 1959 and soon after that he and Midge bought 'Pippins' in Ryde Place, Lee-on-the-Solent, for the now unbelievable sum of £3,600. At last they had the security of the comfortable base for which every naval family craved. The way things turned out it was to be the only permanent home they ever owned.

* * * * * * * *

In the summer of 1959 John paid a short visit to the USA to examine the content of the American nuclear training programme. The three others in the party were all senior to him and specialist engineers. He was quick to form a judgement that the syllabus was overbearingly heavy in academic and theoretical content for the needs of officers not directly concerned with the operation of the nuclear plant. On his return he submitted a minority report to this effect, with the caveat that he was fully aware that nothing could be done to change the existing arrangements in the short term.

John arrived at Greenwich in September for what he already knew was going to be an academic year of unremitting toil for one who had left school nearly fifteen years earlier. He and another CO, Peter Herbert, were joined by four young seaman officers, two of whom were Al Kennedy and 'Kipper' Walker. They had all been specially selected as having the best chance of being able to cope with the academic pressure, having passed out top in their initial training for submarines. Also on the course was the next wave of engineers and *Dreadnought*'s first doctor, Roger Lambert, who was later to die while still serving as a Surgeon Vice Admiral.

John remained in college during the week, returning home to 'Pippins' at the weekend, laden with homework for completion by the following Monday. If there was ever a period of disharmony in the thoroughly secure Fieldhouse marriage, it occurred at about this time. Midge had suffered post-natal depression after the birth of Amanda and felt very much in need of a considerate and attentive husband. John realised that he had an academic crisis on his hands and that, unless he passed the course, his career would be in jeopardy. In these circumstances, his canny Yorkshire instinct caused him to devote all his energies to what he believed to be his overriding current priority. With the benefit of hindsight, this can be seen as the sort of passing glitch likely to beset any marriage. Whatever the degree of Midge's resentment, she remained fiercely loyal to John and wholeheartedly shared his ambitions for the future.

Back at Greenwich, Walker, who had a room on the same corridor, recalls their stringent routine. After a working day of formal lectures, those living-in would have an early supper in plain clothes in the Painted Hall before returning to their rooms for further study. At 10.45pm there would be a general movement towards the bar for a nightcap before closing time. After that, work would often continue into the small hours. Despite the pressure, there was plenty of time for lighter moments. Although John had the elevated status of a CO, he maintained an easy relationship with his fellow students. Amongst his *bon mots* was a piece of advice that needed to be treated with caution when applied to others. 'You can say what you like to senior officers as long as you call them 'Sir' occasionally.'

At one time Al Kennedy threatened to become ensnared with a newly promoted Wren officer. 'I should give that a miss' was John's advice of deep experience. 'Either she will have to go on serving to justify the cost of her officer's training or it will cost you a fortune to get her out of it'. Many years later John said this to a friend pursuing a very senior Wren officer: 'Take some advice from me: think hard before marrying a girl with any officer-like qualities!'

The first term brought the course up to 'A' level standard in mathematics, physics, applied mechanics and thermo-dynamics. In the second they covered nuclear reactor theory, including the calculation of core size for criticality. After this the engineer officers left for the States for an eight-month period 'riding' American nuclear submarines. Samborne and Squires joined the seaman officers for the final term's detailed study of *Dreadnought*'s 5SW Plant. To his great credit, Fieldhouse successfully passed his examinations. But when he finally packed his bags to go home, he was more than ever convinced that he had been required to absorb far more knowledge than he was ever going to need. When the next group of seaman officers assembled at Greenwich some time later, their course was reduced to a more realistic single term. This became the accepted norm for all future nuclear training.

On completion of the Greenwich course the appointing plot for the four initial qualified commanding officers began to clarify. Samborne and Squires were already installed as CO and XO of *Dreadnought*, then still in the course of construction. Should anything happen to either of them, Fieldhouse and Herbert were now fully trained. In due course, when promoted, John was earmarked to relieve Samborne, while Peter would stand by *Valiant*, the first all-British SSN. Meanwhile Fieldhouse was given command of HMS *Walrus*, the seventh and final SSK he was to serve in; this being the code used when referring to a conventionally powered diesel-electric submarine.

* * * * * * * *

John's appointment on 29th July 1960 draws attention to something that, in hindsight, could be considered an anomaly in his career pattern. A month earlier he had passed the date on which he could have been selected at the first attempt for promotion to commander. Indeed his friend Peter Kimm had already achieved this goal. Over the next year or so, a few others started to overtake him, including one or two colleagues in submarines. For someone of his exceptional record, this could be said to be surprising. There is no doubt that John would have noticed this and, although it would not have unduly worried him, it would certainly have been an irritant.

On the credit side of this was the opportunity to commission a brand new submarine. *Walrus* was the last but one of the eight Porpoise class which, together with the thirteen Oberon class submarines that followed them, were to become the world's most effective diesel-electric submarines. Of similar size to the T-conversions, they were better equipped in every way and set new standards in the reduction of radiated noise. Fieldhouse quickly established a strong rapport with the directors of Scotts' Shipyard at Greenock, complementing the excellent cooperation that already existed with the foremen and charge hands. At that time Scotts' finishing trades were generally considered to be the best of all submarine builders. Of particularly high quality were the joiners, upholsterers and deck-tilers. Each Scotts boat was an improvement on its predecessor. Until HMS *Otter* was commissioned some time later, *Walrus* was to become the showboat of the Third Squadron for which she was destined. The whole ambience of the internal fit out was one of light and space. On an early visit to the shipyard, Midge had an important input to the selection of the colour scheme.

Reluctantly John and Midge had decided not to abandon 'Pippins'. It seemed the wrong time to offer their new home for let, having so recently completed decorating and furnishing it in the way they wanted it. John resigned himself to having to commute backwards and forwards from Scotland on night trains at weekends. Occasionally Midge sallied north, being there over the period of the February 1961 commissioning ceremony. Cocktail parties in the evening followed days at sea on trials. There was little time for preparation and First Lieutenant Dick Husk recalls that the captain's wife showed her true spirit and devotion to the common cause by helping the duty watch to scrub out on return to harbour. She also introduced the attractive concept of covering the periscope wells with chicken wire mesh and filling the spaces with welcoming flower arrangements.

Part of the trials programme was to fire gyro-angled torpedoes on the range in Loch Long. One of these headed for the shore and landed close alongside a startled Laird who was fishing. Despite this, the workup inspection went off extremely well; an operator in the Faslane telephone exchange reporting that he had overhead a conversation in which Captain SM3 had reported to FOSM at Gosport that he could find absolutely nothing wrong with the submarine whatsoever. Later the admiral himself spent the tactical phase of a Londonderry exercise at sea in *Walrus*. Again everything went splendidly as they penetrated the screen, 'sank' the target and avoided detection by the 'Boys in Light Blue' overhead. However, 'Baldy' Hezlet's comments on departure were not entirely complimentary: 'Well that all went very well, but I do think you and your officers smoke far too much'.

Another important visitor off Londonderry was the new Navy Minister, Lord Carrington. He and a senior civil servant were winched down onto the casing from separate helicopters. Fieldhouse received his guest with due ceremony and they set off together for a tour of the inside of the submarine. Husk waited for the second helicopter and was surprised to discover that it contained the Minister! It didn't seem to matter and they all met up in the wardroom some minutes later.

Throughout her first commission *Walrus* was employed on a succession of trials and routine training tasks. Lieutenant Commander Dick Sharp, who conducted a series of trials, was unequivocal in his praise for the cooperation he received on board. This came from all quarters, but there is no doubt in his mind that the pattern was set by the example of their ever-courteous Commanding Officer. Husk recalls a similar but slightly different perspective.

> An accident of appointing had thrown together a ship's company of exceptional quality. The lower deck was led by a team of senior rates who were quite splendid. I have never come across a team like them

> either before or since. The Coxswain and several other senior rates subsequently became officers. The junior rates were also very good indeed.

Husk is not the only person who has mentioned one of John's recurrent habits. He was an inveterate snacker! Before turning in at night, for instance, it would be normal form to visit the galley to see what the chef had laid out for the morrow's breakfast. In this way a bacon sandwich or delicious plate of mushrooms on toast could be knocked up very easily. As both officers were comfortably built, it would seem that they were partners in crime on these occasions.

After the statutory annual foreign visit to Horsens in Denmark, Terry Thompson relieved Dick Husk in November 1961. He, too, was delighted by the atmosphere he found on board, particularly having himself come from an A-boat with a totally impossible commanding officer. In March 1962 *Walrus* left to take part in the usual fleet training period in Gibraltar. This was marred by a catastrophic explosion in one of the diesel engines whilst snorting. Component parts and bits and pieces of cylinder liner were ejected in all directions, but mercifully there were no injuries. The boat proceeded to Gibraltar for an investigation, followed by a lengthy period of repairs. Fieldhouse sought permission for some of the crew to be flown home on leave, but this was turned down because of the cost involved. Later, when *Walrus* returned to Faslane, she lay idly alongside while the due leave was taken. Shortly before John was relieved in August by old shipmate 'Olly' Sharp, the boat paid an enjoyable courtesy visit to Santander.

In June 1962, Fieldhouse had been selected for promotion to Commander, to take effect in the following December. At that time lieutenant commanders had twelve opportunities for selection, coming at six monthly intervals between a seniority of three and nine years. At the age of 34, he had spent five years in the rank but was still one of the earlier members of his term to be promoted. This was an impressive though not exceptional achievement. The high regard in which he was held as a submariner was indisputable and he was already trained and labelled as the commanding officer in-waiting of a nuclear submarine. Yet of the wider navy beyond submarines he knew very little, and those who controlled its fortunes knew even less of him. At this time of rapid expansion into nuclear propulsion, shortly to be followed by a decision to go for the Polaris nuclear deterrent, FOSM needed all his best officers in submarine appointments. To his disadvantage, it was to be some years before Fieldhouse could be spared for a general service posting. One fact is irrefutable. From the moment of his promotion to commander, John's career entered a state of overdrive. He started to climb the next part of ladder in seemingly effortless strides; hardly pausing for breath, it seemed, until he reached the very top.

CHAPTER FIVE

Rising Star

1962 – 1967

IT WAS NOT SURPRISING THAT Fieldhouse's first job as a commander was on the staff of Flag Officer Submarines. He was appointed Flotilla Material Officer (FOM), a job with a rather unusual nomenclature. In the early 1960s FOSM, in his role as the submarine 'Type Commander', had a large staff and far reaching responsibilities. As well as his operational and training roles he had direct access to the Ministry of Defence (MoD) to provide professional input into the formulation of requirements for new boats, weapon systems and equipment. For this purpose FOM acted as a direct link between the submarine staff at Gosport and the Naval Staff in Whitehall.

The Directorates of this formidable organisation situated on the fourth and fifth floors of the MoD Main Building formed a breeding ground for the more senior ranks. Indeed it was almost impossible for anyone to reach the top without having first served an apprenticeship there. This was normally done as a commander who, having arrived from a sea appointment where he had been in a position of near deity, found himself as a 'desk officer' with no subordinates. John was destined never to serve in Whitehall in the rank of commander, but his many visits as FOM gave him a valuable insight into its complex procedures.

In a complete turn up for the books John had an office job that was very close to home. Sarah had been born in a private nursing home in Gosport in November 1962 and for a period of almost two years the Fieldhouses were able to enjoy a normal life with family and friends. One of the closest of these was Gill Oddie who held John and Midge in great affection because of their kindness to her over the period of the death of her first husband. She has provided a snapshot of typical 'Pippins' hospitality. After some form of entertainment elsewhere, there would be an impromptu gathering at the end of an evening with Midge exploiting her natural gift for playing the piano. Over a nightcap or two there would be much enlivened conversation, song and laughter, often ending up with bacon and eggs at 1.00am. It was fortunate that they had friendly neighbours and that the children were good sleepers!

Although John was to see more of 'Pippins' during this job than at any other period of his active service life, his work often took him away from home for short periods. Apart from his regular visits to the MoD, he travelled far and wide to shipyards and to research, development and design authorities involved in producing equipment for future generations of submarines. It was a period of great expansion during which many of the new Oberon class SSKs were accepted into service; in which HMS *Dreadnought* started her long series of acceptance trials; in which HMS *Valiant* was brought forward towards completion; in which the agreement to build the Polaris armed Resolution class ballistic missile SSBNs was signed. Indeed it was John's Admiral, Rufus Mackenzie, who had his time as FOSM cut short in order to lead the new Polaris Executive, charged with the timely introduction into service of what was to become Britain's largest ever peace time defence programme. Further around the corner was the design concept of a higher performance SSN to follow the Valiant class. His work also included liaison visits to the USA and days at sea in diesel boats undergoing trials of new weapons and equipment. He had a special responsibility for the policy regarding the fitting out of submarines allocated for covert surveillance operations.

As commanding officer elect, he was deeply interested in *Dreadnought*. Britain's first SSN was the test platform for important new equipments. Pre-eminent amongst these was the revolutionary Type 2001 sonar. The transducers for this were wrapped around the lower half of the snub-nosed bow, with coverage over an arc of 135 degrees on either side. Until it could be fully tested at sea, little would be known about its true capabilities, both in its impressive active mode, and passively against the background of the submarine's high radiated noise. The all-British Valiant class was being fitted with its main machinery mounted on a resilient 'raft', making it altogether much quieter. These developments had a spin-off into tactical concepts governing the employment of these highly sophisticated SSNs. FOM was the staff officer most immediately concerned with monitoring these and many other material issues from a user's perspective. His background as an experienced CO enabled him to work comfortably and productively at the interface of operations and technology.

Sharing an office with John at HMS *Dolphin* was Peter Usher of the Royal Corps of Naval Constructors, then serving as a commander in naval uniform while seconded to the staff of FOSM. Amongst his tasks was to inspect and advise on the material state of running submarines. He was also on board to supervise the tests connected with *Dreadnought*'s first deep dive. Coming from totally different professional backgrounds, this pair had many a lively discussion on matters of common interest. Soon afterwards, Usher left the Corps and achieved distinction with the country's leading private warship building group, Vosper Thornycroft; later becoming Chairman. There is little doubt that John derived benefit from this useful liaison, particularly in his later post as Controller of the Navy.

Dreadnought began a long series of sea trials in December 1962, but it wasn't until May 1964 that she was commissioned in Barrow-in-Furness; ready at last to join the active Fleet. It had been a long hard slog for all those connected with coaxing her into service and even before the White Ensign had been hoisted for the first time there had been a trickle of departures from the original ship's company. Tubby Squires had been promoted to Commander and had been relieved as XO by Barry Wallace. Al Kennedy, the navigator, had left to start his Perisher. Soon there would be new faces appearing everywhere. Peter Samborne had been an ideal person to steer *Dreadnought* through the tortuous first few years of building and acceptance trials. The worth of his technical expertise at the heart of the project in its early stages had been incalculable. Although promoted to captain, this was to be the peak of his professional career. Meanwhile it was time for Britain's first SSN to move forward into a new phase of evaluation as an operational fleet unit in the hands of a fresh Commanding Officer.

* * * * * * * *

John Fieldhouse assumed command of *Dreadnought* at Gibraltar in July 1964. She had arrived after visiting Bermuda and Norfolk, Virginia, where the opportunity had been taken to show her off in the USA. One of the disadvantages of nuclear powered vessels was the strictly limited number of ports that were prepared to accommodate them. In the interests of safety, approved berths needed to be in secure and remote locations, away from areas of public access and high-density habitation. In western democracies there was also the recurring possibility of demonstrations against all things nuclear. Gibraltar harbour, with its outer moles, was one of first British ports to be cleared, making it a more than welcome home from home for *Dreadnought*. The added advantage of Gibraltar was its proximity to deep water and varied sonar conditions, essential prerequisites for her lengthy periods of evaluations and trials.

Having already served with him, Spam Hammersley was delighted to welcome his new CO. As one of a handful of the original team, he himself was nearing the end of his time on board. But rather than Spam, it was a junior engineer officer, Ned Purvis – later Vice Admiral – who was on watch in the manoeuvring room at the time of the handover. To demonstrate the high standard of training of the engineering staff, all of whom had spent many months in American nuclear submarines, Samborne inflicted a full range of emergency breakdown drills on the nuclear reactor plant. Purvis remembers having to be fully on his toes to remain within the stringent nuclear safety requirements demanded by Admiral Rickover.

For all his technical brilliance, Samborne was not a complete people's person, and John had arrived at an opportune moment. A somewhat cliquey wardroom atmosphere was broken down and a more relaxed style of leadership was introduced. The 'one man band' concept of command practiced in the smaller SSKs was entirely inappropriate in the more complex nuclear boats. John saw the need to delegate more freely to the highly trained team around him, offering encouragement, advice and support whenever it was needed. As far as their new CO was concerned, those serving in *Dreadnought* had no justification for feeling elitist unless they were seen to be delivering the high quality performance expected of them.

Inevitably, the boat was always full of visitors. After John's death, Jeremy Larken, later to distinguish himself in command of HMS *Fearless* in the Falklands War, wrote some notes to Midge about the times his and John's paths had crossed over several years. Jeremy recalls a period of sea riding in the Mediterranean in preparation for his own appointment to *Valiant* as Navigating Officer.

> *Dreadnought* gives the impression of a vast high-tech space capsule, full of cheerful, dauntingly competent people, revolving around the masterful presence of John. There appeared to be a remarkable harmony between *Dreadnought* and her boss. Physically, even, they were somehow much akin, and the submarine seemed to adopt a measure of his personality (each seemed alarmingly intelligent). For me *Dreadnought* retained this persona for the rest of her service. John liked being in the wardroom, presiding of course at the end of the long athwart ships table, the natural focus. From here he directed, mainly by inference and tone, and talked – with that easy, diverting touch which was a hallmark. He was master already of the art of making his world revolve around him – in a magnetic way which led people both to enjoy being part of it and to do their very best. A masterful tease, often puckish, he was – and blessedly remained – the perpetual assassin of pomposity and humbug.

Another of Larken's observations seems strangely out of place in the light of the distinction Fieldhouse subsequently achieved right across the Navy.

> Back in Gibraltar, late evening in the wardroom, John just returned from a dinner for the assembled ships' captains (having, one suspected, been man-of-the-match). This is his kingdom, and we his own trainee barons, wayward and irresponsible, but definitely his family. Masterly as always, he confides with an engagingly-assumed modesty the innate superiority of the submarine species. Nursing (I am sure) a gentle nightcap, he says 'I wondered what I was doing there; they're all much older than me, and really I had nothing to say to them.'

Dreadnought returned to Faslane for summer leave before taking part in NATO exercise 'Teamwork' in the North Atlantic. By November she was back in Gibraltar and it was there that Senior Technical Officer Spam

Hammersley finally left, six years after he had originally joined the programme. Together with John Grove, who had had already departed, he had borne the overall responsibility for the navy's first operational nuclear plant and its complex protection systems. His personal contribution had been immense and it was no surprise that Fieldhouse decided to give him an impressive send off. Rather the worse for wear after a leaving party that had ended up in the Senior Ratings mess, Spam was put ashore at the end of the outer mole immediately prior to *Dreadnought*'s departure. From this vantage point he watched the boat slip and proceed sedately out of harbour. But instead of turning to port and heading out into the Straits of Gibraltar, she increased speed to arc in a wide circle around adjacent Algeciras Bay. Minutes later she was 'on the step' at 20 knots; flashing closely past where he stood in a final farewell gesture. Uniquely, because of her hull shape, it was possible to increase *Dreadnought*'s surface speed from 17 to 20 knots by causing her to hydroplane, the condition known as 'on the step'. This was achieved by partially flooding the after ballast tanks, adjusting the control surfaces and allowing the stern to sink, thereby giving the boat the characteristics of a semi-submerged submarine. When fully submerged at depth, the maximum speed was over 28 knots, and of course this could be maintained indefinitely.

At the end of 1964 *Dreadnought* sailed to Rosyth for a routine period of maintenance and docking. Emerging in late February, she returned to her base at Faslane where she was part of the Third Submarine Squadron. In accordance with usual practice, she was programmed to undergo a routine Captain SM's inspection. Brian Hutchings, who was soon to leave the Navy to pursue a career in industry, was Captain SM's deputy at the time, responsible for making the necessary arrangements. He recalls the unusual circumstances in which the inspecting officers went off to sea knowing very little about the capabilities and limitations of the boat they were inspecting. It became a matter of looking on in admiration as *Dreadnought* strutted her stuff with a series of high speed 'angles and dangles'. He was particularly impressed by the way in which everyone quietly got on with their jobs with a total lack of fuss or excitement. Hutchings, himself something of a high flyer who had been the first Porpoise class Commanding Officer, rates Fieldhouse as the most outstanding submarine CO of his generation. Interestingly he places Sandy Woodward second in line behind him. Sandy, who was five years younger than John, had been *Porpoise*'s initial First Lieutenant and was then standing by as XO of *Valiant*. Both he and John were destined to create history together later.

In May, *Dreadnought* made a short visit to Southampton where a berth had been specially cleared for nuclear use. This was very important to John because of the many members of the ship's company who had families and friends living in the south of England. But being in harbour never meant it was possible to give the crew unrestricted leave. A heavy workload and burden of responsibility always fell upon the nuclear plant watchkeepers who were required to remain at their posts whenever the reactor was critical. It was only possible to shut down the reactor when totally dependable shore electrical supplies were available, and this could normally only be done within the strict discipline of dockyard ports or naval bases. Despite the obvious benefits to crew morale, there was an added public relations benefit in opening up new ports for nuclear visits.

From Southampton, *Dreadnought* proceeded to Gibraltar to prepare for another important operational evaluation. Some of those most concerned with the navy's tactical development saw the SSN as an integral part of the surface fleet. In war, an aircraft carrier task group needed the best possible protection from an enemy's submarine threat. In a fast moving force, the chances of escorting destroyers or frigates gaining early contact by hull mounted or variable depth active sonar were close to negligible. A useful new dimension was the introduction of helicopters fitted with retractable 'dunking' sonar. At least this device produced detection opportunities in undisturbed water beneath the surface 'layer' in which sound waves often became distorted. But its effectiveness was limited by the number of aircraft available and the relationship between static 'dip' time and speed of advance. The answer to a maiden's prayer, it seemed, lay in the SSN, with its massively capable active sonar in the 'direct support' role.

This tactic, though noble in concept, was flawed in its underlying principles. The SSN was a capital ship in its own right, capable of operating independently for weeks on end and projecting power and influence at short notice anywhere in the world. The submarine lobby likened this role to asking a General to polish his Batman's shoes. Despite the enhanced range of detection, it was felt that blasting away on the very distinctive Type 2001 sonar would serve as a beacon to attract enemy submarines rather than to deter them. An added complication was that a fully integrated SSN needed a frigate permanently allocated as a 'link-ship', both to relay contact information and to prevent mutual interference. However tight the procedures, there was always a chance that one's own priceless submarine would be attacked by friendly forces in the heat of any action. In order to obtain a balanced judgement, 'linked' procedures had to be thoroughly tested, and John did everything in his power to give them a fair trial. After this valuable spadework, the role continued to be practiced for some years, but the full potential of the newer, quieter SSNs was to be realised in a purely passive role.

The programme was interrupted by a short break at anchor in Palmas Bay in Southern Sardinia in early June. Later that month the crew much enjoyed a five-day visit to Malta. On return to home waters in July 1965, another milestone was passed when the Dutch authorities agreed to a port visit to

Rotterdam. Authorisation was received very late, but in the event the Embassy reported that 'the visit went very well and created an excellent impression, there being no sign of any public demonstration or protest.' It was there that Dick Heaslip relieved Barry Wallace as XO. Himself newly selected for promotion to commander, Barry had seen service under both of *Dreadnought*'s first COs. With Samborne there had been underlying tensions, often requiring the XO to adopt a conciliatory role. With Fieldhouse, there was a happier atmosphere with the whole crew working together as a cohesive unit.

A highlight of John's period in command was that summer's Clyde Fleet Review. An impressive array of warships was anchored off the Tail of the Bank near Greenock, with Britain's first nuclear submarine taking pride of place at the head of the line. The Queen had launched *Dreadnought* in 1960 and this was an opportunity for Her Majesty to come on board and meet the crew for the first time. There were so many VIPs in the Royal party that they had to be split up into two equal groups to be escorted round. A separate tour was arranged later for teenagers Prince Charles and Princess Anne. That evening commanding officers were bidden to dine in the Royal Yacht *Britannia*. Heaslip is not the only person to recall that Fieldhouse was an officer not exactly noted for the smartness and crispness of his uniform. A considerable effort was made to brush him down and get him over to the Yacht in good order for this special occasion. On his return a few hours later, his first reaction was to ask for a plate of sandwiches. 'I'm absolutely starving', he exclaimed. 'They kept whipping my plate away before I had hardly started!'

A dark shadow was to descend over Fieldhouse's last few months in *Dreadnought*, but it was certainly not one of his making. In August 1966 the boat entered Rosyth Dockyard for a detailed examination of some hairline cracks that had appeared in the welds on her pressure hull. Thus began a period of great concern and uncertainty because of the implications of this defect on the whole nuclear submarine programme. *Valiant* had entered service the previous month, with *Warspite* shortly to follow. The first of the four Polaris submarines, *Resolution*, was already in an advanced stage of construction. During the long period of tests and repairs in dry dock the CO kept closely in touch with the ship's company's morale, but the boat's day-to-day administration was best left in the capable hands of the XO and other heads of departments.

Two highly productive extra tasks helped him to pass the time. He was called to the personnel department of the MoD to advise on the manning and training policy for future classes of submarine. Unlike the double manned Polaris concept, the heavy demand on the nuclear attack boats (SSNs) placed a great strain on the overworked single ship's company. To provide a second crew was rightly considered to be too manpower intensive. The study led to the provision of the SSN 5th Watch, the principle of which was to use all hands during harbour maintenance, allowing one watch to be rested during periods at sea.

He also spent a month writing a tactical manual, some of which remains unaltered to this day. For many years the submariners' 'bible' had been a highly classified document known as *The Conduct of Submarine Operations*. Not unnaturally, its contents applied solely to the long established diesel-electric boats (SSKs). Guidance was now needed for SSNs, which had come to be referred to rather grandly as Fleet Submarines. As the only CO around with the necessary experience, John was summoned to *Dolphin* to take on this task, and *The Conduct of Fleet Submarine Operations* was duly born. With the family ensconced at 'Pippins', this gave John good opportunity to spend more time down south. For some time Midge had been imploring him to give up smoking. Cancer scares were starting to circulate and she was particularly concerned about the adverse effect on their young children. It was on one of many journeys over the Forth Rail Bridge to return home that he finally decided to make a clean break with a lifetime's habit. His parents had given him a golden cigarette case and lighter for a twenty-first birthday present. In an expansive and impulsive gesture, he opened the train window and ceremoniously committed them to the deep.

As *Dreadnought*'s repairs neared completion in April 1966, it was time for Fieldhouse to hand over to a new commanding officer. It had not been in his best interests to spend over seventeen years without break in a submarine environment. Up until then he had served in four boats in a subordinate role and had held four commands. Dotted about in between had been various periods of training and staff appointments. For someone whose card had already been marked for the higher ranks, he needed to be given a much wider range of experience and responsibility. When the opportunity came, he was to grasp it without blinking.

* * * * * * * *

Even then, the broadening of John's horizons started in a rather surprising way. In June 1966 he flew to Halifax, Nova Scotia, to attend the Canadian Advanced Maritime Warfare Tactical Course. It had been explained to him that this was part of a larger plot to give him a plum appointment in general service – Executive Officer of an operational fixed-wing aircraft carrier. This job would not become available until the spring of 1967, so, in another time-filler that was of much more use to him, Fieldhouse joined the Joint Services Staff College (JSCC) at Latimer in Buckinghamshire on 5th September. Here three dozen or so middle ranking officers, with a smattering of United States and Old Commonwealth counterparts, gathered together to study staff work in a tri-Service setting. Some New Commonwealth officers also attended all but the higher classified part of the course. Indeed, Colonel

Juxon-Smith of Sierra Leone departed suddenly to become President of his country in a military *coup d'etat*.

Because of the generous weekends, most of the naval students, being homeowners, chose to spend the working week in Latimer's country house atmosphere. John was no exception and used a car-share system to travel to and from 'Pippins' with friends. Like others, he soon discovered that the competitive atmosphere tended to put those in dark blue uniform at a disadvantage. Without exception, the JSSC was their introduction to formal staff training, whereas other officers had already passed through their demanding single service Staff Colleges that were seen as prerequisite to command and promotion. Where the navy gained was that many of them had experienced command already, none more so than John with his track record in Britain's first nuclear submarine.

Fellow student Blake Parker, who later returned to Latimer as the senior naval member of the directing staff, felt that 'John made an immediate impression on his peers. He was a charming and confident man and was a credit to the naval presence on the course.' This was one of many periods of deep controversy between the services. In the face of escalating costs and bitter infighting in Whitehall, the Navy had recently lost its future fixed-wing aircraft carrier building programme. Likewise the RAF had lost the sophisticated TSR2 aircraft thought likely to fulfil the same role when deployed from 'island' bases. The Army sat comfortably on the fence, content with the case for a strong continental strategy at the lower end of the scale of NATO's deterrence. A bright light on the Royal Navy's horizon was the imminence of its takeover from the Royal Air Force of the nuclear deterrent, but at what cost to its other aspirations?

The course advanced through a series of lectures and syndicate studies, culminating in showcase visits hosted by individual services. The highlight was a visit to the army training ground at Hohne in West Germany where members were accommodated in an imposing castle. It was an important time for making contacts across the Services divide, for this was a cross section of officers who, in their turn, would be pitted against each other in tomorrow's confrontations, both in the MoD and elsewhere. Parker tells of how Fieldhouse totally defused a difficult discussion with a throwaway comment causing paroxysms of laughter. 'Can anyone tell me why Army officers all wear different coloured socks?'

It is interesting that slowly, yet perceptibly, John was beginning to stamp his authority upon a wider audience. For the first time, his name was being mentioned in circles far removed from the submarine service that had dominated the whole of the early part of his working life.

CHAPTER SIX

Career Lift Off

1967 – 1968

FIELDHOUSE FLEW TO MALTA to join HMS *Hermes* at the end of March 1967. The XO of a fleet carrier was a big job by any standards, so much so that the responsibilities were later to be divided between two Commanders in the somewhat larger HMS *Ark Royal* and HMS *Eagle*. With the air group embarked, this ship was an overcrowded home for over 2,000 men. As second-in-command, the XO was responsible for general administration, cleanliness, discipline, welfare and morale. He was also head of the seaman department and President of the wardroom mess. The overriding aim of all on board was to be at all times ready to operate aircraft. These consisted of squadrons of Buccaneer and Sea Vixen fast jets and a flight of turbo-prop Gannets in the airborne early warning role. There were also the helicopters needed for plane guard and general communications duties. Although recently fully modernised, *Hermes* was working at the edge of her capabilities, being only just large enough to handle her modern inventory of jet aircraft within acceptable safety limits. An environmental and work ethic more different from the submarine world was very difficult to imagine.

It was John Fieldhouse's good fortune to be serving under Captain Terry Lewin. Already singled out for promotion to Flag rank, Lewin was an officer of exceptional charisma and professional standing. A priceless bond of friendship and mutual respect was formed during their busy six months together, made more important in the light of subsequent events. Much of the detail of this period had been expertly chronicled in Richard Hill's authorised biography *Lewin of Greenwich*. Having been in touch with several officers and men in the ship's company whilst researching for this book, Hill made this observation:

> You do not get sailors referring to their ship as 'Happy Hermes' without good reason. That phrase occurred several times in correspondence. Even more telling was the expression 'dream team' applied to the Lewin – Fieldhouse combination.

Following an extensive refit and workup in home waters, *Hermes* had left the UK in January for a nine months overseas deployment; the first four in the Mediterranean and the next five East of Suez. This was the maximum period of peacetime family separation permitted under new Admiralty Board guidelines. It was a happy coincidence that John's appearance on board marked a decided up turn in the ship's fortunes. Since arriving in the Mediterranean, there had been a number of serious flying accidents involving the loss of three aircrew, two Sea Vixen aircraft and one helicopter. A further Sea Vixen had been damaged in a flight deck parking incident. These disasters had undermined the confidence of the air group, and it had needed all Lewin's leadership skills to restore equilibrium. In the aftermath of this process, the ship sailed for NATO exercise 'Dawn Clear' involving major USN participation. The arduous flying programme went well and, although no one could have foreseen it at the time, there were to be no more serious accidents for the remainder of the commission.

Meanwhile Fieldhouse launched himself into his imposing new round of responsibilities. Manpower intensive seamanship evolutions were entirely outside his experience, and his first efforts at taking personal charge of the arrangements on deck for refuelling at sea from a tanker fell far short of acceptable operational standards. In later life he mentioned to a friend that he had sat in his cabin that evening with his head in his hands, wondering how he was ever going to be able to cope. 'Suddenly the penny dropped', he said. 'I realised that it was my job to stand a little further back while highly competent lieutenant commanders demonstrated their talents.'

An already accomplished delegator, he lost little time in gaining the confidence of his Captain and of willing colleagues and subordinates. Little escaped his eagle eye and his quiet style of leadership permeated throughout all ranks, rates and departments. A major asset, which was never to leave him, was his natural flair for casual conversation. In the course of a working day he would stop and chat to scores of individuals. Anyone he spoke to was left in no doubt about their importance to the whole *Hermes* family. A seemingly kindly exterior was tempered by a rock hard centre. There was never any doubt that those failing to measure up to the standards he required would be severely censured. He ran the wardroom mess with quiet but unquestionable authority. In the event of unseemly conduct by young aircrew officers, for instance, everybody knew that the squadron CO would be sent for and invited to take his own appropriate action. Discipline remained taut during his period as Commander, but, due to excellent morale, the punishment return was well down on normal 'big ship' expectations.

1967 was proving to be a troubled year for a variety of reasons. The day *Hermes* left Phaleron Bay after a visit to Athens, the 'Colonels' seized control of the Greek government. The ship was ordered to stand by at 24 hours notice for the possible evacuation of British nationals. Two weeks were spent continuing with flying training in the vicinity of Cyprus, where the RAF had excellent diversion airfield facilities at Akrotiri. When the *coup d'etat* proved to be bloodless, *Hermes* was released to continue her planned deployment to the Far East. On 3rd May John made his fourth transit of the Suez Canal, the other three dating from 1945 when he was a midshipman. Richard Hill paints a gloomy picture of the local political situation in Lewin's biography.

> The area into which *Hermes* was steaming was, in fact, more volatile than either the eastern Mediterranean or the Far East. All around the Red Sea and Arabian Peninsula, political, military and propaganda machines were stirring. In Egypt, the regime of President Nasser was strongly anti-western, naturally anti-Israeli and in rivalry with Saudi Arabia. In the Gulf of Aqaba, four regimes – Egyptian, Israeli, Jordanian and Saudi – jostled uneasily, as indeed they had fifteen years before ... and in the Aden Colony and Protectorate, at the southern end of the Red Sea, the forthcoming British withdrawal, announced as taking place sometime in 1968, had led to violent jockeying for position amongst rival contenders for power.

All these developments had to be seen in the context of super power political manoeuvring in the on-going Cold War.

Hermes arrived in Aden on 6th May where Lewin was fully briefed on the ship's politico-military role. Together with HMS *Victorious*, shortly to leave for home, an opportunity was taken to support the RAF in a series of exercises and operations ashore. While in the area, the ship came under the control of two senior officers of rapidly growing stature. Admiral Sir Michael Le Fanu, as Commander-in-Chief Middle East, had his headquarters ashore as the tri-service commander. Rear Admiral Edward Ashmore, as Second-in-Command Far East Fleet, directed the naval forces and was to use *Hermes* as his Flagship on several occasions during the carrier's eastern deployment. Together with Lewin and Fieldhouse, all four would become First Sea Lord and would serve successively at the axis of naval power for the next two decades. Indeed all would go on to be selected for or serve as Chief of the Defence Staff in varying circumstances.

After an abortive operational commitment 220 miles northeast at Mikalla, the carrier was detached on 19th May to undertake a period of self-maintenance in the tranquillity of the Maldive Island anchorage at Gan. On 28th May, when the political situation in the Gulf of Aqaba had deteriorated rapidly into the threat of an Arab-Israeli War, she was ordered to return to Aden at best speed. Predictably this uncertain situation had caused a knock on effect of anti-Western feeling throughout the Arab World, but considerable pains were taken to demonstrate Britain's resolve to stand back from any sort of military intervention in the conflict. On 5th June the Israelis carried out pre-emptive strikes against Egyptian, Jordanian and Syrian air bases, triggering the Six Day War.

Within days local tension at Aden had eased and *Hermes* was released to continue her passage to Singapore. On 13th June she replenished at sea from RFA *Reliant*, an evolution that highlighted the enormous needs of 2,000 men for food, drink and stores. In moderately severe monsoon weather, 376 heavy loads were embarked in nine hours using two heavy jackstays. There were ironic cheers when some barrels of beer fell into the water from a badly loaded container. Having despatched her air group ashore, she secured alongside in the Singapore naval base on 22nd June for a well-earned maintenance period. All night leave was given to the ship's company for the first time since Athens over two months before, and the crew streamed ashore to sample the delights of the much admired Tiger Beer, brewed locally. Throughout the period at sea Fieldhouse had been a central figure in the many activities organised to foster team spirit and uphold morale. While flying training continued in bursts of high intensity, there were many opportunities for flight deck sports and impromptu concert parties. An excellent ship's newspaper, the *Hermes Herald*, kept all amused and well informed.

Charter flights at reasonable cost had been organised to bring some of the families out to Singapore. Mark was then nearly twelve and doing well as a boarder at Cumnor House Preparatory School. Able to offload the younger girls on her parents-in-law, Midge joined John for a very welcome three weeks break. They stayed in some luxury with old submarine friends Bob and Joy Garson, who had a large and well-staffed house near the Changi Memorial, off the Bukit Timah Road. Several years senior to John in age, Bob was then serving in the military intelligence command ashore. On 30th June, while both couples were relaxing at home, a call came through with the news that John had been selected for promotion to Captain. John himself was outdoors, idly chipping a golf ball around the garden. When Bob shouted the news and asked him to come to the phone, there was an instinctive reaction; 'Don't be ridiculous. I'm not even in the promotion zone!'

The fact of the matter was that he had been selected at the first attempt, and would have served the minimum time possible as a commander when his promotion became effective in six months time. This news gave good cause for celebration, neatly made possible by the occasion of the shore base HMS *Terror's* summer ball that very night. An interesting point about this promotion was that it arose solely from submarine service recommendations. John had not been in his current post long enough for a report from Lewin to have filtered through.

All good things had to come to an end and *Hermes* sailed from Singapore on 17th July. Once clear of land, the air group was re-embarked after its weeks ashore at the RAF base at Changi. Rear Admiral Edward Ashmore and his Staff rejoined for an extended period of exercises off the US naval base at Subic Bay in the Philippines before the ship proceeded to Hong

Kong. True to form, the commission continued with plenty of variety. On the first evening there was a reception on board for 250 guests. The following day *Hermes* helicopters were deployed in support of the police and army ashore, ensuring a quick resolution of what turned out to be an isolated incident. Happily there was the opportunity for all to have a good 'run ashore'.

At about this time Lewin and Fieldhouse became aware of a problem that was likely to have a disastrous effect on the existing plans for the current commission. Recent events in the Middle East had caused the Government to bring forward the withdrawal from Aden to the end of November 1967. It had long been planned that two carriers would be required to provide air cover following the withdrawal of RAF aircraft from their base ashore. *Eagle* had already arrived on station and the second one was to be *Hermes*, but on return to eastern waters after giving home leave later in the year. With the Suez Canal closed for traffic, the new schedule would not now allow her sufficient time to return home as long planned. With commendable ingenuity, a way was seen to overcome a dilemma that would otherwise have had a devastating effect on the ship's company's morale. Approval was obtained to steam the ship home round the Cape in a non-operational state. Propulsion plants and other machinery would be shut down in succession, allowing for the completion of all planned maintenance while on passage. In this way time could be found for the air group and all hands remaining on board to be given ten days leave before it became necessary to depart from Portsmouth in time to meet the new date for the Aden withdrawal.

Before any of this could happen, there was a final surge of exercise activity with units of the Far East Fleet. *Hermes* proceeded by way of the Philippines, the Singapore areas and Sunda Strait to the Cocos Keeling Islands. Apart from the flying programme, the emphasis was on anti-submarine operations. There was one relatively minor accident when a Wessex helicopter lost power and ditched during the hours of darkness. Flotation bags kept the aircraft afloat and it was later recovered by the ship's crane in a simple but impressive display of seamanship. When Ashmore hauled down his Flag to fly to Mauritius he was able to report that:

> *Hermes* has achieved a very high standard in the operation of her aircraft and a professionalism that has been a pleasure to watch while my flag has been flown in the ship.

A courtesy visit to Fremantle proved to be a fitting climax to the current Far East tour. The Western Australian port had always been one of the most favourite of all runs ashore for the Royal Navy and this visit proved to be no exception. There were 12,000 visitors to the ship over the weekend and a dance ashore for *Hermes* and *Minerva* was graced by 1,000 female partners. Despite his own heavy social programme, Lewin himself was in excellent spirits, having recently heard confirmation of his forthcoming promotion to rear admiral. On 4th September, after a memorable six-day visit, *Hermes*' started her non-stop 11,800-mile passage home.

The pinnacle of achievement within the navigation branch was successfully to navigate and handle a fleet carrier. Rex Phillips had just taken over as Navigating Officer and recalls how he benefited from a typical Fieldhouse gesture on his first night at sea in his new job. *Hermes* was due to top up with fuel at 2.00am. As usual, the RFA tanker was acting as guide, but on this occasion she was steering a reciprocal course, causing the carrier to approach from ahead. There was a limitation on the amount of helm that could be used because of its effect on the angle of heel – always a consideration because of the enormous weight of jet aircraft, even when firmly secured on deck. Phillips' task was further complicated by having to dash backwards and forwards between the screened radar display to check his ranges and the front of the bridge where the visual picture was rapidly unfolding before his eyes. Lewin was sitting inscrutably in the captain's chair, not wishing to interfere but instantly ready to intervene. Fieldhouse was at the back of the bridge, quietly watching the situation as he awaited the start of replenishment. At this moment of high drama, Phillips caught John's eye. The trademark smile, a reassuring nod of the head and the four words 'It will be alright' did wonders for Rex's confidence. Minutes later *Hermes* was slotted in neatly alongside the tanker. From that moment onwards the new Navigating Officer never looked back.

The return passage in maintenance mode took 25 days. On arrival at Portsmouth on 2nd October, John was able to snatch a few days at home with the family in the busy turnaround period during which almost everyone received ten days leave. Meanwhile he had put his mind to absorbing some key personnel changes, not least the breaking in of Doug Parker, his new Captain. Parker was a highly experienced and decorated aviator, but unlikely to be in the same league as Lewin, his distinguished predecessor. On sailing at the beginning of November, Phillips discovered at the last moment that it would be his task, rather than the captain's, to 'con' the ship from the outset when proceeding to sea. In Spithead, the ship's company lined the flight deck to cheer ship for RMS *Queen Mary*, which was proceeding on her final voyage to a resting place in California. Once out in the Channel, the air group was re-embarked and course was set for a speedy return to the Indian Ocean. Flying exercises were conducted within range of the mid-Atlantic diversion airfield at Ascension Island. Little did Fieldhouse know that he would be visiting the island in exceptional circumstances fifteen years later.

High drama attended the arrival of *Hermes* in Mombasa on 1st December. It had been clear during the latter part of the non-stop passage that Captain Parker was far from well. As the ship approached the fairway buoy, he left the bridge and went below without explanation. When he did not return within a few minutes, Phillips became concerned. Maintaining steerage way up the channel, he telephoned Fieldhouse, who was still in his cabin aft, to report what had happened. At that moment, Parker was already in the capable hands of the Surgeon Commander who was in the process of informing John that his charge would be unable to continue. 'It's OK, Pilot,' came the reassuring directive. 'I'm on my way up to the bridge.'

With a total lack of fuss, *Hermes* berthed at head and stern buoys an hour or so later, marking the effective start of John's short period of aircraft carrier command.

Subsequent events need to be seen in the context of the wider operational situation. Two days earlier the last British troops had left Aden. Meanwhile a strong naval task force consisting of the carrier *Eagle* and the embarked Royal Marine Amphibious Group (code name 'Operation Monitor') remained in the area under the command of Rear Admiral Edward Ashmore. *Hermes* was shortly due to relieve *Eagle* as his Flagship. The choice of a new Flag Captain now briefly reared its head. Parker was out of the equation for the time being and was invalided home for urgent medical treatment. His replacement by an experienced carrier captain such as Ian McIntosh, who had recently left *Victorious*, was considered. In the event, Ashmore knew and liked Fieldhouse, and asked for him to be appointed. On 7th December he formally assumed command on promotion to Acting Captain. Luckily he was due for formal promotion in 24 days time, so had all the appropriate uniforms on board. Arrangements were already in hand for his relief, Commander Geoffrey Sayer, to join the ship. On 11th December, accompanied by the frigate HMS *Phoebe*, *Hermes* sailed north to join the Task Group.

The opportunity was taken to carry out a rare two-carrier exercise. This involved long-range strike and attack, interceptions and jamming and proved to be valuable in settling the aircrew into the operational mode they were required to assume. On 14th December Ashmore transferred his Flag and *Eagle* and *Dido* departed for Singapore for Christmas. With things generally quiet in Aden, notice was extended for the Task Force to remain within four days steaming. This enabled the Royal Marines to be landed from *Bulwark* for a few days shore training at Masirah where there were excellent flying diversion facilities. Thereafter, the ships proceeded to Khor El Kuwai at the entrance to the Persian Gulf for Christmas. A 'shamal', or severe tropical storm, rendered this carefully selected anchorage untenable, but an alternative was found further south along the Omani coast. There were no facilities ashore apart from bathing, but two days were set aside for traditional seasonal celebrations.

On Christmas morning the Padre conducted a well-orchestrated festival of lessons and carols in the hangar, but lunch itself was something of an ordeal for both Admiral and Flag Captain. Before sitting down *a-deux* in the

Admiral's cabin, each had separately been escorted around the mess decks to meet a cross-section of the ship's company. In the event, not a single word was spoken throughout the meal. Both had had several sips of naval rum and neither was prepared to risk drawing attention to their advanced state of inebriation!

On the evening of Boxing Day the Task Force sailed south in order to be within 24 hours steaming of Aden by 29th December when the end of Ramadan rendered the risk of disturbances affecting British and other western nationals appreciably greater. The new British Ambassador arrived in Aden on New Year's Eve. Having noted that the situation ashore was peaceful, he approved the return of the Task Force to Masirah, which allowed for further flying training and an opportunity for the Royal Marines to stretch their legs again ashore. On 8th January 1968, Flag Officer Aircraft Carriers, Rear Admiral Derek Empson, arrived on board with his Staff to take over as 'Operation Monitor' Task Force Commander. By 15th January the tension following the withdrawal from Aden appeared to have eased, and *Hermes* was detached to Mombasa for a period of maintenance and to give shore leave. Captain Parker met the ship on her arrival there on 19th January and reassumed command.

As he prepared to leave the ship and fly home, Fieldhouse would have been entitled to reflect that he had fully grasped an outstanding professional opportunity. His six weeks in command of a fully operational fixed-wing aircraft carrier had added an entirely new dimension to his experience. As Flag Captain he had held additional responsibilities. In his autobiography *The Battle and the Breeze* Ashmore reviews the scene from his own perspective:

> *Hermes*, as always, was a very happy ship. Time in an aircraft carrier is not particularly restful, even for the admiral. With everyone else busy day and night when flying is on, I had a guilty conscience sitting in my cabin aft, and would often go into Flying Control to learn something more about this extraordinary business of landing very heavy, vastly expensive aircraft on a small deck, mostly done by young men of 22 or 23.

He also reported favourably on Fieldhouse:

> His ship wore my flag as flagship of the Naval Task Force standing by to evacuate our people from Aden. In a semi-operational environment, with some non-diversion flying in difficult conditions to do and with the problems associated with Christmas at sea in a big ship in peacetime to contend with, this officer's qualities for command were well tested. I was impressed with his showing and the leadership and judgement he consistently displayed under heavy responsibility. He handled his ship confidently and well and in tactical command of the

> Task Force on my behalf showed a good grasp of the principles and practice of controlling a group of ships.

In barely ten months John had succeeded in shedding his 'submariner only' image. From that time forward he would be seen increasingly by those in the highest authority as an officer of outstanding all-round ability who needed to be given every possible encouragement to prepare himself for the inevitability of further promotion to higher ranks. Empson also reported on 'the first class spirit and standards that existed throughout *Hermes* and on the cheerfulness and courtesy of the ship's company.' But let a more junior officer, Phillips, have the final word.

> Like Lewin before him, Fieldhouse was a natural leader. He had a wonderful touch with people and during our time together I never once heard him raise his voice in anger. He was held in deep respect by a ship's company who would willingly have followed him anywhere.

CHAPTER SEVEN

Polaris Squadron

1968 – 1970

IT WAS A SUNDAY MORNING early in 1968, and the newly promoted Captain was enjoying his leave having recently flown home from tropical Mombasa. John and Midge felt on top of the world as they motored along the sea front at Stokes Bay on their way to St Ambrose Church in HMS *Dolphin*. John was delighted with the prospect of his new job. His reporting officers had been saying for years that he should have a Ministry of Defence appointment, and this had now happened in the most agreeable way possible. Since the recent withdrawal from Aden, Admiral Sir Michael Le Fanu had moved on to become First Sea Lord. He had been impressed by what he had seen of Fieldhouse in HMS *Hermes*, and had asked for him as his Naval Assistant, who, with his Secretary, would hold the two key posts in his private office. Midge was equally delighted, looking forward to flat hunting in London and to the prospect of being able to take in some of the capital's expanding culture.

As they passed through the main gate, there was a message for John to have a private word with Flag Officer Submarines after church. This sounded ominous, which indeed it proved to be. It was a fairly short conversation. Rear Admiral Michael Pollock, later to be First Sea Lord, was one of the rare non-submarine officers to hold the appointment. Many years earlier, as Gunnery Officer of HMS *Norfolk*, he had achieved the rare distinction of shooting a barrel off one of his own eight-inch guns! During his few weeks in office he had decided that the Polaris force needed new dynamic leadership. There was to be no choice in the matter. Fieldhouse was to prepare himself to go to the Clyde and take over as Captain SM Tenth Submarine Squadron. Midge recalls disgracing herself by bursting into tears in the car beside him as they drove away.

Much has been written about the bringing to fruition of the Polaris programme. It was, quite literally, the largest British peacetime defence contract ever known, completed within the forecast time and budget. An independent management structure with sweeping powers had been set up following the December 1962 Nassau agreement. The then FOSM, Rear Admiral Rufus Mackenzie, had been appointed as Chief Polaris Executive and had put the wheels in motion for a frantic period of research, design, development, shipbuilding and shore construction. The boat chosen for the task was essentially a dissected Valiant class SSN with a centre section consisting of the sixteen-tube A3 Polaris weapon system then being fitted into the latest batch of United States submarines. Under the terms of the agreement, the UK would be entirely responsible for providing its own missile warheads. There were also formidable personnel problems to be overcome, both in the selection and training of the multiple submarine crews, and of the additional people needed for the many support facilities ashore.

The first of class, HMS *Resolution*, had been laid down in February 1964, launched in September 1966 and accepted into service in October 1967. *Repulse*, *Renown* and *Revenge* were following along closely behind her. At the time of the Pollock/Fieldhouse conversation there were more dates looming critically on the horizon. Following a general workup period for both crews, *Resolution* was currently in the USA preparing for her missile test firings, known as the Demonstration and Shakedown Operation (DASO). In a few months time, in June 1968, she was due to deploy on her first deterrent patrol. In July 1969, by which time *Repulse* would be in the patrol cycle, the Royal Navy was due to accept responsibility from the RAF for deploying the nation's independent strategic nuclear deterrent. *Revenge*, the last of the four SSBNs, would enter service in December 1969 and deploy in 1970.

Until then, John had had no direct connection with the Polaris programme. Now he was to become deeply involved at a time of great importance. The two shipbuilders, Vickers at Barrow-in-Furness, and Cammell Lairds at Birkenhead had already largely fulfilled their part of the bargain. A magnificent new base named HMS *Neptune* stood at Faslane on the east bank of the Gareloch, with its deepwater berths, engineering and other support services, Polaris school, floating dock and accommodation facilities. It had been built on a grand scale, not only as a home for the Tenth Submarine Squadron SSBNs, but also for Third Squadron SSNs and SSKs. Over the hill on the eastern shore of Loch Long was the Armament Depot at Coulport, with its own berth for loading and off-loading the 32-foot long missiles. Towards the entrance of the Gareloch and around Helensburgh had grown vast estates of married quarters and a school in which to absorb the rapid influx of young families to the area.

This package of Herculean proportions had been achieved by teamwork involving many different agencies. It was now the duty of the submarine service to deliver and maintain a fully credible independent nuclear deterrent at sea. This task was to become more complex due to imminent changes in the maritime balance of power of the Cold War. The Soviet Navy was in the process of introducing into service new classes of highly sophisticated nuclear submarines, both SSBNs for its own deterrent purposes and SSNs to counter Western deterrent deployments.

In order to keep the Polaris force at sea for as long as possible, each boat was to have two entirely separate crews, known as Port and Starboard. In terms of cost and shore time, the 1,200 officers and men of the new Tenth Submarine Squadron was the most highly trained group of people the RN had ever known. It was also the least experienced in terms of sea time in the vehicle it was required to man. Only a handful of individuals had seen previous service in *Dreadnought* or *Valiant*. Although the COs and XOs had commanded diesel-electric submarines, the steep learning curve started at the top and permeated through every rank, rate and specialisation. Nearly all the men of the Polaris weapon system departments, for instance, had been recruited direct from general service and were about to enter a submarine of any sort for the first time. The two crews of *Resolution*, at that time the only runner, had passed through acceptance trials and workup, and had reached the DASO stage largely through their own ingenuity and with little supervision. A Squadron CO had been appointed in 1967, but he had neither the experience nor the robust health needed to create the desired impact on the rapidly expanding programme. The clarion call for Fieldhouse arose from the perception that the best man available was now required to provide the necessary impetus to weld the squadron into a cohesive whole. On 1st April 1968 John became the first ever Captain SM to have commanded a nuclear submarine. Although he would be expected to 'ride' his boats for short periods as often as he wished, his command would be exercised from an office in the Clyde Submarine Base ashore.

Meanwhile, Midge was enduring a typical dose of naval domestic upheaval. 'Pippins' was prepared for letting as the family packed up to move north. The new house being built for them on base was still a building site, so the Fieldhouses moved into No 1, Bannachra Drive; the best of a group of older quarters in nearby Helensburgh. Mark was now nearly thirteen and Head Boy at his prep school, but Amanda and Sarah, at nine and five, would be accompanying their parents to Scotland to attend a local day school. This was to be Midge's first experience of supervising John's new entitlement to a retinue of staff in the home. Things were a bit cramped for a cook and steward at first, but became better when they were able to move into the official Captain's House, which had the appropriate accommodation.

Wearing his SM10 hat, John was directly responsible to FOSM at Gosport for the general administration and training of the submarines and their crews, their preparedness for what amounted to a state of war, and for the Polaris School within the Faslane Base complex. Once the boats were actually deployed on nuclear deterrent patrol, they came under the command and control of C-in-C Western Fleet at Northwood, Middlesex. Britain's main fleet was organised into a number of task forces, and the C-in-C exercised this ultimate responsibility on behalf of the Government from a cell deep inside his underground headquarters in his capacity as Commander

Task Force 345. The small CTF 345 team, headed by a submariner commander, controlled the continuous low frequency broadcast which boats were required to read at all times in order to be instantly ready to receive the firing signal. Through this network flowed intelligence reports, instructions needed to ensure evasion and to avoid mutual interference, dummy firing signals to test the weapon system, targeting changes, weather reports, news bulletins and, on Saturdays, the weekly football results. Not least were the regular short messages or 'familygrams' for each crewmember from his next of kin. These were censored in the 'off crew' office so that bad news could be filtered out if that was the recipient's wishes. The most frequent subject for mention in these 'one way' missives was the state of the family car!

In his second hat, as Queen's Harbourmaster, Clyde Dockyard Ports, John reported to the Commodore Clyde, the overall Base Commander. To enable the navy to exercise jurisdiction over waters of such importance, the Gareloch, Loch Long and the Holy Loch, where the US Polaris squadron was based, had been designated by Act of Parliament as a 'Queen's Harbour'. It was an area bounded by 60 miles of coastline in which it was necessary for safety purposes to coordinate the movements of shipping, in particular nuclear submarines. Effectively, this duty was discharged on a day-to-day basis by John's able deputy. A useful perk of his office was a fast motor boat which could be used for visiting such places as the USN base in the Holy Loch, or for the occasional off duty family picnic, Scottish weather permitting.

Squadron duties took up almost all of John's time and energy. It was inevitable that the COs of the Polaris boats were largely his contemporaries. Mike Henry, of *Resolution* (Port), had been a term behind him at Dartmouth, on the same Perisher, and had beaten him to promotion to commander. This had caused a certain atmosphere in informed submarine circles that had been laid to rest by John's early promotion to captain. Yet it was Mike's strong and ambitious personality that had created the waves that had led indirectly to John's appointment. As the first CO to be selected for the programme, Mike had thrown himself wholeheartedly into his important mission, but possibly with a higher degree of egotism than some of his superiors felt to be appropriate. Despite some excellent and necessary cooperation at many levels, particularly between XOs, Dick Husk (Port) and Francis Ponsonby (Starboard), disharmony had grown between his and Ken Frewer's starboard crew. In *The Impact of Polaris*, published in 1999 and edited by Captain John Moore, Henry wrote this about *Resolution*'s crews:

> Individually we were long time friends; collectively we just did not get on, and I am ashamed to say that we, the Captains, were not innocent of this discord. I believe and hope that it did not extend to the crews of the other three submarines.

This serves as a generous admission of a personal failing that had thrown something of a shadow over those early, exciting and intensely busy times. One of the root causes of the problem was Mike's insistence and contrivance that the port crew should do everything first, thereby engendering an aura of superiority. Perhaps Ken, another fine but less demonstrative officer who held equally strong but differing views on various subjects, should have insisted on the starboard crew leading on some of the major milestones. Following on behind, and watching the situation with interest, were the older and wiser COs of *Repulse*, Phil Wadman and John's term mate, Tony Whetstone. Benefiting from this experience, they worked carefully on the inter-crew relationship and had no intention of falling into the same trap. In *Repulse*, *Renown* and *Revenge*, the port crew were first to sea and conducted the contractor's sea trials. The starboard crew then became the first to workup, for DASO and to deploy on deterrent patrol. As can be imagined, John played an important part in smoothing over these troubled waters. Under his quiet yet forceful leadership, a feeling of great togetherness and mutual dependence developed between all Polaris crews. Whatever the nature of their early glitches, the two crews of *Resolution* were the pioneers who made a decisive contribution to the eventual success of the whole programme.

In June 1968, shortly after her arrival in Scotland, Midge admits to having put up something of a black mark. Also writing in *The Impact of Polaris*, she recalls joining a group of wives to wave *Resolution* off on her first patrol.

> One young wife was in tears, and I tried to comfort her, saying, 'It won't seem too long. You'll see the time will pass very quickly.' 'Oh, that's fine for you isn't it?' she said sharply. 'Your husband will be home every night for his whisky and soda and his supper. Heaven knows what mine will be doing.' I took the lesson to heart and thought very carefully before coming out with more platitudes to any of the wives.

Both John and Midge played a major part in establishing a community spirit and there were many instances of both base and 'off crew' families supporting those whose men were away at sea. For the remainder of John's career, and to the present day, Midge's own touch on the tiller of personal relationships has been exemplary, earning her the affection and respect of service families everywhere.

With his uncanny knack of cutting through quickly to the heart of any problem, John moved fast to establish a standard workup programme, to be carried out by both crews before proceeding to the USA for DASO. At that time, workups for all submarines in home waters were conducted on the Clyde by the Staff of Captain SM3 who commanded a mix of other nuclear and conventional submarines. The basis of these was to undergo a full range of safety and breakdown drills, combined with the use of aggressive tactical and attacking procedures associated with SSNs and SSKs. As *Resolution* had already discovered, SSBNs required a different operational philosophy. Theirs was a mission of endurance, patience and stealth; of avoiding contact with others rather than deliberately seeking out the heat of the action. John's protégé, Alan Kennedy, was one of the *Repulse* XOs. On his selection for promotion to commander, he had been relieved early in order give his successor as much experience as possible before deployment. On a temporary basis, he was swept into the Squadron Staff where, under John's guidance, he established and set to work a new Polaris submarine workup programme. The last six crews all benefited from this, and from John's personal conduct of their successful workup inspections.

Following the individual crew workups, Fieldhouse attended the DASOs at the United States missile range facility at Cape Kennedy. This was a period of great pressure for the Polaris weapon system departments, during which an experienced American team took each SSBN crew, both USN and RN, through a concentrated two-week period of drills and procedures culminating in a live missile firing. During this time, the submarine operated on a daily basis from the USN facility at Port Canaveral. For the firing itself, a specially prepared telemetry head replaced the warhead on a standard A3 missile. This was then fired down the Atlantic range to a 'target' near Ascension Island in the South Atlantic. Thanks to the latest computer technology, a printout of the precise accuracy of the 'shot' was available before the boat's return to harbour. Due to high quality personnel and sound training practices, British boats always achieved extremely good results at their DASOs.

The day of the firing also placed pressure on the CO, not least because of the number of VIPs embarked to witness the action. On these occasions John Fieldhouse played a major part in hosting and shepherding the guests around the submarine, allowing the CO and his officers to concentrate on the business in hand. A typical example was the missile-firing day of *Revenge* Starboard in June 1970, at the very end of John's time as squadron commander. On board were no less than seven admirals and five captains. The admirals, four British and three American, had an accumulative total of 19 stars, on the basis of four stars for an admiral, three for a vice admiral and two for a rear admiral. The home team included C-in-C Western Fleet, Admiral Sir William O'Brien, and Vice Chief of Naval Staff, Vice Admiral Sir Edward Ashmore.

The most memorable DASO of all was that of *Renown* Starboard the previous summer. This was conducted amidst scenes of the greatest excitement as astronaut Neil Armstrong and his team departed from Cape Kennedy in some style for man's first landing on the moon. Fieldhouse felt fortunate to have found himself on duty in Florida at exactly the right time to witness the blast off and to join in the widespread celebrations attending the success of this singular achievement.

A sad episode occurred soon after this when *Renown*'s starboard crew was shaking down in the outer Clyde exercise areas, preparing for the boat's first patrol. The CO, Commander Ken Mills, ordered a return to periscope depth from deep at a moment when it was later judged to have been unsafe to do so. A collision with a passing merchant ship resulted, causing superficial damage to the boat's upper works. The chances of this occurring were very small, but in slightly different circumstances there might have been a major nuclear incident. A Court Martial was convened following an immediate Board of Inquiry. In accordance with normal practice, Fieldhouse acted as prosecutor and pressed his case with some vigour. Mills was found guilty of hazarding his ship and relieved of his command, the boat sailing on patrol with a newly appointed commanding officer. John's conduct at the trial had been both professional and humanitarian. Ken recalls that, after the verdict, he demonstrated a commendable generosity of spirit by changing sides and delivering a glowing character reference. He would have been the first to admit privately that the possibility of an accident when returning to periscope depth from deep formed the substance of any submarine CO's worst recurring nightmares.

A regular highlight was the return of a boat from deterrent patrol. Until it surfaced in the Clyde approaches, nothing would have been heard from it since the day it had sailed many weeks earlier. With the mail, newspapers, fresh milk and senior squadron staff, John would join by fast despatch boat off the Isle of Arran. His cheery face would be the crew's first contact with the outside world as he walked through the boat, chatting away to all and sundry. Meanwhile the off crew was at instant readiness to step on board as soon as the boat berthed, and the full resources of the base would be available to ensure a smooth and timely handover. Although none of the families knew the exact date of a boat's return, a 'bush telegraph' system spread the word around very quickly. There was always a good crowd of wives on the jetty, many of whom had even found time to visit local hairdressers!

Fieldhouse took over the squadron with *Resolution* preparing for her first patrol and the other three still in the builders' hands. By the time he left, three were in the patrol cycle, shortly to be joined by the fourth. During his stewardship, the Royal Navy assumed responsibility for the nation's independent nuclear deterrent, which was to remain credible and unbroken for the rest of his life and far beyond. His considerable personal and management skills had played a large part in all of this, and many of the procedures he initiated lived on largely unaltered until the end of the Polaris era. On 28th August 1996, some years after his death, *Repulse* returned to base after the 229th and final patrol. Prime Minister John Major was himself there to meet her. These words were included in his speech as he unveiled a plaque to commemorate the occasion:

> The years of the Polaris Force have seen some dramatic changes in our world. In 1968, when *Resolution* began her first patrol, East West tension was running very high. The Soviet Union had invaded Czechoslovakia and the Vietnam War still raged. And yet, in 1994, I was able to sign an accord with President Yeltsin agreeing no longer to target our nuclear forces at each other's territory. Today, the West enjoys a co-operative relationship with Russia unthinkable even ten years ago. But throughout those turbulent years, the Polaris force has always been there, always ready, always prepared, always the ultimate guarantee of this country's security ... As Trident takes over from Polaris, so the Vanguard class takes on the torch from *Resolution* and her sisters.

During his last twenty years of active service to Queen and country, John Fieldhouse was never far removed from the focal point of delivery of the nation's submarine launched nuclear deterrent. As a junior captain, he commanded the Polaris Squadron at the time of its formation and at the initiation of the patrol cycle. As Flag Officer Submarines, he held responsibility for its administration, manning and training. As C-in-C Fleet, he exercised full command on behalf of the Government. In his Ministry of Defence appointments he had varying degrees of interest and responsibility for the Trident replacement programme. These lofty ideals were far from John's mind as he prepared to return once more to the mainstream navy.

CHAPTER EIGHT

More Sea Time

1970 – 1973

THE CAREER PATTERNS of the younger and most highly thought of Post Captains invariably required a job ashore to be followed by one at sea, and *vice versa*. This meant that the Whitehall appointment John needed to complete his inventory would have to be further delayed. On his relief by colleague Peter Herbert at the end of June 1970, the family returned south as he started a three-month round of courses for COs about to take up sea commands. This package was centred on the tactical course at HMS *Dryad*, near Portsmouth, where he was brought fully up to date with the latest warfare practices. On 17th October he took up his appointment as Commanding Officer of HMS *Diomede*.

Diomede was the last but two of the 26 highly successful Leander class general-purpose frigates built for the Royal Navy. At that time, she was still at Yarrow's shipyard on the Upper Clyde, some months short of completion. The rider attached to John's appointment was that he would assume the additional role of Captain F 3rd Frigate Squadron when his ship was ready to join the Fleet. There is little doubt that John would have preferred to have taken over a fully running organisation, but he did not know then that a far larger prize awaited him.

Meanwhile Fieldhouse settled down to enjoy his second experience of commissioning a new warship direct from shipyard hands. Again it was domestically inconvenient because, like HMS *Walrus* ten years earlier, she was a product of the Clyde. A short unforeseen delay meant that contractors sea trials were deferred until January 1971. When this important milestone arrived, there was no Admiralty approved shipmaster available. John was delighted to be invited by the shipyard to assume command, welcoming the added responsibility and ship handling opportunities. The trials went well, but, when at anchor at Lamlash in the outer Clyde, the senior Yarrow's management decided to go ashore by boat without informing the Master. On their return, John delivered a good-natured admonition to Deputy Managing Director Bob (later Sir Robert) Easton. This was the beginning of a long and fruitful friendship. Bob recalls that

> John made it his business to understand shipbuilders. He respected people for what they were, be they the managing director or the lowest

> paid member of the work force. It was a difficult time for industrial relations and I asked him if he would mind talking to the powerful and militant union leaders. He never hesitated and was unusually successful in holding their interest and respect.

Bob later succeeded Sir Eric Yarrow as Chairman and Managing Director of the de-nationalised shipyard, and their paths were to cross again when John became Controller of the Navy. Still under the Red Ensign, *Diomede* sailed for Portsmouth on 1st April for her weapon system setting to work trials.

The commissioning ceremony was held in Portsmouth Dockyard on 21st May. It was an impressive occasion with the ship's company paraded on the jetty abreast the ship, accompanied by the Commander-in-Chief's Royal Marine band. Also there were many of the crew's families and a small number of dignitaries, including Lady Mills (wife of Vice Admiral Sir Charles) who had performed the launch in April 1969. Proceedings opened with the Captain reading his Commissioning Warrant. Little did Fieldhouse realise that a few years later he would be signing such documents himself. The stirring words he read that day are repeated here.

> The Admiralty Board on behalf of the Defence Council having directed that Her Majesty's Ship *Diomede* is to be commissioned at Portsmouth on Friday 21st May 1971, or as soon afterwards as circumstances permit, you are to proceed forthwith to commission her for General Sea Service. On commissioning, you will be under my full command. You are to bring to my immediate notice, and to the notice of the appropriate local authority, anything which gives cause for dissatisfaction with the ship or any part of her, and any other matters of importance, particularly those relating to the welfare of the Ship's Company. May God's blessing be upon the ship and company hereby entrusted to your command, and may your joint endeavours to uphold the high traditions of the Royal Navy in the service of Her Majesty The Queen be crowned with success and happiness. Given under my hand this 26th day of May 1971.
> *WD O'Brien, Admiral, Commander-in-Chief Western Fleet*

This was followed by the ceremonial hoisting of Colours and an ecumenical Order of Service. Then the Captain was piped on board for the first time, enabling him to receive the official guests for a reception on the flight deck. A buffet lunch was laid on for all those who attended.

The next hurdle was the shakedown and Basic Operational Sea Training (BOST) at Portland. In this finely tuned process under the control of the Flag Officer Sea Training, ships were put through a rigorous programme of drills, evolutions and weapon system practices; all closely monitored by a highly skilled sea riding workup staff. Everyone from the CO down was kept under constant pressure as complex breakdown and action 'damage' situations were injected into an already busy programme. Weapons Electrical Officer

Commander Anthony Wheatley, who himself later reached Flag rank, remembers the quiet confidence with which Fieldhouse coaxed his young and inexperienced team through this minefield of uncertainty. 'Just remember,' he told the ship's company, 'you can't win at Portland. You can only draw.' In the event the 'Diomedes' did rather better than that, obtaining a 'Good' assessment at their workup inspection. 'Goods' were handed out very sparingly and 90% of ships had to be content at best with a 'Satisfactory'. Of incalculable value at this time had been the support of experienced Executive Officer Roger Heptinstall. As an additional task, the ship had been charged with conduct of a management trial, aimed at reducing the complement while increasing efficiency. This placed a heavy burden on the XO and the hard worked Heads of Departments, but their collective efforts eventually led to the production of a 'bible' known as *Practical Management in Ships*.

By the time the ship arrived at her homeport, Chatham, for delayed summer leave, John knew of the navy's exciting new plans for his immediate future. He was to be relieved early in order to be available to take over command of NATO's Standing Naval Force Atlantic. It was with mixed feelings that he assumed his squadron commander's responsibilities and prepared to enjoy his final few months in *Diomede*. On 8th October she was back at Portsmouth for a thoroughly enjoyable sea day for families. From there she made a traditional return to Glasgow to welcome on board the Yarrows' work force so that they and their families could admire the results of the Yard's labours. The ship continued to Newcastle, always a popular run ashore for a ship's company containing a considerable number of 'Geordies'.

Now that Fieldhouse had honed himself and his team into a state of operational efficiency, he was given an opportunity to put his diplomatic skills to the test. For the first time since Franco's dictatorship, it had been decided that the RN should pay an operational visit to a port in mainland Spain. *Diomede*, accompanied by the submarine HMS *Sealion* arrived in the Spanish naval base El Ferrol on 22nd October for a week's programme consisting of two short periods in harbour, punctuated by a couple of days of fairly simple exercises at sea. Roger Heptinstall has clear memories of this unusual visit.

Despite the strongest warnings, conduct ashore was deplorable. It was *Diomede*'s first-ever foreign visit and it seemed that cheap booze was causing havoc amongst the younger sailors. On the first evening several fights broke out and chairs were smashed in bars. Far more worrying was that the trouble continued into the second day; despite leave restrictions and an increased Shore Patrol. Matters came to a head when the Head of Chancellery at the British Embassy telephoned from Madrid to say that a diplomatic complaint had been received from the Spanish authorities. In consultation with Fleet Headquarters at Northwood, Fieldhouse was instructed to redeem the situation as best he could. On this unhappy note, the ships sailed for the pre-planned exercises.

An explanation for this extraordinary state of affairs came to John's notice when he was in the Ministry of Defence some two years later. Apparently, an unfriendly element of the Madrid administration had sent in the Spanish equivalent of the SAS to incite lawlessness amongst British libertymen!

The joint exercises went off very well, but the success of the visit hung on the single thread of the ships' reception on return to harbour. In the event, the mayhem ashore subsided and all the top people attended *Diomede*'s final party, seeming to enjoy themselves immensely. The Spanish Admiral spoke effusively about the Royal Navy, with John making the right diplomatic noises in return. There was the usual exchange of complimentary signals when the ships sailed the following morning.

Curiously, Fieldhouse wrote rather differently about this venture in his official Report of Proceedings. Presumably this extract refers to the second visit to El Ferrol and not the first one!

> Despite the fact that the local so-called 'Barcardi Rum' could be bought for the equivalent of 60p a bottle in the local bars, the ship's companies behaved themselves with credit. The only incident ashore was the strange case of a skirt, which was reported to have been removed from somebody's car by a British sailor. This matter was resolved by the Welfare Fund paying up in full.

After a tactical exercise in extremely rough weather north of Scotland, *Diomede* returned to Chatham on 17th November for a maintenance period. Three weeks later Fieldhouse handed over his command. He must have felt a genuine degree of sadness as he rang off main engines in his own ship for the last time after six sea commands. He could draw solace from the thought that his sea-going career was far from over.

* * * * * * * *

In 1972 the Standing Naval Force Atlantic was a relatively new organisation. With the lower deck gift for absurd abbreviation, it had come to be known as 'Sniffle'. For the purposes of this narrative, SNFL will do. During the mid-1960s, the expansion of Soviet naval forces highlighted the need to practice improved tactics and procedures between the alliances various navies. Initially, ships were assembled for training periods in groups known as the Matchmaker Squadrons. This led to the formation of a permanent NATO force, a structure that has remained largely unaltered until the present day.

Four ships gathered together for the first time as SNFL at Portsmouth on 13th January 1968. The initial group of destroyers and frigates were from the Netherlands, Norway, the UK and the USA. Norway's involvement was of a temporary nature and Canada soon became the fourth 'permanent' member. The Federal Republic of West Germany also provided an almost continuous presence with a rather smaller frigate without a helicopter. The policy was for ships to rotate every six months in order to give the NATO experience to as many people as possible. Additionally, ships from other nations, such as Denmark, Norway and Portugal, would contribute in their own adjacent waters. SNFL ships were fitted with a large NATO emblem on each side of their funnel. Personnel wore a small badge on the left breast of their formal uniform. A typical annual deployment pattern consisted of about eight months in the Eastern and three months in the Western Atlantic areas. Although the squadron remained in being, it was the practise for ships to return to homeports over the Christmas and New Year holiday periods.

In full command of the force was the US Supreme Allied Commander Atlantic (SACLANT) in Norfolk, Virginia. This role was delegated to UK Commander-in-Chief East Atlantic Area (CINCEASTLANT) at Northwood, Middlesex, for the major part of the time while the squadron was operating in European waters. CINCEASTLANT, like his American NATO superior, doubled up as the national Fleet Commander. In sea command, on an annual rotational basis, was a ship-riding Commodore from the 'permanent' nations. The first Commodore had been a British officer. Three years on, it was time for the RN to have a second bite at the cherry.

There can be no surprise that John had been singled out for this appointment. With his star in the ascendancy since his days in HMS *Dreadnought* and *Hermes*, his reports as a junior captain had been predicting his promotion to Flag rank as a matter of 'almost certainty'. Here was a rare opportunity for him to combine command of an international squadron with an important insight into the mysterious ways of NATO. Fieldhouse flew to Florida where the 1972 Squadron assembly took place at Port Everglades, Fort Lauderdale. On 20th January, at an elaborate change of command ceremony, he hoisted his Broad Pennant in the Leander class frigate HMS *Jupiter*.

With his inbred deep perception, Fieldhouse was quick to 'get under the skin' of the SNFL experience. Essentially it was a public relations exercise, where the outward signs of concord and togetherness were initially more important than outright operational efficiency. He was happy to accept that the speed of the convoy was that of its slowest ship. By working and playing together for a number of months, a highly commendable all-round standard could be achieved. The inevitable competitive spirit engendered between ships should at all times be without rancour. Understandable suspicions between nations must be swept away and, above all, ship's companies must learn to laugh together as opposed to at each other. The Commodore's main tools in achieving these aims were the individual commanding officers, and he lost no time in cultivating their friendship and loyalty.

A week later the force arrived at San Juan, Puerto Rico. It was here that the Flag was transferred to *Jupiter*'s sister ship HMS *Aurora,* earlier delayed by a main engine defect before leaving her UK homeport. Having fulfilled her useful role, *Jupiter* departed. Sadly, no official report of Fieldhouse's tenure in command of SNFL has survived. Of considerable interest, however, are two other documents. One is the lucid 'Report of Proceedings' submitted by the CO of *Aurora*, Commander Guy Liardet – later himself to become an admiral. Not surprisingly this lacks any comment on the Commodore himself, but it nevertheless provides a valuable insight into the composition and activities of the squadron. Over thirty years later, Liardet has helped to fill in some of the gaps with personal memories. The other document is a splendid *Cruise Book* covering the period 1st January to 1st July. Containing many photographs, this high quality publication was produced in USS *Charles F Adams*.

The layout of compartments in *Aurora* was identical to those in *Diomede*, with the relatively spacious captain's cabin being made over for the Commodore's use. The CO moved into the navigator's cabin behind the bridge, had his breakfast there, but lunched and dined with his boss in familiar surroundings. Despite a considerable difference in age and rank, the two built up a strong and productive relationship. A rare altercation occurred on return from a social event ashore on an evening before sailing. John stood at the entrance to his cabin and invited Guy in for a nightcap. Mindful of the morrow's demands, he politely made his excuses. 'If the Captain asks you for a drink, you have a drink', said John with some authority. 'I am the Captain' replied Guy with unarguable finality!

Ships of the Leander class had not been designed to carry senior officers for any length of time or act as Flagships. A particular problem was the lack of officer's accommodation, but this had been alleviated by increasing bunk space by four berths and offloading junior officers under training. Also, some young seamen had been landed to create space for additional communications ratings. Luckily the Commodore's personal entourage was quite small. His Chief of Staff was a German commander who piled into the wardroom with all the other officers. The next two weeks were spent mostly at sea using local US weapon training facilities in and around Roosevelt Roads, Puerto Rico. Caribbean weather and tropical uniforms made life acceptable to all and John's staff celebrated his 44th birthday at Charlotte Amalie in the US Virgin Islands.

The Force contained an impressive mix of weapon system capabilities. In order of size, USS *Charles F Adams* was a modern computer assisted, missile-armed destroyer optimised for anti-air warfare. The Dutch general-purpose frigate HNLMS *Evertsen* was a Leander design variant incorporating many new features that made the 'Auroras' envious. HMCS *Skeena*, with its large Sea King helicopter, excelled in the anti-submarine role. FGS *Braunschweig* was well equipped for basic gunnery. The helicopter inventory consisted of the Canadian Sea King and the Dutch and British Wasps. *Aurora*'s main problem was that her communications department was severely tested due to the additional weight of signal traffic. Despite inferior equipment, particularly teleprinters, an inexperienced team somehow managed to muddle through. In common with others who have commanded basic Leander class frigates in NATO squadrons, Liardet reported his ship generally outclassed in the equipment needed for modern warfare. Most of these ships were later to undergo expensive mid-life refits to prepare them more effectively to handle the needs of the missile/computer age.

The squadron then sailed south to Curacao in the Netherlands Antilles. *Evertsen* led the group into Willemstadt, it being John's practice to transfer to the ship of national prominence for the entry into harbour. By this time the ships were beginning to work together well, using NATO as opposed to national procedures. Social commitments ashore helped to cement relationships at all levels. In port receptions were held in *Aurora*, *Evertsen* or *Skeena*. *Charles F Adams*, a dry ship, of course, generously provided an excellent range of canapés. The American wardroom was also an open house for officers looking for steaks and snacks after parties. Without any apparent effort on his part, Fieldhouse soon had the COs pulling together as a 'band of brothers', with loyalty spreading downwards through all levels. 'Cross decking' was practised for many activities. At Willemstadt, for instance, individual boat's crews were made up by men from different navies. Liardet reported that 'one will often hear a member of the force defending his friends of another nationality against any slights or attacks from one of his own countrymen not belonging to SNFL'.

While still in tropical waters, a trial was conducted with the chartered tanker SS *Erna Elizabeth*. She represented the type of ship that would have to taken up from trade to provide refuelling services to warships in the event of tension or war. This fully tested the ingenuity of navies not accustomed to replenishing at sea by the astern method. After a further call at San Juan, the Force arrived at Charleston, South Carolina, on 9th March for a two week assisted maintenance period. Here, individual ships were responsible for their own arrangements and *Aurora* benefited from the efforts of the Chatham based mobile Fleet Maintenance Unit. The next port of call was Halifax, Nova Scotia, first known to John as a junior submarine officer in 1950. Undeterred by heavy snow, the Canadians laid on a predictably heavy social programme. A week there was followed by a visit from 6th to 10th April to the vast naval base at Norfolk, Virginia to celebrate the 20th anniversary of the setting up of the NATO Atlantic Command. The cruise book contains a delightful photograph of the commodore being welcomed by 'Miss Norfolk' and 'Miss Hospitality'. Not unnaturally, the NATO squadron took centre stage for this formal occasion attended by a formidable range of dignitaries. Liardet was full of admiration for Fieldhouse's impressive stamina in coping with a seemingly endless programme of official and social events.

With the Western Atlantic leg of the deployment now complete, the Force made a nine-day working ocean passage to Lisbon. There they prepared for exercise 'Night Search' in company with the Portuguese frigate *Almirante Pereira da Silva*. For the more sophisticated structured exercises with national navies, the squadron was used either in its normal Blue role – as NATO forces – or in the Red role to represent Soviet opposition. At intervals throughout the deployment, submarines, maritime patrol aircraft and replenishment ships were made available for training or support purposes.

In early May, SNFL entered the Mediterranean for the first time in its history, but without calling at Gibraltar. This move was inspired by increased activities in those waters by Soviet maritime forces, including the guided missile equipped helicopter carrier *Leningrad*. As *Skeena* and *Almirante Periera da Silva* went their separate ways, the squadron was joined by the Turkish *Izmir* and Greek *Themistocles*. 'We must try and prevent them from shooting at each other' observed Chief of Staff Commander 'Fred' Lacher with typical dry German humour.

A port visit to Izmir itself was followed by one to Piraeus, last seen by Fieldhouse when in HMS *Hermes*. The *Cruise Book* contains photographs of groups of sailors touring the Acropolis, although inevitably many more man-hours were spent in downtown bars. With typical generosity John found time to entertain Ken and Jane Mills on board for dinner. After his misfortune in HMS *Renown*, Ken was enjoying a shore appointment in Athens. The next treat awaiting the Squadron was a passage of the man-made Corinth Canal. Three miles long, 75 feet wide and with steep walls rising in several places to 200 feet, it provided a unique and impressive experience. On arrival at Naples on 19th May, the Italian Ship *Alpino* was in company. Yet more culture and bars beckoned, together with the added activity associated with the presence of a major NATO headquarters. A short loop to the north to visit La Spezia completed a hectic Mediterranean agenda.

Before entering Lisbon again for a maintenance period, *Braunschweig* took her departure. All longstanding members of the Force received the dubious honour of a high-speed sail past the column of ships remaining. This provided an occasion for much good-natured banter between ships' companies. High pressure hosing down was a common feature, as were an exchange of toilet rolls and uncomplimentary slogans. These seemingly juvenile pursuits released tension and caused much enjoyment.

After nearly six months away, it was *Aurora*'s turn to head for home waters. Following a top up at the NATO fuelling jetty at Campbeltown, the

Squadron arrived at Glasgow for the Clyde Week International Fair. Midge had travelled north for the occasion and a Pipe Band on the jetty ensured a rousing welcome. The *Cruise Book* mentions that Glasgow was a city 'where thousands turned out to visit our ships and where we found the friendliest girls of any port we visited.' Fortified by these lassies' attentions, the Force sailed to provide the opposition for the final stages of a submarine Perisher course.

Mike Henry recalls a typical example of John's thoughtfulness and personal kindness. During this busy period in Scotland, he made a brief return to Faslane where Mike was then commanding the Tenth Submarine Squadron, residing in the official quarter initially built for the Fieldhouses. In the course of conversation Mike mentioned that the hot water system seemed to have been fitted in such a way that the flow of water worked against the laws of convection. 'Oh, I know how to fix that', offered John brightly. Minutes later he clambered into the boiler house in a pair of borrowed overalls and made the necessary adjustment. In a recent interview daughter Amanda was asked about her father's DIY skills. Unhesitatingly she replied 'There was never any doubt in my mind that Daddy could fix anything!'

After a night in Rothesay Bay and completion of the Perisher running, SNFL set off for a visit to the Pool of London. Again there was a heavy social programme, including a visit from HRH Princess Margaret. By then, those ships still left from the January assembly were nearing the end of their six months tour of duty. *Aurora*'s last commitment was to an exercise run by the French and a visit to Lorient. On 21st July she left the squadron at Devonport and returned to Chatham for some much needed leave and maintenance in her homeport. During the first half of 1972 SNFL had steamed 30,000 miles, visiting 18 ports in 10 countries, taking part in three major and many minor exercises. Liardet reported on how operational efficiency had benefited considerably from the 'in company' time with ships from other nations and from the unusual challenge of assuming flagship duties.

* * * * * * * *

It is not intended to write at any length about Fieldhouse's second half year in command of SNFL. The high incidence of work and play continued very much as before. What changed were the ships, the operating areas and the people.

HMS *Norfolk* was one of the newer batch of County Class destroyers, armed with improved Sea Slug anti-air missiles, a twin 4.5-inch gun and a dunking sonar-fitted Wessex helicopter. With excellent accommodation and improved command and control facilities, these ships were far better equipped than the Leander class to act as Flagships. To avoid confusion, the

Christian name John appears sparingly in the next few paragraphs, as the ship's CO was Captain John Cox.

Fieldhouse hoisted his Broad Pennant in *Norfolk* on 21st July 1972; just four days after Cox had assumed command. It was bad programming for these two strong characters to arrive on board almost simultaneously. Cox, who had already made his name as a Commander Sea Training at Portland and whose previous appointment had been Naval Attaché in Bonn, would have preferred to have settled in and shaken down according to his own agenda. Fieldhouse needed to carry on very much as he had done before; building up confidence throughout the force; coaxing his new group of ships gently along towards an achievable NATO standard. Cox wore his heart on his sleeve and was a more naturally forceful leader, accustomed to demanding instant action and quick results. Like Fieldhouse, he was a man of compassion, warmth and humour, but he displayed these qualities in a very different style. Perhaps the two Johns were too close in age and experience to be able to enjoy a totally harmonious relationship. Predictably, their main concern was to get on with the job in hand. Cox proved to be an exceptionally effective and supportive Flag Captain. Fieldhouse was quick to recognise his qualities and it was no surprise that Cox was selected when it was next the UK's turn to provide the SNFL Commodore. For an officer coming up towards selection for a Flag, as he was, there was no more prestigious sea appointment. *Norfolk* provided facilities beyond the wildest dreams of the *Aurora* months and, in the hands of an unusually strong team, the Flagship and Squadron immediately began to run on oiled wheels. In due course Cox himself became a vice admiral. Ben Bathurst, the XO, was a future First Sea Lord and at least two other officers achieved Flag rank.

The programme continued with a succession of weapon training periods, more advanced exercises, surveillance operations and port visits with all their attendant official and social activity. As the Force settled in and headed north, an unscheduled stop was made near Trondheim. In glorious weather, the Commodore arranged a banyan in a remote rocky inlet as a bonding opportunity for his diverse international team. From there the squadron proceeded through the spectacular leads of the Lofoten Islands to Tromso, entering the Arctic Circle and the land of the midnight sun. This was to be their closest point to the Soviet Northern Fleet bases, known to Fieldhouse in his earlier submariner days. Short visits to Narvik, Trondheim again, Stavanger and Newcastle followed in quick succession. At the end of August, SNFL entered the Dutch naval port of Den Helder for a ten-day period of recreation and yet more social activity. The major NATO exercise 'Strong Express' started in mid-September, after which ships assembled in Rosyth for the post-exercise discussions. In October the squadron steamed up the River Weser to the ancient West German city of Bremen. Cox, whose own German language skills were very useful, remembers that Chief of Staff

Fred Lacher organised an excellent wine tasting and dinner there for the international 'band of brothers'. The squadron then returned to Rosyth for a welcome maintenance period.

At the beginning of November, SNFL was in Antwerp for a scheduled visit from NATO's Military Committee. This was an august group consisting of the Chiefs of Defence Staff – or equivalent – of all fifteen NATO nations, and it was imperative to put on a good show. Bathurst recalls that it had been decided to give the occasion an international flavour, starting with welcoming all these distinguished officers with a fully integrated SNFL Guard. *Norfolk*'s Chief Gunnery Instructor, nicknamed 'Chief Sitting Bull', took on the thankless yet eventually successful task of introducing sailors in six different uniforms to the mysteries of RN ceremonial arms drill. Having negotiated this hurdle, the VIP group repaired to the wardroom for luncheon. This was an elaborate affair, with each course having been prepared in a different ship. The generals and admirals were feeling quite contented by the time they had polished off the Dutch cheese and American ice cream. There was nothing the Military Committee appreciated more than a manifestation of NATO solidarity that involved themselves being made a fuss of.

This was followed by a period of Danish operations and a popular five-day visit to Copenhagen. Ships sailed from there for another exercise in the Norwegian Sea, culminating with a few days in Bergen. The annual programme was completed by participation in a Joint Maritime Course in early December. After a final visit to Rosyth, ships companies must have been more than thankful to return to their homeports for Christmas.

For Fieldhouse, the pace of events over the last year had been unrelenting. Whilst the ships themselves had joined SNFL for a maximum of six months, its embarked Commodore had been working and playing hard for a whole year without a significant break. Without achieving *Aurora*'s impressive mileage, *Norfolk* had made fifteen port visits in six different countries with a heavier load of operational commitments. Throughout this period Fieldhouse had been untiring in his efforts to inspire his disparate group towards a state of greater efficiency and to create the best possible atmosphere within the small NATO community.

* * * * * * * *

The outgoing SNFL Commodore had one more part to play. On 19th January 1973 he handed over to his Dutch successor in a change of command ceremony in Portsmouth Dockyard. Fieldhouse received the official guests including Dr Joseph Luns, the Secretary General of NATO, General J Steinhoff, Chairman of the NATO Military Committee and Admiral Sir Edward Ashmore, Commander-in-Chief Eastern Atlantic. After prayers by SNFL chaplains, the formal handover took place. As the NATO flag was transferred, the Commodore's Pennant was struck in HMS *Falmouth* and broken in HNLMS *Isaac Sweers*. Speeches were followed by a reception in the largest ship of the newly formed squadron, HMCS *Protecteur*. In excellent shape after Fieldhouse's stewardship, the SNFL bandwagon continued to roll along its way.

For John, it had been a remarkable year of both achievement and preparation for the higher commands that were to follow. He had successfully grasped a unique opportunity to exercise sea command of a group of ships; fulfilling an important Cold War role far and wide across the North Atlantic and Mediterranean, earning the admiration and respect of officers and men of many nations. His diplomatic skills, practised earlier in El Ferrol, had been displayed many more times on the international stage. Last, but not least, he had become a significant player on the NATO stage.

Young Commander

HMS *Dreadnought* 'on the step' off Gibraltar

JF receives HM The Queen at the Clyde Review

Hermes (foreground) and *Victorious* during withdrawal from Aden

Hermes salutes *Queen Mary* as she departs on her final voyage to Long Beach, California

The Polaris Squadron less one boat on patrol

The ultimate deterrent

HMS *Diomede* commissions at Portsmouth

and dips her nose into a heavy sea

Squadron Staff
celebrate the
Commodore's
Birthday

Welcome for the
Commodore at Norfol
Virginia

Aurora arrives at
Charleston,
South Carolina

HMS *Aurora* transiting the Corinth Canal in Greece

Princess Margaret visits in the Pool of London

HMS *Norfolk* , JF's second NATO Squadron flagship

A favourite family portrait of JF as an Admiral

CHAPTER NINE

Introduction to Whitehall

1973 – 1974

A NEW PATTERN had started to emerge in the structure of Fieldhouse's blossoming career. His command of the Polaris squadron had been governed by the short-term needs of the navy. It had been a simple matter of putting the best person available into an important job at a particular time. In order to do this, John had been deflected from a chance to serve in the MoD as a junior captain; and this had been further delayed by his subsequent sea postings. For some time it had become apparent to the Naval Secretary, who scrutinised officers' reports and handled their appointments, that he had a genuine 'high flyer' on his hands; someone with the ability to reach the very highest ranks of the service. His selection for command of the NATO squadron had been the first indication that John's jobs had started to be very carefully tailored to ensure that he would be given the best possible chance to prepare himself for these inevitable responsibilities. On hauling down his Commodore's Pennant he had the broadest sea command experience of any captain in the RN or any other navy. He had already been piped onboard three conventional submarines and one nuclear, a fixed-wing aircraft carrier, the leader of a frigate squadron and the Standing Naval Force Atlantic. All that was now blocking his path to further promotion was the lack of an incumbent's security pass to the MoD.

* * * * * * * *

On 19th February 1973 Fieldhouse took up his appointment as Deputy Director of Naval Warfare (DDNW), knowing that by the end of the year he would be moving up into the Director's chair. A few months earlier, a rather younger Sandy Woodward had also joined the crowded ranks of London's 4,000,000 commuters. In his book *One Hundred Days*, Woodward wrote:

> Each day I made my way to the fifth floor of the Ministry of Defence Main Building in Whitehall. Gone were the glorious vistas of the seascapes I had lived with for so long, the great Scottish lochs, the Western Isles, the open sea and the sky. Instead, if I looked out of my office window, I could gaze straight down into the spectacular granite cleavage of the massive Goddess of Fertility who guards one side of the North Door of the building.

Sandy was an assistant director in the Plans Division, whose offices at least had an outside view. John's office was down the corridor and around the corner; facing into the inner well of the building; short on natural light. He barely had time to peer around before he was confronted by his first ministry crisis.

Commander John Webster (later Vice Admiral), then serving as a subordinate desk officer, recalls that it was a rather busy morning. The Third Cod War was just about to start off Iceland and proposals for Rules of Engagement (ROE) were required to be before the Chiefs of Staff for approval that evening. Working the clock backwards, this meant that the Assistant Chiefs required a completed document by lunchtime. ROEs were the Deputy Director's responsibility, but Webster found Fieldhouse totally unflappable. After a brief discussion, the more junior officer was sent away to produce a first draft and return for a further meeting two hours later. A few minor amendments arose from the second meeting and the tight deadline was met with an absolute minimum of fuss. Fieldhouse's calmness and sound judgement left a lasting impression on Webster.

Captain Derek Reffell (later Admiral) was then a DNW Assistant Director. He welcomed John's 'refreshingly unconventional approach' to the conduct of day-to-day business. Some might think that the action man of so much sea-going activity would have found it difficult to settle into a pin stripe suited MoD environment. In fact, he took everything in his stride without any difficulty. His father had been a supremely effective Whitehall mandarin, and it was not long before it became apparent that his son had inherited many of Sir Harold's political skills. As Dick Heaslip (later Rear Admiral) put it 'He didn't only have the attributes of command at his fingertips. You could also see the ink on his hands.'

DNW took its place with the Directorate of Naval Plans (DN Plans) and the Directorate of Naval Operational Requirements (DNOR) as the three working groups forming the 'power house' of naval policy initiatives. Indeed the three Directors, all senior captains, had come to be known as the 'Three Wise Men'. Each team consisted of four or five captains and about a dozen commanders; mostly with recent sea experience and some of whom were being groomed for future stardom. These, together with some other, smaller Directorates, such as the Directorate of Naval Air Warfare (DNAW), reported to rear admirals at the Assistant Chief of Naval Staff level, either to ACNS(P) – policy, or ACNS(OR) – operational requirements. Naval aviation was a particularly 'hot potato' at that time as the RN grappled with the introduction of the Sea Harrier as the replacement fixed wing aircraft. Current operations were handled by the Directorate of Naval Operations and Trade (DNOT), reporting to ACNS(O) – operations. In their turn, these two-star admirals reported to the three-star Vice Chief of the Naval Staff (VCNS), who had a seat on the Admiralty Board. The Chief of Naval Staff

(CNS) was the four-star First Sea Lord. These various groups of officers were just some of many making up the Naval Staff in Whitehall. In support were large numbers of civil servants organised into Defence Secretariats. Similar but larger structures existed for the other services, and presiding over all were Government Ministers and the Defence Central Staff.

The nature of Fieldhouse's job can best be described by outlining the interaction between the domains of the Three Wise Men. DN Plans peered deep into the distant future, looking at strategic policy and at the size, shape and cost of the fleet needed to implement it. DNOR brought these ideas forward into realistic proposals for the procurement of ships, weapon systems and equipment. DNW looked at how best to operate ships and equipment entering service, providing a link with and feedback from the fleet on operational procedures and tactics.

DNW was a relatively new Directorate, the brainchild of Edward Ashmore, who was then nearing the end of his time as Commander-in-Chief Fleet. In his haul down report as Flag Officer Second in Command Far East Fleet, where he first met Fieldhouse in HMS *Hermes*, he expressed his disquiet about the over-specialisation of seaman officers. He recommended that there should be a radical overhaul of the system with a view to producing people with a broad warfare qualification; rather than expertise in gunnery, torpedoes and anti-submarine (TAS), communications, navigation or other disciplines. He felt that 'officers nowadays knew more and more about less and less'. A new approach was needed to react to the missile age the world was entering.

Ashmore had been best placed to initiate these changes when he left the Far East to become VCNS. Captain Lance Bell Davies had been selected as the first DNW Director, and his successor David Hepworth was in post on John's arrival as the Deputy. The fact that they were all submariners was no coincidence. Within the limitations of their chosen arm, submarines officers were trained in all warfare roles, having no axe to grind over the breaking up of the surface navy's tribalism. So these were interesting days in DNW as the Fleet adjusted to a new junior officer structure. In its simplest terms, each frigate was to have two Principal Warfare Officers (PWOs); able to work watch and watch in the operations room for extended periods; trained to react instantly to any form of threat.

The post of DDNW has been described by some as being something of a non-job. Because of the clearer cut roles of the various assistant directors, the files on anything unusual seemed to end up on this desk. As has been seen, Rules of Engagement were a particular responsibility, as were such things as Economic Zones and the International Law of the Sea. This mattered little to John Fieldhouse. He was biding his time; spreading his huge breadth of operational experience liberally around; soaking up the atmosphere and learning how things really 'clicked' in the strange recesses of the MoD. He knew that Hepworth would be leaving in a few months time and that he would be stepping up into the Director's shoes. Once he himself became one of the Three Wise Men, he would be in a position to exert influence and mould policy.

* * * * * * * *

It is time for a brief update on the Fieldhouse family situation. With Lee-on-the-Solent too far from London for daily commuting, John and Midge rented a furnished flat in Blackheath, an ideal base for use during the week. From there they returned to 'Pippins' for most weekends. In the summer of 1973, Mark was eighteen and coming to the end of his time at Marlborough. He had not had the easiest of passages through public school; but had plenty of character and entrepreneurial drive. On leaving school, it was first decided that he should become an articled clerk and train as a solicitor; but he was not destined to follow an ordered existence of that sort. Because of his restless nature, it was to be some time before he was able to settle down and direct his energies towards the type of employment that really suited him. There was genuine family relief when he went into partnership with a friend to form a motorcycle courier service. Meanwhile Amanda was fourteen and had moved on from Rookesbury Park to St Swithin's School, near Winchester. Sarah was ten and a half, and still at Rookesbury. As to be expected by anyone who knew their parents, both girls were lively and bright; with Sarah beginning to show the greater academic promise. In those days, fees at the best private schools were just about within the reach of Service families because of the navy's generous education allowance. Like many other couples in similar situations, John and Midge placed the highest priority on the quality of their children's education. In later life, both Amanda and Sarah felt that they had missed out on a large slice of family life through having been packed off to boarding schools at too early an age, but attitudes had changed by the time they were faced with the prospect of bringing up their own children.

John's father, Sir Harold, was then a well-preserved 71 years old, and he and Mabel were frequent visitors to 'Pippins'. Midge's close friend Gill Oddie remembers a conversation she had with Harold at about that time. With a mixture of pride and solid Yorkshire humour, he revealed his two remaining ambitions. One was for his elder son to be made an admiral. The other was to become involved in a juicy divorce scandal! He was to achieve the first of these sooner than anyone believed possible.

* * * * * * * *

John became the Director of Naval Warfare on 1st November 1973. A contemporary report states that he 'brought his unusually wide command experienced to bear on all the many aspects of Naval Staff business – from officers training, management and security through seamanship, exercise policy and tactical doctrine to the higher principles of maritime warfare and strategy.' Of particular interests amongst his projects was the 1974 tactical symposium on 'Passive Operational Procedures for the Fleet'. Held at the Maritime Tactical School at HMS *Dryad*, it considered some important work undertaken by the recently deployed Second Flotilla, establishing guidelines for future progress.

Had he thought about looking back, he would have had every reason to be grateful for the opportunity he had been given in HMS *Hermes* to increase the diversity and substance of his career. Six years on, his two mentors from those days had become increasingly involved in shaping his future. Terry Lewin had been a close and interested observer from his lofty perch as VCNS, before leaving to take over from Edward Ashmore as Commander-in-Chief Fleet. Meanwhile Ashmore had arrived in the MoD as First Sea Lord, where one of his early moves was to implement a policy first mooted by Admiral of the Fleet Sir Michael Le Fanu, a predecessor, to make some early promotions to rear admiral. In the normal course, captains were required to serve nine years in the rank before they were either promoted or retired. The advantage of having a limited number of younger promotions was that it increased the chances of finding someone of the right age with the necessary experience to aspire to the ultimate height of Chief of the Defence Staff. In the event, three senior captains were selected at about this time, one of whom fell short of expectations.

Matters came to a head towards the end of 1974. John had been at a routine Naval Staff briefing and had shown the temerity to disagree openly with the First Sea Lord. Shortly afterwards he was sent for and given the substantial 'rocket' that doubtless he thoroughly deserved. As he turned to leave the room, he was recalled. 'By the way, John, I have decided that you should be promoted early to Rear Admiral.'

Admiral Ashmore was not noted for the broadness of his smiles when addressing subordinates. But his expression did noticeably change at this moment of deep mutual satisfaction. John found it difficult to believe what he had just heard and when he broke the news to Midge she thought it was a leg-pull. Harold had always been immensely proud of his son's achievements, whilst giving the impression of being mildly surprised by his continuing success. Amanda remembers his reaction. 'Well lad; someone must see something in you. But I'm dammed if I know what it is!'

It was a treasured moment for celebration by family and friends.

CHAPTER TEN

The Second Flotilla

1974 – 1975

AT THE TIME OF HIS PROMOTION, Fieldhouse was two months short of his forty-seventh birthday. He was the youngest admiral in the Royal Navy, having spent seven years as opposed to the statutory nine in the rank of Captain. On 10th December 1974, he succeeded Rear Admiral Richard Clayton as Flag Officer Second Flotilla (FOF2) and hoisted his flag in Devonport Dockyard. At that time, there were about forty Seaman vice admirals and rear admirals on the active list, but only a favoured three were in sea going appointments. For purposes of sea command, administration and training, major war vessels of the surface fleet were split three ways. aircraft carriers and amphibious ships formed the Third Flotilla; cruisers, destroyers and frigates were divided equally between the First and Second Flotillas. All three admirals reported to the Commander-in-Chief Fleet at his shore headquarters at Northwood, Middlesex. The Flag Officers Flotilla (FOFs) were essentially operational commanders. Engineering, maintenance, stores and other administrative matters were handled by separate authorities in Dockyard Ports or Fleet Headquarters.

At that time the Second Flotilla consisted of the helicopter cruiser HMS *Tiger*, the guided missile destroyers HMS *Devonshire*, *Fife* and *Glamorgan*, and the Sixth, Seventh and Eighth Frigate Squadrons. The latter, each consisting of five or six ships, were led by squadron commanders or Captains F in the Leander class frigates HMS *Andromeda*, *Scylla* and *Ajax* respectively. The Admiral's brief was to fly his Flag at sea whenever ships were allocated to a task group for a particular purpose. He was also responsible for carrying out routine inspections of the ships named above and for the fighting efficiency of the whole flotilla. Irregular periods ashore were spent at Flotilla House in Devonport Dockyard.

Because of the need to be constantly on the go, the Admiral had a small and close-knit staff. Of Commander's rank were the Staff Officer Operations (SOO) and the Secretary. Four Lieutenant Commanders served as Staff Warfare Officers (SWOs) for Underwater, Anti-Air, Missiles and Gunnery, and Communications. The latter doubled up as the Flag Lieutenant. There was in addition an RAF Liaison Officer (Squadron Leader) and an Assistant Secretary (Lieutenant). On the lower deck were a number of Fleet Chief Petty Officers for duties as sea-riding warfare specialists, a Chief

Communications Yeoman with his small team of Leading Ratings, a couple of Office Writers and the Admiral's personal retinue of Cooks and Stewards. The total number of about thirty squeezed into the larger part of Flotilla House during working hours. The Admiral had a small but comfortable flat on the upper floors.

It is fortunate that his SOO was the concise and thoroughly efficient Garth de Courcy-Ireland. Shortly after John's death, at the request of an earlier potential biographer, he had assembled his thoughts on paper about their service together. In what amounted to a labour of love, he got out his old diaries and drew heavily on regular letters to his wife during long periods away from home as the Admiral's senior Staff Officer. It is a bonus indeed to be able to quote liberally from this authoritative source with its refreshing contemporary flavour. En bloc, the staff had been inherited from John's predecessor, Richard Clayton. He had been a fine master to serve, but was a confirmed bachelor with a more formal approach to personal working relationships. He was also something of a *bon viveur* who had obtained and handed over one of the best chefs in the Royal Navy. Chief Petty Officer Cook Mick Palmer had started his working life as a butcher's apprentice and was soon to learn all there was to know about meat, or indeed anything else that was served as food at table. It had been part of his regular morning routine to discuss with his Admiral the previous evening's dinner; usually down to the last grain of pepper, before deciding on the next day's menu. When he first called on Fieldhouse, he carried a pile of recipe books under his arm. He was told to go away and produce what he thought appropriate.

It is clear from the moment of Midge's arrival at Flotilla House that there were going to be some domestic changes. First, it became evident that, without sacrificing discipline, there were to be more relaxed relations with the retinue staff, including the use of Christian names on informal occasions. Next, orders went out that, when away at sea, the Admiral was to be fed sensibly, without too much rich food or second helpings. Garth recalls that he and others failed Midge miserably in this respect. A year later, the Staff gave John an exercise wheel for his birthday.

> This was a device with two handles either side of a small wheel and the idea was that, if you got on your knees and rolled the wheel backwards and forwards, the waistline would be miraculously reduced. When he unwrapped his presents somewhere in the Pacific, I sensed that we had failed again. On returning to his cabin after having been called away, the Secretary was on his knees rolling under the lash. We gave up after that!

The mid-1970s was a period of relative calm around the world for the surface fleet. Apart from a destroyer or frigate as Belize guard ship and on duty with the NATO Standing Force, there were few operational commitments. With Ministerial and NATO approval, a pattern had developed whereby FOF1 and FOF2 in turn would deploy regularly with a task group for a period up to nine months overseas. These group deployments provided an opportunity to visit many countries worldwide and to arrange exercises with other fleets and navies. There was also a subsidiary role in promoting the sales of defence equipment. In the winter of 1974/75 Vice Admiral Henry Leach was away with Task Group 317.2, made up of ships of the First Flotilla. From the moment of taking up his appointment, Fieldhouse began planning the detailed programme for TG 317.3, to be known generally as the Group Three Deployment. Exceptionally, this was to be a voyage around the world, the first undertaken by the RN for half a century. It was to be the main focus of his tenure of office as FOF2; but he was to be kept busy by plenty of other activities.

* * * * * * * *

In January 1975 John carried out his 'dunker drill' in the mining tank at HMS *Vernon* at Portsmouth. This was a particularly unpleasant experience in which trainees were immersed several times in a helicopter shell in order to learn how to escape successfully in the event of a genuine 'water landing'. Considering himself to have made something of a hash of the first set of dunkings, he earned increased respect by ordering his tormentors to put him through the whole process a second time.

On 3rd February the Admiral and his Staff embarked in HMS *Fife* (Captain David Hallifax) and sailed from Portsmouth as the Flag Officer directing the Fleet's annual training period, code named 'Springtrain'. A large RN contingent was joined by a Netherlands task group, and a series of exercises were conducted on passage to the Gibraltar area. After four days of weapon training, a ceremonial entry was made into Gibraltar harbour on 14th February. This was followed by a ten day period of social and sporting activities; much enjoyed by ships' companies more than happy to break away from the short nights and inclement weather of an English winter. It was the practice for the Commander-in-Chief to visit his Fleet during 'Springtrain', and Sir Terence Lewin lost little time making his presence felt. Soon after hoisting his flag in HMS *Tiger*, he made this signal to FOF2:

> Continue to administer the Fleet on my behalf, which means I will pass any comments direct to you. For a start I wasn't too impressed by the way Sunset was conducted this evening!

The 'new boy' had been put firmly in his place, and the routine for the ceremonies of Colours and Sunset was tightened up immediately.

Yet Fieldhouse was at his majestic best on this sort of occasion. Drawing on many years of experience, he was a complete master of the art of talking to officers and men, either in groups or individually; of making them feel important in the overall scheme of things, of earning their deep respect and inspiring them to greater efforts. Midge was one of several senior officers' wives who flew out to join their husbands. She was to be at John's side at the Rock on a similar but much more dramatic occasion seven years later.

Before sailing for further exercises in the Mediterranean, FOF2 transferred his flag to HMS *Glamorgan*. This ship was under the temporary command of her XO, Commander Jeremy Larken, already quoted in an earlier chapter. *Glamorgan*'s CO had been taken ill and evacuated to the UK for treatment, and Larken was expecting a replacement to be flown out to Gibraltar. Drawing on his own experience in *Hermes*, Fieldhouse had other ideas and was happy for Jeremy to retain command until the ship's return to Portsmouth at the end of her current deployment. This devotee's words are aptly descriptive and refreshing.

> Once again John's personality moved immediately to the pole position. His authority always having been natural, the fact that he was a very new, very young Admiral simply did not signify for those around him. Essentially, he seemed to have changed little from those *Dreadnought* days. By token of his position, there had to be more formality on the surface. He was now prince of those from whom he had rather mischievously distanced himself after that COs' dinner but ten years earlier. We had made *Glamorgan* a very professional flagship. This he appreciated, even enjoyed, whilst behind the doors of his Flag Mess, of which I and Tony Provest were members, his easy natural ways and enchanting sense of fun and the ridiculous were more evident than ever.

Provest was John's first Flag Lieutenant who was due to leave shortly, having already been selected for promotion to commander.

The period 24th February to 7th March was spent exercising in the Western Mediterranean Basin. Larken recalls that some time was devoted to developing tactics for the new Exocet surface-to-surface weapon system, fitted in both *Fife* and *Glamorgan*. On the first occasion, under David Hallifax's direction in *Fife*, the ships contrived to 'eliminate' their own replenishment group, resulting in David's explicit and laconic signal: 'a bad night for RFAs'! The next day, under the Admiral's surer touch, *Glamorgan* did rather better. These were the early days of John's and David's association; a prelude to their winning partnership in the Falklands War.

There was a short break as the Flagship led two majestic lines of ships into Cagliari Bay in southern Sardinia for one of the RN's most cherished rituals – a formation anchorage. The idea was that all the perfectly stationed vessels should slow down, stop and anchor by executive signal in predetermined positions at precisely the same moment. *Glamorgan* blotted her copybook by overshooting slightly, but the error was quickly remedied. The Admiral was always prepared to accept understandable mistakes as long as corrective action was prompt and lessons learned enduring.

John was already well accustomed to standing back to allow the Flag Captain a full rein in handling his own ship's affairs. Larken recalls a rare occasion of intervention.

> In one of those uneasy steep Mediterranean seas, *Glamorgan* was pitching head to sea in a rocking-horse motion, not quite putting her nose into successive waves. John and I watched a seaman make his way slightly precariously onto the fo'castle, I suppose to make some loose fittings secure. Whilst I observed this spectacle with an unhelpful suspension of decision in my mind, John directed me roundly to have the man withdrawn to safety forthwith.

Glamorgan and three frigates then paid a five-day visit to Naples. As had happened when he was there with the NATO squadron three years earlier, John became heavily involved with a round of official calls and entertainment. One incident on board is a delightful example of John's thoughtful humanity. Captain Charles Baker, the Naval Attaché, and his wife Romy had arrived on board in mid-morning so that Charles could brief the Admiral before his official lunch party. While showing Romy around his quarters, John pulled back the curtain to reveal the spacious dining area. Sitting at the table was a young naval rating studying for an advancement examination. It was typical that John should have thought of offering the use of this peaceful place for such a purpose.

On leaving Naples, there were a couple more days of local exercises before the Admiral and his Staff were landed ashore for return by air to the United Kingdom. This was a routine task for a VC10 of RAF Air Support Command. Accompanying the thirty or so passengers was a considerable amount of personal kit and numerous hampers containing classified books, documents and correspondence. Empty seats on the aircraft were invariably filled by personnel coming and going from the Flagship or other ships in company. This completed John's first sortie as a sea-going admiral. Garth de Courcy-Ireland and the rest of the staff were much encouraged by the successful way things had turned out. The warm reception they had received in *Glamorgan* augured well for later in the year when the same ship would be Flagship for the round the world deployment.

* * * * * * * *

Garth has produced a memorable vignette of events of 26th March 1975.

> The Admiral, Midge and I flew from Exeter Airport to Lee-on-Solent in a Sea Devon of the Communications Flight, piloted by Lt Cdr 'Bushy' Shrub, a famous Fleet Air Arm aviator who flew the Swordfish on special fly pasts. They were going to a change of command ceremony for the NATO Standing Naval Force, which he had formerly commanded and I had business with my opposite number on FOF1's staff. Exeter Airport was little more than a grass

> strip then. We were driven over from Devonport and went straight up to the aircraft, which was standing next to a solitary hut. Midge said, 'We're not going in that are we? It's only a toy', but the Admiral just laughed in his inimitable, disarming way and Bushy handed her on board and strapped her in. On being offered a choice of route, the Admiral chose the scenic one and so we flew to Lee along the valleys and over Hardy's hills and moors, looking at the sheep and cattle on somewhat level terms. Midge grew and remained very silent for the next 45 minutes, something I never experienced again. However I was told that she had recovered full powers of speech by the time of the ceremony and had a great deal to say – not all complimentary – to Roy Mason, the Labour Defence Secretary. The return route from Lee to Exeter was selected by Midge and was well above the clouds.

This story touches on an enduring aspect of Midge's character. She was – and is – a politically minded person with views comfortably to the right of centre, views that she has been always happy to share with those around her. Now that John was an admiral, he felt it best to keep his own thoughts on such matters to himself. In the exalted circles in which they had now started to move, it was perhaps fortunate, in the best interests of the preservation of the skin on his wife's shins, that they usually found themselves seated at opposite ends of the table! Midge enjoys quoting John's remark to her that 'The only thing you and I have in common is our incompatibility!' But around this good-natured banter were the obvious signs that complementary qualities had created a partnership of remarkable strength and solidity.

Midge has a story of her own about life at Flotilla House. It was an ancient building dating from 1690, and the flat had an unusual room layout. To reach the bathroom from her bedroom, she had walk across a passageway. From the bathroom, a door opened out onto a terrace where John's valet was accustomed to hanging out his laundry. One day Midge was in the bath when the outer door opened and this reluctant intruder entered carrying some of John's shirts. With a polite 'Excuse me Ma'am', he scuttled across the room, unlocked the door and went out into the corridor. Later Midge put him at his ease and gave him some useful advice. 'The next time you walk into a lady's bathroom, remember to say, "Excuse me Sir"!'

The incident caused much merriment in the household and Midge was presented with a cartoon with which to commemorate the occasion.

Another incident is typical of John's thoughtfulness and generosity. Leading Radio Operator Jeff Mays, who acted as his driver, was required to drive his master from Devonport to Lee-on-the-Solent, deposit him there and return to Devonport; a round distance of comfortably over 300 miles. On arrival, 'Pippins' was unoccupied; but John invited him into the kitchen and personally cooked him a plate of eggs and chips before sending him on his way. 'Not many admirals would have done that!' was Mays' reaction.

On another occasion, they undertook the round trip of Devonport/Portsmouth/Northwood/Devonport in a single day. This was an impressive mileage for one person, and the Admiral insisted in taking a full share of the driving.

Another LRO on John's staff, Charlie Newby, was standing with a group of other ratings waiting for the shuttle bus to take him to the Naval Barracks after finishing his forenoon watch at Flotilla House. The sight of an approaching staff car flying a rear admiral's flag caused the group to stand to attention and prepare to salute. The car drew up alongside him, the rear window was wound down and the Admiral called across 'Newby. Get in'. The pleasure on being offered a lift was slightly dented by the next utterance from the back seat 'Newby. Your hair!' 'I'm getting it cut this afternoon, Sir' was the prompt reply.

* * * * * * * *

Fieldhouse had already spent a few days at sea in HMS *Tiger* (Captain Mike Stacey) and this was by far his favoured choice of Flagship. Unlike the smaller County class destroyers, *Tiger* and *Blake* had been built with ample tailor made Flag facilities. On the down side, the addition of a flight deck and hangar aft to accommodate four ASW Sea King helicopters had not exactly enhanced their beauty. Unaffected by this, of course, was the ambience on board and the comfortable working and living quarters for all the staff. *Blake* was in the First Flotilla and was often used as FOF1's Flagship. Sadly *Tiger* was soon to enter refit at the end of her current commission, making her unavailable for the forthcoming Group Three Deployment.

On 28th April, FOF2 hoisted his Flag in *Tiger* in Rosyth Dockyard for Joint Maritime Course No 752. Fieldhouse's attendance at JMCs, both in submarines and surface ships, has been referred to on various previous occasions in these pages. They formed an important part of the peacetime navy's training scene and were bread and butter stuff to a FOF's SOO. De Courcy-Ireland's diary contains a thoroughly succinct account, making it all the more appropriate to use his words.

> JMCs were conducted by an organisation called JMOTS (the Joint Maritime Operational Training School), which was a joint RN/RAF organisation previously based in Londonderry, where it had been known as the Joint Anti-Submarine School. On moving from Northern Ireland the scope of the school had been increased to include more anti-air warfare. The school conducted courses on behalf of NATO four times a year, attracting sizeable participation of NATO submarines, ships and aircraft. The course started with three days of shore training either in the ships alongside in Rosyth or over at the school, which was based at Turnhouse Airport on the Edinburgh side of the Firth of Forth. The ships would normally be commanded by one

> of the NATO sea-going commanders and this was FOF2's second one in six months, since Admiral Clayton had done one in November. We sailed from Rosyth on Thursday 1st May for three days of working up exercises in all aspects of maritime warfare ending up in Scapa Flow on the Sunday. There the ships were briefed by the Admiral and his Staff and we sailed late that night to go round a race track in the North Sea for the next five days, being subjected to a near continuous attack from aircraft, submarines, ships and fast coastal craft representing Soviet forces and their weapon systems, before returning to Rosyth, where an attempt would be made to reconstruct what actually had happened and the success and failure of tactics used by both sides. JMCs were advanced maritime training exercises and were used to evaluate new tactics and to assess the effectiveness of new systems against perceived threats. *Tiger* was an excellent command platform and her Sea King helicopters were a very useful ASW asset, but her equipment was antiquated. Nevertheless this was a good exercise for the operational staff which was now getting well used to the Admiral's ways.

On return from Scotland to Flotilla House at Devonport, two key changes on the staff took place. Commander Jake Francis-Jones took over as Secretary and Lieutenant Commander David Brown became Flag Lieutenant. Together with de Courcy-Ireland, these two would complete the inner core of the team now in place for the round the world deployment. The indefatigable Garth had already fully demonstrated his worth at the hub of the operational wheel. As a junior officer, Jake had seen service as Flag Lieutenant to the C in-C South Atlantic, so had already had plenty of experience in anticipating an admiral's wishes and reading his mind. David combined sound professional skills as a warfare officer with a cheerful outlook on life. It wasn't long before he was referring irreverently to his immediate superior as 'de Quincy-England'! He has shared some discerning memories about his Admiral.

> Assisted by the privilege of messing in the 'cuddy', I formed what became for me the most rewarding professional relationship of my entire career. From the outset John's qualities of leadership, professional grip, humanity and integrity seemed to set him apart from other men. He had adopted an 'alternative lifestyle' as a senior officer, a course which cannot have been without risk. He never sought personal publicity, nor aimed to 'cultivate' people in high places. He was deeply professional in things that mattered, but less attached to the formalities and customs associated with a peacetime navy. Above all, he was deeply humble, willing to give his time to all sorts of person. He was supremely gifted in forming relationships and in being able to use few words to brilliant effect. He was devoid of gossip, even in the 'cuddy', and was unusually sensitive to the damage of careless talk.

Another key member of the team needs further mention. An essential ingredient of command was communications; and whenever the admiral was up and about, Chief Communications Yeoman David Morris was never far from his side. To him:

> Fieldhouse was the greatest motivator I ever met, but he did it all naturally without any airs, graces or pomposity. When we got together as a close-knit team, I felt I had found my niche in life. With him, loyalty was always a two way street. He gave all his staff both trust and responsibility. They knew and he knew that what they did was in his name. He smiled a lot and always called me 'lad' informally.

Morris and his small group of leading communications ratings, one of whom doubled up as the Admiral's driver, assumed full responsibility for signal message handling both at sea and ashore.

At the end of May FOF2 embarked again in *Tiger* as host for the annual Staff College Sea Days. These took place from 2nd to 5th June and involved taking a group of ships each day round the same carefully planned track in the Channel. Embarked at differing times were members of the Royal College of Defence Studies and Senior Officers War Course and students of the Joint Services, Army and Air Force staff colleges. This was the Royal Navy's 'shop window' for educating and impressing members of the other Services in as many aspects of maritime warfare as it was possible to contrive in rather constricted circumstances. Garth reported that it all went quite well despite the efforts of early summer fog to disrupt proceedings. On 6th June the ship sailed again for a much more relaxing day with families.

The following ten days ashore were partly taken up with a series of discussions known as the Fleet Tactical Panel, conducted at the Tactical School at HMS *Dryad* near Portsmouth. Garth noted that it was at meetings of this sort that 'the Admiral showed us his knack, whilst deeply submerged in his chair, of surfacing without a ripple to contribute to the subject under discussion both lucidly and to the point.'

Fieldhouse and his Staff returned to *Tiger* on 18th June. The ship sailed from Portsmouth that afternoon to represent the Royal Navy at *Kielerwoche*. This was an annual festival and yachting regatta at Kiel, traditionally attended by warships from many NATO nations. The RN usually sent a ship commanded by a senior captain, but on this occasion it had been programmed as a Flag visit. After a relaxed passage across the North Sea, the ship entered the Kiel Canal and berthed alongside in the port on 20th June. Because the Captain had entrusted this manoeuvre to his soon to be departing Navigating Officer, it was conducted with some difficulty. Garth continues:

> The approach alongside was enthusiastic and the German military band, which was positioned where the bridge should be when the ship

> stopped, found it steaming on past them. The bandmaster shuffled them along the jetty, perspiring freely but still blasting away, keeping them abreast the Admiral, then shuffling them back and forth, as 'Pilot' corrected his excesses and eventually yo-yoed into the proper berth. It was impossible to keep a straight face; something that the Admiral, with his splendid sense of fun and the ridiculous, never attempted anyway.

While in Kiel, the ship took part in no less than twenty-nine sporting events, ranging from sailing to soccer, from rugby and judo to chess. Meanwhile Midge and Garth's wife, Margie, had travelled by ferry from Harwich to Hamburg, where Garth had been driven in a staff car to meet them. The party moved into the comfortable officer's club, in World War II, the German C-in-C's residence, but then still a British Forces recreational facility. There followed a round of lunches, receptions, dinners and balls requiring all of the Fieldhouses' noted stamina. Their one respite was to drive to Lubeck for a picnic and to peer through the Iron Curtain to a very different scene on the eastern side. John was struck by the stark comparison between the prosperous West German farms running up to very wire of the border and the bleak and desolate countryside beyond it. The Admiral disembarked by helicopter on *Tiger*'s return to home waters on 1st July, taking with him some happy memories of a Flagship had had served him more than well. There remained three hectic weeks for closing out the UK end of his business and making final preparations for the Group Three Deployment.

CHAPTER ELEVEN

Around the World

1975 – 1976

THE TASK GROUP SAILED from UK ports on 22nd July. Accompanying Flagship HMS *Glamorgan* (Captain Bob Leathes) was the 8th Frigate Squadron. This consisted of the modernised Batch 1 Leander HMS *Ajax* (Captain John Mackenzie), and the older Type 12s HMS *Berwick*, *Plymouth* and *Rothesay*. A fifth ship, the air direction frigate HMS *Llandaff*, was to join the group at Gibraltar. John Mackenzie was a much respected and experienced CO who had recently held the important post of Commander Sea Training at Portland. He was leader of a happy young team of COs of ships of a certain age which, despite early fears, stood up very well to the long periods to be spent at sea. Attending the group's considerable logistic needs were RFA tankers *Tidespring* and *Gold Rover*, and the stores ship *Tarbatness*. All their masters had years of command experience and could not have been more cooperative. It had been made clear at the outset that the RFAs were to be full members of the group, with their crews entering into all its activities.

It was unfortunate that there were a number of problems concerning *Glamorgan*. On return from the Mediterranean that spring, she had entered Portsmouth Dockyard for a routine docking period, expected to restore her to the best possible shape before a long absence from home waters. Larken left in May, and a new CO and XO were appointed almost simultaneously. Captain Bob Leathes was highly experienced, four years older than Fieldhouse, and serving in his last job before retirement. He was a navigation specialist and, like Mackenzie, an expert ship handler. The Commander was a recently promoted Fleet Air Arm officer, understandably with little feel for a ship's or indeed a Flagship's administration. Through no fault of the new command team, the period in dockyard hands did not go well. It was a time of bad industrial relations, with the civilian workforce working to rule. Some of the maintenance work was below par and, being severely pressed for time, the ship had to be undocked before her underwater hull had received the correct protective treatment. Since last at sea, there had also been quite a number of other crew changes. *Glamorgan* eventually sailed for sea trials on 30th June. This was cutting things fine, leaving insufficient time for a proper shakedown period at the sea training base at Portland, on top of which there were some personality problems. Because of a probable lack of sympathy on both sides, the Admiral's Staff, so comfortable in this ship a few months earlier, found themselves on the receiving end of a rather frosty welcome. In the course of time, things settled down and relationships improved, but for some it was not a happy start to the deployment. It was unfortunate that Leathes chose to opt out of joining the Secretary and Flag Lieutenant as members of the flag mess. The Flag Captain's regular presence at table would have provided the Admiral with a priceless informal link with all that was happening in the ship itself; a benefit that was sadly denied to him.

* * * * * * * *

This is perhaps the moment for a brief summary of the Group's overall objectives. The circumnavigation was built around two major milestones; first to exercise with the Royal Australian Navy (RAN) and Royal New Zealand Navy (RNZN) in December; second to do likewise with the United States Navy (USN) in March 1976, having previously attended the American bi-centenary celebrations. Around these prime commitments were inserted plans to visit several other countries along the way. Whenever it was at sea, the Group was a ready-made test bed for exercising tactical procedures and furthering new concepts of operations. Submarine input was provided by the RN and USN as far as the Mediterranean. The RAN's British built SSKs served as 'targets' in eastern waters. Off Hawaii and California, there was a heavy input of American SSNs. Finally, British and Dutch submarines would join the Group for parts of the homeward passage across the Atlantic. The same principles would govern the provision of maritime patrol aircraft for exercise purposes.

The underlying thrust of the tactical development programme was to advance the good work already progressed in previous deployments. Something has already been written about the changes in the seaman officer structure, with the introduction of the Principal Warfare Officer concept already underway. The Fleet needed to be able to operate in a totally passive environment; to be able to react instantly to any perceived threat. In the missile age, the RN was converting to a doctrine of Standard Operating Procedures (SOPs), in which a variety of actions, such as violently manoeuvring the ship, jamming hostile emissions, and the firing of decoys and defensive weapons, could be taken at a junior level on receipt of the defining information. When self-preservation could be measured in seconds, there would certainly be insufficient time to call the captain or consult the admiral. The presence of a group of ships, often for days on end, provided the tools that could mould these concepts into shape. Since World War II, the surface fleet had become adept at blasting away on its multitudinous radar, sonar and radio equipments, often to good effect. Clearly these skills would still be required in many instances, but an irreversible trend towards a strong and complementary passive ethic was firmly underway. Previous group deployments had made major strides in this direction. Who better than ace submariner Fieldhouse, with his inbred flair for stealth and craftiness, to add new momentum to this changing scene?

In consequence the Staff had prepared in advance a comprehensive set of orders expressing the Admiral's intentions. Outlined were a number of circumstances in which COs were expected to act on their own initiative in accordance with SOPs. De Courcy-Ireland recalls that:

> It took time to get used to and we always seemed to be having to go back to square one as ships lost their way. But we won through in the end when the group was able to leave San Diego in company, settle into a cruising formation for Panama and carry out all pre-planned exercises overnight without a single radio signal or prompting from the Task Group Commander.

John Mackenzie recalls another and no less important objective, arising from the premise that 'all work and no play makes Jack a dull boy'. The Admiral had briefed his COs that every effort should be made to grant as much leave as possible to all hands while in port. He wanted everyone to take full advantage of a once in a lifetime opportunity to visit some fascinating places in their voyage around the world. There was an additional brief for furthering sales of defence equipment to Commonwealth and Third World navies, but the Group Three Deployment was not best placed to make a meaningful contribution. Many of the ships were old and some of the modern equipment, such as *Glamorgan*'s Exocet and *Ajax*'s Ikara missile systems, had been purchased from other nations.

* * * * * * * *

When the Task Group sailed, there still some doubts about whether or not the Suez Canal would be available. It had only recently been cleared of mines and wrecks following the Arab/Israeli conflicts and no RN ships had yet received clearance to make a transit. However, all seemed well as the Group prepared to sail from Gibraltar on 28th July. At this moment another uncertainty intervened. As she was about to slip, *Glamorgan* suffered from severe gearbox overheating, causing her to remain in Gibraltar for investigation and repairs. Fieldhouse decided to transfer his Flag to RFA *Gold Rover*. Although she was the smaller of the two tankers, she was a modern ship with good accommodation and communications facilities. Within two hours, the remainder of the group was steaming on with the Admiral, his 'inner' circle of three officers, the Chief Yeoman and small team of communicators comfortably installed in their new temporary surroundings.

Captain John Fisher, accompanied by his wife Gwen, was a charming host. Under Royal Fleet Auxiliary rules, he had authorised the embarkation of up to 12 wives, extending the invitation of officer's wives of the group in the event of insufficient take-up from his own ship. In a letter home, Garth reported that

> All are most welcoming and it is really rather comfy. I have my own loo and shower, etc and a huge double bed. We are adapting to life at sea in mixed company – sitting down to dinner with the ladies in our respective evening dress, regardless of what might be happening elsewhere.

He felt that *Gold Rover* 'was as effective and adaptable as a Flagship as she was comfortable and friendly'. With a flight deck aft, the Admiral and he were able to visit the other ships, to observe the various planned exercises and to get to know their companies. Mackenzie recalls his visit to *Ajax*. After an hour or so on board, Fieldhouse remarked 'It is good to come to a ship where people talk to each other'. Unsaid, of course, was the inference of comparison with *Glamorgan*. This saddened Mackenzie, who had stood by during her building at Newcastle, had been her first XO and had always been very proud of her. The subject of this comment was soon in business again. *Glamorgan* caught up with the group off Malta, but Fieldhouse decided that he should reward *Gold Rover* by letting her lead the nine ships into Grand Harbour before transferring his Flag.

There followed a busy ten-day period consisting of two short periods in harbour broken up by a four-day weapon-training period, including contact with the carrier USS *John F Kennedy* and the SSN USS *Tulibee* of the US Sixth Fleet. The First Sea Lord, Admiral Sir Edward Ashmore, was on a private visit to Malta and witnessed the second entry into harbour. De Courcy-Ireland noted that that there were still rather too many mistakes as ships strived to settle down.

> At the morning briefing, the Admiral always kept calm; although his manner, transmitted by uncanny means around the group, never left his commanding officers and others in any doubt as to their shortcomings. Only the blind failed to respond to that style of leadership.

On leaving Malta, the group moved up a gear into the real world of the Cold War. A useful reconnaissance was carried out of the helicopter carrier *Leningrad* and other Soviet fleet units by making a silent approach and catching them unawares in their anchorage off Sollum in Libya. On arrival at Port Said, *Ajax* was sent straight on down the Suez Canal to check that it was fully clear of obstructions. Garth and his colleagues enjoyed a beer at a bar

> where the shoe cleaning wallah pinched David Brown's shoe laces and he had to pursue him round the square to recover them. He got no help from Jake or me who cheered on hare and hound as we ordered more beer.

It might seem that little had changed, but 'there were no small boys offering their sisters and the 'filthy' postcards were no worse than the ones I sent the children.' The next day the Admiral was taken off by the Naval Attaché for a round of official calls in Cairo and Alexandria, while others took time off to visit the Pyramids. When *Glamorgan* passed down the Canal on 16th August, the 'gully gully man gave us an excellent show – every bit as good as ever'.

In the Red Sea, Fieldhouse visited *Llandaff* and *Berwick*, whose air-conditioning was rather antiquated. The temperature in *Llandaff*'s diesel engine rooms was about 110 degrees F, but the men working there seemed quite nonchalant about it. Meanwhile, the frigates made short visits to Port Sudan and Djibuti to equal the time the Flagship had spent in Port Said. There followed a period of chasing around the Soviet anchorage off Socotra and seeking out the 'enemy' off the coast of South Yemen. It was there that *Glamorgan*'s Wessex helicopter had a tail rotor malfunction and made a controlled 'ditching' close to the ship. Before it could be recovered, it sank; but not before the aircrew and passengers had clambered into their life rafts, soon to be safely back on board. A replacement was crated up and shipped out to Singapore.

While in the Arabian Sea, the group exercised briefly with 'resident' USN Seventh Fleet warships. Since the withdrawal of the UK Far East Fleet, the USA had felt it necessary to keep a strong naval presence within easy reach of the Strait of Hormuz. A high percentage of the free world's oil supplies passed through the waterway, and it was necessary to deter any attempts by the Soviets to destabilise this politically sensitive area. In the mid-1970s there was not always a full battle group on station, but the events of the next three decades were to see an increasing military focus on this troubled part of the world. Also in the area was an Australian squadron under the command of Rear Admiral David Wells, and much more of these ships would be seen later. Towards the end of the month the group split into two Task Units. Mackenzie led the *Ajax* team to Madras, while *Glamorgan* berthed alongside in Bombay on 28th August. It was time for FOF2 to take his first break from the deployment. Fieldhouse was a busy man with many other matters to occupy his attention. He handed over command of CTG 317.3 to Leathes, struck his Flag, and, together with his Staff of thirty or so, flew home in a VC10 aircraft of RAF Air Support Command.

* * * * * * * *

The next few weeks at home passed in a flash. Not least important was that members of staff were due some summer leave. There followed the usual round of meetings and visits to other ships in the Second Flotilla. The Admiral flew with a small team to Stavanger in Norway to join Captain F7 in HMS *Scylla*, carrying out a formal inspection on the passage back to the

UK. On October 12th, he returned with his Staff to Singapore and rehoisted his Flag in *Glamorgan*. During his absence all the ships had made port visits and carried out maintenance periods in preparation for the next stage of the deployment programme. *Glamorgan*, with *Plymouth* and *Tidespring* had visited Port Klang, near Kuala Lumpur, and Captain F8, with the other four frigates and two RFAs had visited Hong Kong. Meanwhile it was a nostalgic period at the naval base in Singapore. Since the RN's departure in 1971, it had been kept open on a reduced scale as an UK/Australia/New Zealand army/naval base facility. Now all this was about to close down. Both the RN and RAN were there in strength to mark the occasion, the latter consisting of the flagship HMAS *Supply*, together with *Vendetta*, *Vampire*, *Hobart*, *Brisbane*, *Torrens*, *Swan*, *Diamantina* and the submarine *Oxley*.

It had been pre-planned that the group should continue to spread its tentacles widely. *Ajax* led some ships on a visit to Fremantle, thence south about Australia to Sydney. *Rothesay* was detached to take part in Indian Ocean exercise 'Midlink', which would take her first to Gan and then to Muscat. *Glamorgan*, with *Llandaff* in company sailed from Singapore on 16th October. Crossing the Equator later that day, they made a four-day official visit to the Indonesian naval port of Surabaja, last visited by Fieldhouse in his carefree midshipman's days. As always, he was the right man for this sort of occasion. His attitude towards his hosts was totally unpatronising. He went out of his way so show an interest in all the Indonesians' cares and activities.

Following a passage of the Lombok Strait, the ships anchored off Bali on 23rd October to allow the hands ashore for a beach 'banyan'. For Fieldhouse, this brought back happy memories of an earlier visit in HMS *Norfolk*, all of thirty years ago. The next morning, rendezvous was made with the Australian Fleet returning from Singapore to Sydney. A series of exercises were arranged over the next few days as the combined group sailed through the Torres Strait and the Great Barrier Reef of North East Australia. Having been built in Newcastle, England, *Glamorgan* detached for a twelve-day visit to Newcastle, New South Wales, from 5th to 17th October.

After normal courtesies on arrival, Fieldhouse left for a round of calls in Canberra and Sydney where most of the Group Three Task Force had congregated. Meanwhile, Leathes felt unhappy about the Flagship's immediate programme. The great deal of hard work needed in preparation for the Admiral's harbour inspection on 14th October seemed in direct conflict with his wish to grant as much leave as possible so that the crew could enjoy the benefits of being in Australia. It was to the great credit of all concerned that a good compromise was reached. When Fieldhouse returned to Newcastle to conduct the inspection, all went well. His official report stated that 'It says much for the ship's company that they managed to retain a proper balance between their activities ashore and their preparations on board.' This was the verdict as seen from the Star Hotel's perspective.

> *Dear Captain Leathes,*
> My husband, the licensee, and I would like to congratulate you on bringing to our city such a fine crew of gentlemen. We have found the entire complement of men from officers to junior seaman to be well mannered, well attired, and as perfectly behaved as you would have wanted them to be. They are a great credit to you and your country.
> *Yours sincerely Leslie Graham*

Just as *Glamorgan* seemed to be on a crest of a wave, fate intervened again. By 17th October, all ships were at sea for the joint UK/ Australia/New Zealand exercise 'Tasmanex' involving surface, submarine and shore based air forces. The Admiral had set aside the early part of this for his Flagship's operational readiness inspection. This was curtailed when a major defect developed in the port gearbox that resulted in her withdrawing from the exercise and making best speed for Sydney on one shaft for repairs. RFA *Gold Rover* was recalled to harbour to embark the Admiral and a small nucleus of Staff so that he could take his turn as the Officer in Tactical Command (OTC) for the exercise. For this he transferred to *Ajax* in order to make use of her better communications and computerised action information system. 'Tasmanex' consisted of a series of staged maritime incidents conducted along the 34th degree parallel between Sydney and the North Cape of New Zealand. The British and Australian ships anchored in the Bay of Islands on 27th November, not being permitted to enter harbour until after completion of voting for the New Zealand general election. Participating ships, submarines and shore-based aircrew were able to gather together in Auckland for the post exercise discussion two days later. In his official report, Fieldhouse commented on the value of such exercises, particularly for the Antipodean navies which saw all too little of the advanced tactical concepts practised by NATO.

It had been a fragmented period since the Admiral had rejoined the Task Group in Singapore. For much of this time the ships had been widely dispersed, and *Glamorgan*'s latest defect had caused further disruption. December and the early part of January had been programmed as a period of port visits for maintenance and recreation over the long southern Christmas holiday. It was time for the Admiral and his Staff to return again to the United Kingdom.

* * * * * * * *

While the remainder of the team returned home direct by RAF Air Support Command, Fieldhouse and De Courcy-Ireland flew by commercial air via Hawaii to San Francisco. Because of crossing the international dateline, they arrived in Honolulu the day <u>before</u> they left Auckland. There they had a round of meetings on forthcoming Task Force activity before continuing their journey. On arrival in mainland USA, there were taken to the residence of Rear Admiral H P Glindeman USN at Oakland, across San Francisco Bay. This was an important meeting for Fieldhouse in that he was able to establish a close rapport with the Battle Group Commander involved in the major exercise planned for the following March. Exercise 'Valiant Heritage' was to be the operational highlight of the entire deployment, and the contacts made that day were to ensure that the USN was entirely happy to give the RN a substantial share in controlling the proceedings. The two guests retired early that evening and Garth recalled that it was the first time he had ever seen John tired. With Glindeman, they embarked the next morning in the giant aircraft carrier USS *Enterprise*. Garth's letter home called it 'an amazing experience for both of us. As we sailed out through the Golden Gate on the admiral's bridge, we were thirteen decks above the flight deck!' Planning talks continued over 'Valiant Heritage'. Garth's impression was of

> a huge American staff well behind the plot, struggling with mountains of disorganised paper. I remember their Chief Staff Officer asking how I managed to keep up to date with my signals because he was still reading yesterday's! It was a fascinating two days before we got catapulted off the deck in a passenger aircraft with about 12 others en route for San Diego.

The pair flew from there to Los Angeles to connect with an overnight flight to London. Arriving on 4th December, they had completed a combined air/sea circumnavigation inside two months. There was a busy build up to Christmas with as many visits as possible to other ships in the Second Flotilla.

Meanwhile the Group Three ships had fanned out for a series of visits to Australian and New Zealand ports in all of which they had been made exceedingly welcome. After her earlier visit to Fremantle and Sydney, *Ajax*'s post 'Tasmanex' programme took her to Wellington, Melbourne and Adelaide, where she spent Christmas with *Plymouth* and the RFAs *Gold Rover*, *Tarbatness* and *Resurgent*. The latter had joined the group for the specific purpose of providing a mid-deployment top up of practice ammunition. Later, *Ajax* made a second call at Sydney before the group finally left Australasian waters. Mackenzie recalls the good fortune of a particular junior member of his ship's company. In October at Fremantle, a gorgeous blonde had swept this young rating away from the dockside in an expensive sports car. The same lady had been on the jetty to meet him at most subsequent ports, including Honolulu, San Diego and the final arrival in England.

Following the disappointment of missing the exercise, *Glamorgan* had undergone a successful permanent gearbox repair at Sydney's commercial Cockatoo shipyard. From there she proceeded to Hobart in Tasmania for a successful Christmas visit before crossing the Tasman Sea to Bluff and Dunedin in the South Island of New Zealand.

In his final report on the group's southern summer activities, Fieldhouse wrote:

> Throughout the period ship's companies, almost without exception, behaved very well ashore. Despite the breadth of territory covered, they have been excellent ambassadors for the United Kingdom and there have been no untoward incidents with local people. The warmth of our welcome in Australia and New Zealand has been outstanding at all levels and the frequent comment 'Its good to see that Britain hasn't sunk as low as the press would have us believe' has been adequate reward for the effort expended.

* * * * * * * *

FOF2 and his Staff left RAF Brize Norton on 16th January 1976 to rejoin the Group Three round the world deployment. It was a long and tedious journey. An aircraft defect caused a long delay at Bahrain and this was followed by an unscheduled overnight stop at Singapore due to aircrew sickness. At least this was spent in a comfortable hotel, the old *Terror* base having finally closed down. After a midnight refuelling stop at Sydney, they eventually arrived at Christchurch airport in the South Island of New Zealand at 4.00 am, finishing with a three-hour drive to Dunedin. *Glamorgan* sailed on 21st January. Before the serious work began again, ships were programmed to make a number of visits around the South Sea Islands. The Flagship arrived at Tonga on 25th January where David Brown takes up the story.

> This visit was particularly memorable. King Taufa'ahau Tupou IV came across as a man of considerable dignity who nonetheless lived modestly in his small colonial style palace in Nuku'alofa. John's audience, with the High Commissioner and me in attendance, must have lasted for over an hour. Almost immediately, John seemed to have gained the monarch's confidence, for after the initial pleasantries there followed a candid sharing of some of the latter's burdens of office. His anxiety over the Soviet Union's increasing maritime ingress into Tonga's extensive area of interest was but one of the matters discussed.

Garth chips in with another of his colourful contemporary jottings.

> The Admiral, Flag Captain, RFA masters and Flags called on the King; 32-stone and apparently built like a house. As they lined up for a group photograph, the Admiral's inadvertent faux pas was to ask if the man had a wide-angle lens! One of the Princesses was at our cocktail party. She was quite striking – only about 12 stone I should say!

Home entertainment consisted of sumptuous beach picnics and a feast for over 200 officers and ratings was provided by the Royal Family on the island of Pangaimotu close to the anchorage. Princess Pilolevi remained throughout the afternoon and until the last sailor had returned to his ship.

David Brown recalls John's valiant effort to have a private banyan with his personal staff on his only afternoon free of official engagements. Flags ordered a car from the Palace to take them and their modest picnic lunch to an outlying deserted beach. They had to wait some time, but John was very patient and eventually they set off. On arrival, the reason for the delay became apparent.

> Kind people emerged from the trees with garlands of flowers, four of them bearing a large stretcher groaning with the weight of a roast-suckling-pig banquet! Both we and our stomachs were overwhelmed with kindness.

Sandwiches and swimming trunks remained in the car unused. Garth reported that the high life was beginning to take its toll.

> Today was pretty tough. The Admiral was very liverish and there was a pile of work to do. He went to lunch with the King, but I pressed on and missed the Royal Command picnic (another) in the afternoon. We left Tonga on 31st January. Then had an extra Sunday as we crossed the date line (again) so stopped at a Friendly Island (Tiku Nomouka) and had a banyan

On 2nd February *Glamorgan* arrived in Apia, the capital of Western Samoa. A heavy social programme had been arranged and the demands on the Admiral's time were unrelenting. It was a relief to be at sea again, but, before sailing, a report reached the Flagship of a serious fire in HMS *Ajax*.

John Mackenzie has provided a graphic account of this alarming incident. Out of the blue a fire was reported in the main electrical switchboard. Within minutes the ship was filled with smoke and the deck under the torpedo magazine became red hot. It was fortunate that *Ajax* had a highly competent team, with both Squadron Engineer Commanders having served recently on the workup staff at Portland. The fire was fought with great skill and urgency and within two hours the ship was underway again. Emergency cables had been run out in all directions, including through bulkhead doors. Fieldhouse later reported that 'the ship was in a safe condition to float and move, but definitely not to fight'. After consultation, the Admiral decided to go ahead with a pre-planned administrative inspection of *Ajax* the next day, before despatching her to Pearl Harbour for repairs. On arrival there, the USN authorities inspected the damage and called a meeting to discuss three possible courses of action. First was to make and fit a new switchboard – estimated time three months. Second was to carry out a temporary repair involving the removal of all the emergency cables – two months. Third was to fit a replacement switchboard flown out from the UK – estimated time unknown. Mackenzie went to the meeting with the news that a complete switchboard intended for fitting in sister ship *Dido*'s refit 'would be arriving tomorrow'. The Americans were much impressed by the RN's spares supply system and were able to complete a full repair in little over a fortnight. *Glamorgan* was also to benefit from the USN base facilities at Pearl Harbour. Because of her unsatisfactory docking at Portsmouth, the ship had been losing speed through the water. Leathes was able to arrange for a commercial 'bottom scrape', the cost of which would be offset by savings on fuel over the remainder of the deployment.

Fieldhouse was much heartened by *Ajax*'s response to her emergency and enjoyed having nearly all his ships around him, plus the New Zealand frigate HMNZS *Canterbury*, which had joined up for several weeks. After passing through equatorial calms, the group entered stormy waters as it neared Hawaii. An intensive weapon training period had been organised either side of a five day visit to Pearl Harbour, using USN aircraft and an SSN. The Canadian frigates HMCS *Kootenay* and *Restigouche* joined up as well, providing a true international flavour in the run up to 'Valiant Heritage'. The enhanced Group Three sailed from Pearl on 17th February; leaving *Ajax* behind to complete her repairs. After some days of useful weapon training, the ships split up to carry out bi-centennial visits to a number of Californian ports. *Glamorgan* docked in the USN's main Pacific Fleet base at San Diego on 23rd February. The next eight days were a busy time for all. Garth wrote:

> I think it is going to be pandemonium. We have a lot of shore training to do and some evening commitments. The Admiral hasn't got one free day and Midge is coming out!

The new C-in-C Fleet, Admiral Sir John Treacher, also felt it was a suitable time to pay a flying visit to some of his far flung ships. A despairing note adds 'Poor old Fieldhouse! He is taking a terrible hammering. He now thinks his wheel is very good news!' There was much to celebrate over the USA's bi-centenary. At least Midge was there to take a full share of the social strain. Garth concluded:

> One night the Admiral had to go to a stag dinner and Jake, David and I took Midge out to a Mexican restaurant. She was in tremendous form with three squires and we had a hilarious evening.

Exercise 'Valiant Heritage' started on 2nd March. Taking part were 41 ships from four navies centred on the USS *Enterprise*, five SSNs, several squadrons of shore based aircraft and 20,000 men. On the first day *Glamorgan* fired her Sea Slug missiles and totally upstaged the USN by shooting down the target. In the first tactical phase the RN/Commonwealth group played havoc amongst the 'enemy' before being sunk by 'friendly' carrier based aircraft. Fully resurrected, the action proceeded at a furious pace for several days. The climax came when Fieldhouse was put in total command for the final phase. By virtue of his excellent relationship with the Americans, he had pre-planned a masterly 'passive' ruse, so subtle that it nearly succeeded in confusing everybody! The idea was for the carrier group, including *Glamorgan* in tactical command, to remain silent, even while operating aircraft. About 50 miles further inshore was a decoy group of US warships, fully 'active' and posing as the carrier. Aircraft from the *Enterprise* were controlled by the decoy group in such a way to make the 'enemy' believe that the carrier was there. It was gratifying that the shore based air and surface ship missile strikes were launched against the wrong targets, while the undetected *Enterprise* group raced around the southern flank to position itself for a climactic retaliatory air strike on shore targets near San Diego.

In a night of eerie darkness, Fieldhouse and his Staff were down below in the Operations Room. In the absence of any radar, Leathes was on the bridge, totally alert as the custodian of his ship's safety. With all vessels fully darkened, *Glamorgan*'s CO sighted a small white light right ahead which he reported to the Ops Room. At first he thought it was a distant fishing boat, but, with the bearing remaining steady, he began to have second thoughts and asked permission to switch on radar. This was refused, but fortunately Leathes insisted. The disclosure of the radar picture coincided with the arrival on the bridge of an initially irate Admiral. There, in front of their eyes, was an enormous echo at a range of 4,000 yards, none other than the fleet aircraft carrier *Enterprise*! The passive plot in the operations room showed her to be many miles away. Despite this minor glitch, 'Valiant Heritage' had been a great feather in Fieldhouse's cap, it being almost unheard of for a British admiral to determine and control the tactics of an American carrier battle group.

All ships returned to San Diego for the exercise debrief and for a final few days of renewed social activity. During this period the British Consul General in Los Angeles hosted a garden party for British officers after which they were swept away by invited American guests for the weekend. John and Midge's car caught fire on the way back to San Diego. Undeterred, they were transferred to a Highway Patrol vehicle and delivered to their destination none the worse for the experience. On 16th March the deployment group sailed south for Panama. The Fieldhouses flew back to the UK where FOF2 was required to take his place at the C-in-C's half yearly Flag Officers' meeting. On the agenda was the Fleet promotion meeting, in which recommendations were sorted in order of priority. Garth de Courcy-Ireland, who was preparing to fly home on the expiry of his tour, would be delighted to discover that his name was on the next list for promotion to captain. Group Three made its transit of the Panama Canal on 24th March before spreading out to visit individual Caribbean ports. Fieldhouse rejoined by helicopter prior to *Glamorgan*'s entry into La Guaria, the port for Caracas, capital of Venezuela. This was the final entry from Garth's 'diary'.

> I flew home on 27th March: like the Admiral, completing my second circumnavigation working two extra days for no extra pay by going east-about both times. My 16 months with John Fieldhouse were the highlight of my career, the never to be forgotten comradeship with Jake and David, serving John and Midge. What a privilege!

The final leg of the deployment consisted of a twelve-day working passage across the Atlantic. The frigate *Zulu* joined the group and the SSN *Sovereign* provided loyal opposition for the first few days. Later, two RAF maritime patrol aircraft operating from the Azores joined the exercises, together with SSKs HMS *Finwhale* and HNLMS *Potvis*. With the ships nearing home, the Admiral continued to drive them hard in order to derive the maximum benefit from the shortly to be disbanded group's operating resources. Task Group 317.3 entered homeports on 14th April. During just under nine months ships had steamed an average of 45,000 miles; exercised with 11 navies; visited 60 places in 27 countries on 6 continents.

* * * * * * * *

In the context of taking a group of ships around the world, John's remaining months as FOF2 were rather less exciting. Naturally he was able to devote more time to the other ships in the Second Flotilla. He flew his Flag at sea in HMS *Blake*, *London* and finally in *Tiger*, which had emerged from her refit. *Blake* (Captain David Eckersley-Maslin) had been borrowed from the First Flotilla to carry out Staff College Sea Days and a Flag visit to Rotterdam. Captain Richard Hill was then serving as Defence Attaché in The Hague, and recalls that his 'difficult' ambassador was delighted with the visit. Against advice, John invited Hill's low ranking embassy secretary to help even up the sexes at his official lunch party. Having been given an unexpected opportunity to shine, the lady conducted herself with great credit. This was a typical example of John's uncanny way with people, and Hill concedes that it was absolutely the right decision.

This simple story of kindness to a stranger ends two chapters on John's Flag command at sea, considered important for two very different reasons. The first is that de Courcy-Ireland's observations were contemporary. Verbatim quotes from letters to his wife contained the 'gut' feeling of a busy and devoted staff officer; sometimes written in his cabin at sea; often from a far flung port or anchorage; always providing a clear and instinctive picture of what was happening at the time. For this reason, Garth's portrait is more accurate and sincere than many of the memories of others, often distorted by passing time.

The second reason impinges not so much on the veracity of this narrative, but on the effect on the man himself. This vital part of Fieldhouse's career put him in line for consideration as a future Commander-in-Chief Fleet. Four and a half years after hauling down his Flag, this became a reality. Less than a year after that, he was required to lead the nation's armed forces into a totally unexpected war. He did so almost exclusively from his shore headquarters at Northwood. But the experience he had gained in leading a task group in 'Springtrain' and Singapore, 'Tasmanex' and Tonga, 'Valiant Heritage' and Venezuela, gave him the capacity to 'enter the minds' of subordinate commanders; charged with the loneliness of having to make crucial decisions in hostile places; thousands of miles from home.

CHAPTER TWELVE

Submarine Admiral

1976 – 1979

WHATEVER HE MIGHT BE called upon to do for the remainder of his career, it was Fieldhouse's destiny to become Flag Officer Submarines. All his seventeen predecessors since World War II had received decorations for gallantry in that conflict – although some of them had been 'drafted in' from general service when no specialist admiral had been available. John was already the first submariner to have reached Flag rank without wartime service in boats. Now he was to be the first FOSM to have commanded a nuclear submarine and the last to fly his flag at the historic base at Fort Blockhouse – HMS *Dolphin*.

Fieldhouse took over his new command from Vice Admiral Sir Iwan Raikes on 27th November 1976. 25 years earlier they had been CO and 3rd hand together in HMS *Aeneas*. Shortly after that he had moved up to First Lieutenant and had met Midge for the first time in Londonderry. More recently, as Naval Secretary, Raikes had been involved in the process of singling out John for his early promotion to rear admiral. They provided an interesting contrast in style as they completed their handover. Raikes was a 'dyed in the wool' traditionalist, whose father had commanded the Submarine Service, and who was about to retire after a distinguished career. Fieldhouse was the first of the new generation. Although he had strong links with the past, he was an active product of the Cold War and the nuclear age, both inexorably linked to current submarine practice. In HMS *Totem*, in the 1950s, he had taken part in Britain's first-ever structured surveillance operation against the Soviets. His subsequent commands of *Acheron*, *Tiptoe*, *Walrus* and *Dreadnought* had given him unparalleled experience. In his leadership of the Polaris force in its formative phase, he had acquired another priceless dimension. Nor was he unfamiliar with the 'nuts and bolts' of keeping the submarine show on the road. He had served at various times on the staff at *Dolphin*, in such diverse roles as rating's training, exercise planning and material development. He had even produced the first draft of the SSN bible, *The Conduct of Fleet Submarine Operations*.

From the outset, a matter of utmost importance occupied his mind. It was the fundamental issue of where and how FOSM should most effectively exercise his command. Raikes had been determined at all costs to maintain the *status quo* by remaining at *Dolphin*. His 'over my dead body' attitude towards any move had succeeded in putting off a decision until after his departure. As well as being base for what had become the First Submarine Squadron, the Fort Blockhouse complex had long been the administrative and training heartland of the Flotilla. What had changed in recent years was that the centre of gravity of submarine operational control had moved to the Fleet Headquarters at Northwood. It had been apparent for some time that changes were going to be needed. Fieldhouse was seen as having the freshness of mind to grasp the situation and tackle it head on.

At the end of 1976, the Submarine Flotilla was nearing a peak of effectiveness in fulfilling a wide range of roles. There were then nine SSNs in commission. Following the one-off *Dreadnought* and the five Valiant class, three of the much-improved Swiftsure class had entered service. Three more were due at intervals of 15 to 18 months, to be followed by the even more sophisticated Trafalgar class. As the older boats were paid off, there were plans for a rolling order of battle of 16 SSNs, plus the Polaris force.

When Fieldhouse became FOSM, all 21 SSKs of the Porpoise and Oberon classes were either in dockyard hands or available for operations. Despite the age of some of the boats – *Porpoise* had been commissioned in 1958 – they were still the quietest and best ocean capable conventional submarines in the world. *Onyx*, the last to be built for the Royal Navy, had entered service in 1967. Plans to replace them with a smaller number of a new design of SSK were still in early stages of discussion. These were heady days for the submarine command for a number of reasons. Operational concepts were on the move due to the alarming expansion of the Soviet Navy. New platforms, technology and weapon systems placed a heavy burden on all aspects of personnel recruiting, training and retention. The on-going replacement of conventional hulls by nuclear leviathans presented a daunting challenge to the engineering community and to all those others concerned with maintenance, dockyard and nuclear support. However, it was the first of these issues that was to decide where the Admiral's day-to-day presence was most needed.

Through the process of evolution, operational control of submarines had become fragmented. Clear-cut, not open to any argument, were procedures for the command and control of the nuclear deterrent. The Polaris chapter outlines that this was exercised by the Commander-in-Chief Fleet at Northwood in his capacity as CTF 345. It had never been intended that FOSM should be a link in this chain that needed to be kept as short and simple as possible. Just three authorities, with their numerous in-built safeguards, were involved: Her Majesty's Government, CTF 345 and the deployed Polaris force itself. The remainder of the Submarine Flotilla was controlled from FOSM's headquarters in *Dolphin*, with one most important exception.

British submarine participation in the Cold War, other than for nuclear deterrence, needed very special handling. Parts of the North Atlantic were fast becoming 'open house' for submarines of many nations. On the Soviet side, Yankee class SSBNs continued to transit from their Northern Fleet Bases to patrol areas off the United States eastern seaboard. The newer Delta class SSBNs, with their increased missile range, were able to reach their targets from the greater security of Arctic waters. SSNs of increasingly sophisticated types, including the latest high performance 'Alphas', came and went at irregular intervals to the Mediterranean and elsewhere. In the NATO arena, USN, RN and French SSBNs deployed from European bases to their highly classified patrol areas. Surveillance operations by USN and RN boats continued in the Barents Sea, the Mediterranean and, by SSKs, in the Baltic. Additionally, acting on superior Western intelligence, SSNs were diverted from other tasks to react to Soviet deployments. It was an amalgam of activity that required very careful control, both of measures to avoid mutual interference and of aggressive moves to place our submarines closely alongside those of the potential enemy. For obvious reasons this process of 'water space management' needed to be located near TF 345, within the Fleet HQ. Thus a new organisation known as TF 311 had been established to control submarines engaged in irregular Cold War operations, reporting direct to C-in-C and run by an experienced nuclear submarine CO. Although he was kept fully informed, FOSM's presence at Gosport isolated him from day to day involvement in these important activities.

Fieldhouse wore a second NATO 'hat'. Following his earlier full-time job as Commodore of the standing surface ship squadron, he assumed the role of Commander Submarines East Atlantic (COMSUBEASTLANT). This was an appointment largely concerned with planning for war, with staff work being led by a US Navy captain attached to his command. Meanwhile he was quick to develop a relationship with his American superior and counterpart, by visiting COMSUBLANT at his headquarters in Norfolk, Virginia.

* * * * * * * *

For the time being, Fieldhouse enjoyed being amongst his own people at *Dolphin*. Captain Robin Heath had welcomed him there as his already established Chief of Staff. They had served in *Totem* together and, later, Robin had been one of the first COs of *Renown* when John had commanded the Polaris squadron. One of John's sayings had stuck firmly in Robin's memory. 'Never fight a battle until you are reasonably sure you can win it.' Chief Staff Officer Engineering was Captain John Jacobsen. After leaving the first commission of HMS *Valiant*, John had served at Bath as the Nuclear Safety Officer to the Director General (Ships), a two-star equivalent civilian responsible for the design and construction of all naval vessels. During

Fieldhouse's Polaris command, Jacobsen had been responsible for qualifying all the squadron's nuclear Engineering Officers. For the first time, the Staff from the top downwards had a thorough knowledge of the idiosyncrasies of nuclear submarines. Jacobsen recalls that his boss

> had a wonderful presence and an entirely natural quality of command. As an engineer, you had to know your facts. He was quick to detect any flaws in your opinions. You knew when he was angry, but he was always completely in control of his emotions.

Things too were highly satisfactory on the domestic front. 'Pippins' had been let and the family moved into the admiral's residence at Dolphin House in Alverstoke. With its tennis court and pleasant garden, Midge remembers it as a thoroughly comfortable family home. Chief Cook Palmer of the exceptional culinary skills had moved with them from Devonport. On and off, he was to remain a member of the household for fourteen years.

John had also arranged to preserve the continuity of his private office by taking Jake Francis-Jones with him as his Secretary. They had established a strong bond over the previous 18 months, much of which had been spent living and working together in close proximity at sea. Jake remembers John as being 'astonishingly clever without ever showing it. He made everyone around him feel an important member of the team.' A specific memory is when a more junior officer became almost impertinent at a routine staff meeting. John inclined his head and said very quietly 'You mustn't get cross with me, you know!' In the Royal Navy the relationship between an admiral and his secretary is often more personal and enduring than equivalent partnerships in other services. Jake felt that he could not have done his job successfully if they had not been genuine personal friends.

Jake recalls an occasion when John was summoned to attend a meeting of the Nuclear Powered Warship Safety Committee. HMS *Valiant* (Commander John Coward) had had an alarming incident while close in the trail of a Soviet Echo II class submarine off the coast of Syria in the Eastern Mediterranean. Without warning, a salt water services pipe situated in the reactor compartment fractured, causing rapid sea water flooding to above the level of the pressuriser. Despite a serious trim problem on slowing down from a speed 18 knots, *Valiant* was brought under control, surfaced and the reactor shut down. In this hapless state, she was quickly joined by a gaggle of Russian warships. Meanwhile, the fault was isolated, the reactor compartment pumped out and thoroughly flushed through with fresh water. Having reported what amounted to a major nuclear incident, Coward was instructed to remain where he was pending expert technical analysis and further instructions. Even the possibility of sending a towing vessel was mooted. As the man on the spot, leaning heavily on his own judgement backed up by the advice of his own engineering staff, the CO felt it was safe to flash up the reactor, dive and extricate the submarine from her position of some embarrassment. In the event, it proved to have been a perfectly safe course of action and *Valiant* reached base without further incident; but Coward received a rebuke from the Commander-in-Chief and was in danger of being disciplined for exceeding his authority.

Fieldhouse, who had succeeded as FOSM since the date of the incident, listened carefully to the technical discussion, but became increasingly irritated by the committee's patronising tone. Eventually he found the right moment for a somewhat icy intervention that brought the proceedings to an abrupt conclusion. 'Gentlemen', he said; 'those of us who serve in submarines live closer to the consequences of our actions than any of you could possibly imagine.'

His confidence in his CO was fully justified. Coward led the frigate HMS *Brilliant* with great tenacity during the Falklands War and himself later became Flag Officer Submarines.

In June 1977, the Fleet assembled at Spithead for the Queen's Silver Jubilee Review. A total of one hundred and eighty ships rode at anchor, including representatives from foreign and Commonwealth navies and the merchant fleet. This was a much smaller gathering than that of the Coronation Review of 1953, but it was still a considerable display of naval force by any standards. Flying his Flag in the ageing HMS *Ark Royal* was the new Commander-in-Chief Fleet, Admiral Sir Henry Leach. Fieldhouse hoisted his Flag in the new SSN HMS *Superb*, and, as a fleet Flag Officer, was much involved in the various ceremonies and social activities surrounding the occasion. The highlight was the C-in-C's dinner for The Queen in the hangar of *Ark Royal*. Two hundred and fifty people attended, including all Flag and commanding officers of whatever rank.

A story has come to light from a reception hosted by Fieldhouse in *Superb's* Control Room. Next to the chart table was a loudspeaker, plugged into a VHF frequency, used by submarines in the anchorage for administrative traffic. During a lull in the conversation an impressive flow of expletives crackled over the ether, causing obvious embarrassment to some of the Admiral's guests. There followed a brief exchange between officialdom and miscreant: 'Report name of stupid person responsible for last transmission. Over'. 'I'm not that stupid. Out!'

At the end of the year, there was a rise in the temperature of the smouldering dispute between the UK and Argentina over the sovereignty of the Falkland Islands. This had being going on since 1820, when the Argentinians first laid claim to what they called Las Malvinas. Since 1833, the islands had been occupied and administered by the British. Under principles enshrined in the United Nations Charter, the UK had continued to defend its right to sovereignty on account of the determination of the population to remain British. Since 1976, Argentina had been governed by a military junta. This had led to a number of aggressive gestures in an area relatively close to the South American continent, but 8,000 miles away from the source of any meaningful military reinforcement from home.

As a prelude to continuing talks at the United Nations, the Labour Government's Foreign Secretary, David Owen, felt that it would be important to negotiate from a position of strength. First he reversed an unwise decision to pay off the naval patrol vessel HMS *Endurance*. Next, as the situation deteriorated, he asked for an SSN to be sent covertly to the South Atlantic. This incident is covered in some detail in Richard Hill's authorised biography of Admiral of the Fleet Lord Lewin, who was then serving as First Sea Lord. On Admiralty Board advice, a balanced force was despatched in November. The frigates *Phoebe* and *Alacrity*, together with RFAs *Olwen* and *Resurgent*, provided a more visible deterrent some 1,000 miles from the Falkland Islands. The SSN *Dreadnought* patrolled in a covert posture close inshore, unseen and unheralded; but probably 'known about' through the circulation of sensitive information through diplomatic and intelligence channels. Rules of Engagement had been drawn up and approved by Ministers. In the event, there was no further trouble during that Antarctic summer. Lewin, Leach and Fieldhouse had all been involved in this incident in one way or another. It was an interesting precursor to events of 1982, which were to see them as Chief of Defence Staff, First Sea Lord and Commander-in-Chief respectively.

Meanwhile Fieldhouse's main interest had been in the impressive performance of his old command, HMS *Dreadnought*; now becoming quite elderly with more than her fair share of material problems. When the crisis developed, she was already taking part in another routine deployment. On recall, she returned to Gibraltar at her best speed of just under 30 knots. There she fully stored for war before leaving for the Falklands. Christmas was spent patrolling off Port Stanley. When she finally arrived in her homeport of Faslane in February 1978, she had been away for seven months, having spent only seventeen days in harbour. This demonstrated, not for the first or last time, the unique capacity for endurance and power projection of the fleet submarine. But Fieldhouse never thought of the SSN as a political platform in isolation. He had always thought that its strength lay in its devastating contribution to a balanced mix of maritime forces.

* * * * * * * *

The move of FOSM's staff to Northwood took place during the Christmas leave period of 1977/1978. For many it was a nostalgic moment and inevitably there were some minor hiccups. What had gone forever was the autonomy of an independent submarine command. But Fieldhouse encouraged his team to make the new organisation work as smoothly as possible. On arrival he assumed direct control of CTF 311, and he soon found that the advantages of being in the forefront of the submarine operational scene outweighed all the disadvantages. One of the latter was the loss of the comforts and convenience of Dolphin House. John and Midge had to make do with a nearby married quarter. Another was the relatively soulless atmosphere of suburban Northwood and of the Fleet Headquarters itself. Although most of the staff was located in part of a large new office block, all sensitive activities took place in safety from nuclear attack deep underground. Robin Heath recalls that he was often required to deputise for his Admiral who liked to spend as much time as possible visiting his squadron commanders and their submarines. The main change from his days as a Captain SM was the growing number of 'nuclears'. The First Squadron of SSKs was based at *Dolphin*. The Second and Third Squadrons, with their mix of SSNs and SSKs, were based at Devonport and Faslane respectively. The Tenth Squadron of SSBNs remained at Faslane, very much as he had left it. There was also an additional Captain Submarine Sea Training located in the Clyde. Like many FOSMs before him, John made it business to visit all the boats in his command and to go to sea in as many of them as possible.

Jim Ring's book *We Come Unseen* (published in 2001) is a fascinating insight into the Submarine Command of the Cold War Years. Ring's novel approach to his subject was to examine the careers of six officers who entered Dartmouth in 1963/64. Of the generation after Fieldhouse, they had served their apprenticeships as watchkeepers both in diesel-electric boats and in the earlier nuclear submarines. When John became FOSM, they had all completed their Perisher and had moved on to SSK command. All known to him personally, these were amongst his 'band of brothers'; the inheritors of the skills he himself had helped to pioneer in the 1950s and 1960s. Later, when he became C-in-C, they were all nuclear submarine commanders. *We Come Unseen* tells of some stirring episodes by these COs, one of whom commanded HMS *Conqueror* which sank the Argentine cruiser *General Belgrano*. Their exploits in close contact with the Soviets required the highest professional standards from all on board which, in comparison with the remainder of the Flotilla, were in no way exceptional. The 1970s and 1980s, when Fieldhouse held high command, were periods of high achievement by British submarines in the prosecution of the Cold War. Much of this was highly sensitive and received little or no publicity in the rest of the Navy or the other Services. A cloak of security still envelops these operations and, like the escapades of the Special Air Service and Special Boat Squadron, it is not yet possible for the full story to be told.

It was at about this time that John became involved in a private venture that was to give him much pleasure and relaxation over the coming years. GP Dr David Black and his wife Thelma, who lived in Alverstoke, had been family friends for many years. After a visit to the London Boat Show, a plan was hatched for joint ownership of a small cruising yacht. After some deliberation, they bought a 28-foot 'Seal' and gave it the somewhat improbable name of *Hoi Polloi*; berthing it first at HMS *Dolphin* and later at the nearby Joint Services Sailing Centre on the site of the old coastal forces base, HMS *Hornet*. It proved to be an entirely happy arrangement. Now that his sea-going days were over, John could look forward to a form of relaxation afloat of his own choosing. When the children were younger, the family had driven to Spain for a number of enjoyable 'bucket and spade' holidays. Now that they were grown up and beginning to go their separate ways, *Hoi Polloi* became available for the occasional weekend in local waters and for longer excursions across the Channel. At first John sailed under the burgee of the Royal Naval Sailing Association. Later, in 1987, the co-owners acquired a more comfortable 'Moody 34'. By this time, John was Chief of the Defence Staff and a naval member of the Royal Yacht Squadron, proud to sail the new *Hoi Polloi* under the White Ensign. He was never much of a racing man; preferring the more relaxing joys of cruising. Midge enjoyed the social activity involved, but would be the first to admit that she was not a natural small boat sailor.

On 1st April 1978 Fieldhouse was promoted to Vice Admiral, one of fourteen in the Royal Navy at that time. This was a strictly routine matter, based solely on seniority and selection. It had no affect on his employment and he carried on to complete a full term in his current job. Later that year, Lewin informed him that he was to be next Controller of the Navy. Midge recalls that John regarded this with some foreboding and expected it to be his final appointment before retirement. It seems more likely, however, that it was part of a master plan to give him the Admiralty Board experience he needed before being propelled towards even higher places.

CHAPTER THIRTEEN

Controller

1979 – 1981

FIELDHOUSE TOOK HIS SEAT on the Admiralty Board for the first time on 1st April 1979. His naval colleagues were all well known to him. One of his mentors, Admiral Sir Terence Lewin, was nearing the end of his time as First Sea Lord and Chief of Naval Staff. In July of that year Lewin was promoted to Admiral of the Fleet in preparation for his role as the next Chief of the Defence Staff. The new professional head of the Royal Navy became Sir Henry Leach, under whose command Fieldhouse had so recently served at Northwood. Other naval members were Admiral Sir Gordon Tait (Second Sea Lord), and Vice Admirals Sir Anthony Morton (Vice Chief of Naval Staff) and Sir James Eberle (Chief of Fleet Support), who left shortly afterwards to take over from Henry Leach at Northwood. The Admiralty Board was under political management, usually chaired by the Permanent Under Secretary of State for Defence for the Royal Navy, a junior minister below cabinet rank. Other members were the Chief Scientist (Royal Navy), the Second Permanent Under Secretary of State (Administration) and the Deputy Under Secretary of State (Navy). The Secretary of State for Defence was the nominal chairman of the Admiralty Board. At that time he was the Right Hon Fred Mulley MP.

At first sight, this may have appeared to be an unwieldy management team, but, as a single service board, it seemed to work satisfactorily. Normally meetings were held on Thursdays. Except on very special occasions, naval members wore plain clothes. The First Sea Lord sometimes chaired a smaller group of admirals to discuss non-political issues such as senior officers' promotions. Despite his obvious political flair, evident during his time as a naval staff Director, Fieldhouse did not feel entirely at home in Whitehall. 'I joined the navy to go to sea, not to drive a desk at the MoD,' he told a friend, adding; 'but there comes a time when you have to pay back for the good times you've had.' Certainly there had been many of those all around the world, but nostalgia was entirely understandable now that his sea-going days were over.

On the credit side was the excellent arrangement of John's small private office. His Secretary, Captain David Allen, filtered and controlled the endless reams of paper that came and went in all directions. He was a large man with a 'monkish' appearance, well versed in the machinations of the ministry. At first he had to tread warily with his new boss, but he soon became John's personal friend and kindred spirit. He had an often-outrageous sense of humour and shared his master's priceless gift of being able to defuse an awkward situation with a few well-chosen words. His benevolent presence in the outer office was the harbinger of a considerable amount of leg pulling and laughter. The contrast between his mastery of the Whitehall scene and his private life was considerable. At heart, Allen was a countryman. He farmed his own sheep at Shapwick in Somerset and loved country pursuits. This was the beginning of a well-forged partnership, ideally suited to the conduct of ministry business. When John returned to the Admiralty Board later as First Sea Lord, it was no surprise that he chose to have David once more at his side.

As his other senior member of personal staff, Fieldhouse inherited from his predecessor a most excellent Naval Assistant in the person of Captain John Burgess. John was an astute Marine Engineer Officer who had started his career as an artificer apprentice. His depth of experience in engineering matters, including the nuclear field, provided the best possible practical support. Who better than he to elaborate on the structure of his master's job and on the impressive 'journey' they took together?

> The office of Controller covered complex responsibilities under two distinctive hats. As what used to be called the Third Sea Lord, he was a member of the Admiralty Board and had the functional role and title of Controller of the Navy. He task was to establish the material needs of the Fleet, and to ensure that design, development and procurement systems were in place to match the Board's requirements. He was the principal advisor to the Board on material matters.
>
> He was also Controller Sea Systems, one of three Service Material Chiefs, and directly responsible to the Chief of Defence Procurement, a five-star civilian who sat on the Defence Council. In this task Controller was responsible for all naval procurement, to a multi-billion pound budget, and for the coordination of those systems with those of the other two Services. The two tasks were, and are today, complementary one to another, and indistinguishable in day to day terms; but the lines of responsibility on the one hand to the Admiralty Board, and on the other to the Procurement Executive were clear and distinct.
>
> The Controller's post has always been filled by either Seaman or Engineering sub-specialists; but there is no doubt that a seaman with wide operational and Naval Staff experience, which John Fieldhouse and his predecessor Dick Clayton brought to the job, held a considerable advantage. These were men of stature, and the high regard in which John in particular was held both in the MoD and throughout the Fleet gave added authority to the Controller's teams. Of course a Seaman Controller needs good technical men supporting him, and in Lindsay Bryson and Ted Horlick, John had two of the

> very best. [Bryson later succeeded Fieldhouse as Controller of the Navy.]
>
> Controller's tasks took him far and wide, and he would always be accompanied by his Naval Assistant, who John liked to call his Business Manager. Much of the time in the Whitehall office was taken up in processing the countless papers calling for decisions, or in long meetings and discussions with colleagues, but whenever possible and at least once a week, Controller would visit his outlying establishments in Bath or the south coast, or the factories and shipyards carrying out the defence business. John's deep understanding of the Navy and of the problems of procurement meant that he was always warmly received, and of course lobbied hard, for everyone knew he carried real clout back at the Ministry. His own warmth and often-avuncular manner, and his relaxed good humour, left everyone feeling good. Only later when they shook their heads did they discover that their throats had been cut!

Dartmouth term mate Simon Cassels was also enjoying a highly successful career. When John arrived as Controller, Simon was a rear admiral serving as Assistant Chief of Naval Staff (Operational Requirements), a post that resulted in much professional contact between them. Simon had seen little of John since their teenage days and was privately concerned that he might not have the ability to measure up to the demands of his weighty responsibilities. He recalls that after a few weeks his mind had been completely put at rest. In his view John quickly assumed the aura and stature of a highly respected Admiralty Board member and Whitehall warrior. John Burgess continues:

> Midge has said that John did not really enjoy his time as Controller. As a fighting seaman he certainly felt the many frustrations of the MoD's workings, and he always walked out of that Whitehall building feeling mightily relieved, but he knew how important his work was. Even before it was confirmed officially, he must also have had a shrewd idea of where he was going afterwards, and the experience and friends he made in the material business would stand him in good stead in later years. No one could say which Controllers made the greatest impact, for several went on to greater things as did John himself. The success of Fieldhouse in this stage of his career may be measured both by his later achievements and by the fact that at least one of great companies that he worked so closely with hoped that, on retirement from the Navy, he might become its Chairman. There is no greater compliment than that.

With its two great Directorates of the Ship and the Weapons Departments, and the Above Water and Underwater Research Establishments, the office of Controller of the Navy was very much engineering orientated. Although Fieldhouse himself possessed many of the instincts of an engineer, it was essential that he should be closely supported by a 'no nonsense plumber' in whose judgement he had implicit trust. Burgess fulfilled this role to perfection, soon becoming an integral member of his wider family. Despite his seniority, the Business Manager was also required to perform the traditional role of personal aide or Flag Lieutenant. On the memorable occasion when the Admiral first appeared dressed as a naval ADC to The Queen, his tailor had sewn the attachment fitting onto the wrong or left shoulder of his jacket. With a bit of improvisation, the aiguillettes were reversed and no one seemed to notice the difference! Burgess additionally felt it prudent to keep spare collar studs and cuff links in his brief case on the assumption that, if they were there, they were unlikely to be needed. As First Sea Lord some years later, Fieldhouse required someone with special qualities to fill a particularly irksome management appointment. He had no hesitation in dipping down and selecting Burgess for promotion to Rear Admiral to fulfil this task.

John Burgess recalls the first meeting of staff in the Controller's private office. With disarming candour, Fieldhouse revealed that 'I have no secrets, no mistresses or anything of that sort. Everything that I know, you will know, and I expect the same openness in return.' He also started a routine that was to continue throughout all his three senior appointments in the ministry. He liked to 'walk the offices'. This consisted of regular visits to each member of staff, however junior, at their desk or workstation. There he would briefly discuss their hopes and fears; their homes and families. He would make it his business to be informed about such things as bereavements, illnesses, house-moving problems or even difficulties in settling a child into a new school. If appropriate, these matters would be relayed to Midge who would follow them up in more detail in her own time. With the couple's personal interest and total lack of pomposity, it is of little wonder that everyone thoroughly enjoyed working for them.

For the second time as a Flag officer, Fieldhouse had taken over from Admiral Sir Richard Clayton. Clayton was a man of high intellect with an unbelievable capacity for absorbing and dealing with paperwork. His working style was to expect to find three huge piles of files on his desk on arrival every morning. Generally, one required immediate attention; the second needed action before the close of play; the third needed to be thoroughly read and dealt with by the following morning. The staff only tried this on once with the new Controller, who quickly introduced sweeping powers of delegation, down to Secretary and Assistant Secretary level. Matters positively needing his attention were brought to his notice when required. Others were dealt with by subordinates who had authority to act for him; who made it their business to know precisely what was in his mind. Despite these measures, he could rarely avoid taking papers home; usually briefing material for the next day's programme. Burgess was surprised to receive a complaint from Midge about some nasty scratches on one side of her body. Apparently they had been caused by the sharp metal edges of a certain type of file that John had chosen to take to bed with him to read! On the domestic front, this was his only appointment during fourteen years as an active flag officer without an official residence and retinue. The family took a small flat in Putney for use during the week, returning to 'Pippins' most weekends. The only luxury commensurate with his lofty status was the permanent use of an official car and driver. This was essential for his many visits up and down the country and for transporting classified papers to and from his home.

* * * * * * * *

Burgess recalls the impressive clarity of John's mental processes. Almost by instinct, he was able to relate material issues to their appropriate operational requirements. It was not just a matter of determining how much a particular piece of kit would cost to develop, to run and maintain. He would balance this wholly important data with such thoughts as 'How much will this help to steal a march on Admiral Gorshkov in the prosecution of the Cold War?' If the answer was 'not very much really', he would move on to consider other priorities. In the continuous debate on the procurement of future ships and equipment, Fieldhouse made use of all the avenues of professional advice available to him; not only from his own department, but also from the office of the Chief of Fleet Support, the Defence Secretariat and the Naval Staff. His signal contribution was to stand comfortably astride the operator/engineer interface and to weigh priorities with clarity of mind and decisiveness. Naturally his proposals were subject to the approval of his Admiralty Board colleagues, but they soon came to respect and rely upon the unerring soundness of his judgements. In one important respect, he and his naval colleagues never wavered. Whatever pressures might be brought to bear from the submarine and air lobbies, there would always be a continuing demand in the navy for a maximum number of suitably equipped surface ships.

On a visit to the USA, Burgess remembers being impressed by his master's ability to open doors that would have been firmly closed to lesser mortals. Fieldhouse had several friends within the powerful submarine community. Admiral Joe Williams, a previous COMSUBLANT, had moved on to a retirement job on the Board of the Electric Boat Company at Groton, Connecticut; the lead building yard for all classes of American nuclear submarine. On a visit to him there, Fieldhouse was asked if he would like to have a close look at an Ohio class SSBN; the leviathan built to accommodate the huge new Trident ballistic missile system. This request was referred to maverick Admiral Hyman G Rickover, who predictably turned it down. However, Admiral Al Whittall, the four-star Chief of Naval Materiel in the Pentagon, overrode Rickover to ensure that the visit went ahead. At that time

USS *Ohio* was in the water in the final stages of fitting out, while the second of class, USS *Georgia*, was 'hull complete' and available for inspection on its building platform. With the UK about to go for Trident as a replacement for Polaris, this was a very timely and useful concession. Up until that point it had been unheard of in the US for the first of class of any type of ship to be available for close inspection by a representative of a foreign navy, however close the link or enduring the special relationship. There is no doubt that Fieldhouse was held in great respect in the US Navy because of his pioneering role as a UK nuclear submariner.

Although they were on the other side of the fence as they competed for lucrative contracts, Fieldhouse maintained warm and friendly relationships with the recently nationalised shipyards and with defence equipment companies. By 1979, it had become increasingly evident that shipbuilding in Britain would be unable to survive at its previous level. A world-wide reduction, particularly in the number of merchant ships required, intense overseas competition – much of which was heavily subsidised – and continuing restrictions on capital investment all contributed to the creation of conditions which would bring about the closure of many shipyards. The number of employees in UK yards fell from 87,000 in 1977 to 41,000 in 1985 when the warship building yards were privatised. During this period, the stronger yards prospered while the weaker ones went to the wall. Pre-eminent amongst successful yards was Yarrow Shipbuilders Ltd at Scotstoun, where Fieldhouse had stood by *Diomede* and where his old friend Bob Easton had recently become Chairman and Managing Director. This sole survivor of the proud tradition of Clyde warship building became the lead yard for the RN's first truly 'all missile' ship. The Type 22 frigate was also the first warship to be built to metric standards. Between 1979 and 1988 ten of these ships were completed at a steady rate of one a year. The last two, *Cornwall* and *Cumberland* were amongst the most versatile frigates ever to enter service in the RN. As First Sea Lord, in the light of the experience of the Falklands War, Fieldhouse had absolutely insisted that the last batch of Type 22s should be fitted with a gun to enhance their general purpose capability.

An enormous adjunct to Yarrow's status was its fully owned subsidiary the Yarrow-Admiralty Research Department (YARD). From a new site in the centre of Glasgow, opened in 1976, it made a major contribution in the fields of warship design, the use of computer services and improvements to support facilities in dockyards and naval bases.

Towards the end of John's period as Controller, the MoD approved the Naval Staff Target for an entirely new concept of frigate to be built in larger numbers to complete the replacement of the ageing Leander class. In contrast to the Type 22, this was a smaller, less expensive and less manpower intensive general-purpose frigate. Yarrow took the lead in designing the first ever RN warship of modular construction. Large units were fully outfitted before being moved to the building slip for incorporation into the main structure. This gave construction teams easier access to their work and substantially reduced the build time. It was not until 1984 that the order was placed with Yarrow for the first Type 23 frigate, to be called HMS *Norfolk*.

Peter Usher, with whom John had shared an office when they were both Commanders on FOSM's staff, was another useful contact in the shipyard world. Peter was then Deputy Managing Director of Shipbuilding for Vosper Thornycroft (VT) at Woolston. VT had made major inroads into independent warship design, doing particularly well with foreign orders for third world nations.

VSEL at Barrow-in-Furness, known to most as 'Vickers', had a peerless tradition of decades of submarine construction. As lead yard for all new classes, it had entered an entirely new world with the introduction into the RN of nuclear power. George Standen's memories go back to the early 1960s. At the same time as the USN training of the first *Dreadnought* personnel, Standen had led a small team from VSEL, Rolls Royce & Associates and the Admiralty in Bath to the Electric Boat Company in Groton, Connecticut. By standing by the commissioning of USS *Scorpion*'s S5W Nuclear Plant, they gained the necessary experience to set up a Dockside Test Organisation (DTO) for *Dreadnought*, which became the forerunner of the facility used for all Britain's nuclear boats. The DTO, responsible for all nuclear documentation, test results and safety standards, required the closest possible cooperation between ship's staff, construction and support agencies; all of whom operated the plant throughout its test programme from the date of first fill of the primary circuit to operation under full reactor power. The culmination of this activity was the 'fast cruise', for which the CO and ship's team assumed full responsibility.

Fieldhouse had been a regular visitor to Barrow since his earliest nuclear days; from 1962 – 1964 as FOSM's Flotilla Material Officer; 1964 – 1966 as the second CO of HMS *Dreadnought*; 1968 – 1970 as the Captain SM of the Polaris squadron and from 1976 – 1978 as Flag Officer Submarines. He was often entertained by the leader of the Vickers' submarine team, Leonard Renshaw (later Sir Leonard and Chairman of the Company). As Standen states, 'There was always a very close rapport as John and Midge were fully gathered into the Vickers fold.' SSNs *Spartan* and *Splendid* were both accepted into service during John's time as Controller. Following along next in line was the first of the new class, HMS *Trafalgar*. Launched with great pride by Midge in 1981, she was to join the fleet in 1983, when her husband was First Sea Lord.

Despite his total commitment to the long-term future of nuclear submarines, John had long been an advocate of a balanced submarine

Flotilla that contained, as a replacement for the Porpoise and Oberon classes, a smaller and extremely quiet diesel electric submarine. The operational case was based primarily on the need to plug the Greenland/Iceland/UK gap in time of war; to integrate with SOSUS and other long-range passive sensors in intercepting and attacking Soviet submarines breaking out into the North Atlantic. Because of financial constraints and conflicting priorities, the first of class, HMS *Upholder*, did not enter service until 1990. Although four submarines were built, the Cold War had ended and they were taken out of service early because the expense of running them could no longer be justified. Enhanced passive sonar performance continued to dominate anti-submarine warfare thinking. This had led to the development of towed arrays, in which multiple transducers could be placed outside the immediate influence of a platform's own noise, be it a submarine or, exceptionally, in some of the new Type 22 frigates.

It is inappropriate to measure the effectiveness of a Controller by the orders placed for new ships and weapon systems during his period of office. To reach this stage was the culmination of an elaborate process involving numerous agencies over a period of many years. Because of this, a Controller's principal contribution may lie in the early stages of a project which may not even go out to tender until after he has left office. Likewise, he may be seen to take the credit for a predecessor's hard work. Because everything he did was subject to the most severe financial stringency, Fieldhouse is known to have thought of himself as nobody's friend. He had to fight hard for the money the navy needed for its ships and equipment, both within the Navy Department and across the Joint Services divide. Despite his excellent relationships with shipyards and equipment contractors, he had to fight them too before arriving at favourable contracts. Perhaps what he liked least about his job was that it isolated him from day-to-day contact with the men of the active fleet. There is no doubt that somebody of his calibre was required to fill this important office, and for him it served as a means towards a highly satisfactory end.

John was made a Knight Commander of the Bath (KCB) in the New Years' Honours of 1980. At that time this was standard recognition and reward for an officer of his rank and status. His great pleasure lay in the implicit recognition of Midge's enormous contribution to the success of his career. Harold, himself a knight of many years standing, was delighted that his elder son had joined the club. But an even greater joy awaited John when he was informed by First Sea Lord Sir Henry Leach that he was to relieve Sir James Eberle in May 1981 as Commander-in-Chief Fleet. Short of entering the highest echelons of the politico/military arena, this was the best of all jobs in the Royal Navy. As he prepared for yet another rapid promotion, he cannot possibly have foreseen that within a year he would find himself commanding British forces in a bloody conflict.

CHAPTER FOURTEEN

Fleet Commander

1981 – 1982

LIEUTENANT COMMANDER JONATHON BAND first met the new Commander-in-Chief when he was summoned to the Controller's office in the MoD to be interviewed as a possible Flag Lieutenant. He found him

> sitting behind his desk, peering over his glasses with what I later came to know as the famous Fieldhouse 'look'. He quickly put me at my ease, but it soon became apparent that there was a very tough edge to him. We talked about me, my command of HMS *Soberton*, what I felt I could contribute as his Flag Lieutenant and what I thought about the Navy. Right at the end, he asked 'So what about your family?' Having been married for two years with one small baby, I replied 'This would be a chance to see something of my family and I would want to have them with me.' His reaction was 'Well, that sounds very sensible.' I didn't know at the time about the strong bond between John and Midge and the fact that they were almost always together. I must have given the right answers because I was offered the job very soon afterwards. In the event they were both very welcoming, and having Sarah with me at Northwood worked very well.

On his arrival in post, these were Jonathon's first impressions.

> He had an incredible knack of relaxing people and getting straight to the point; but there was always time for a bit of humour and banter. He had a tremendous grasp of his subject and a great sense of balance. It became a real privilege to work for him. I learnt so much from his natural way of gaining people's confidence. I soon came to know him as a top operator; devastatingly effective.

This was the beginning of a highly satisfying relationship. As these words are written, Jonathon is the current Commander-in-Chief Fleet; living with his wife Sarah in the home John and Midge came to know so well. 'When I first came back here as an admiral, I had to pinch myself to make sure it was really me. To remind me of my time as Flag Lieutenant, I still get the occasional call from Midge asking me for somebody's telephone number!'

*   *   *   *   *   *   *   *

Flagship HMS *Glamorgan* leaves Portsmouth for the round the world deployment

JF with his deployment COs

JF and his COs are received by the King of Tonga

USS *Enterprise* (centre) and HMS *Glamorgan* (bottom right) with other ships off the coast of California during Exercise 'Valiant Heritage'

HMS *Dolphin*, home to Flag Officer Submarines and the First Submarine Squadron

Controller of the Navy visiting Vosper Thornycroft

Ships at Gibraltar immediately before the Falklands War

The Falklands Command Team at Northwood
From left: Herbert, Moore, JF, Hallifax, Curtiss and Hammersley

The new Commander-in-Chief Fleet arrives at Northwood

The Prime Minister with JF and Midge at Admiralty House
Lewin at right

Hermes at war

HM The Queen and JF with Curtiss and Trant

Staff and retinue at Admiralty House

JF meets Woodward on return from South Atlantic

SS *Canberra* returns to Southampton with 3 Commando Brigade Royal Marines

Fieldhouse succeeded Sir James Eberle as Fleet Commander on 5th May 1981. He was wearing the uniform of a full admiral for the first time, one of just six on the active list of the RN. There is a delightful photograph of him on that day; bending slightly forward in characteristic pose; talking to a submarine rating in the Guard of Honour. It looks as if that young man had been made to feel one of the most important people in the whole world. Northwood held very few surprises for John. It was only a little over two years since he had served there as FOSM. He was thoroughly familiar with the command structure, the communications set-up and the rabbit warren of narrow underground corridors. The main difference was that he was now master of all he surveyed. He spoke of it as 'the best job in the Navy' and it certainly had far reaching powers and responsibilities.

The title Commander-in-Chief Fleet embraced all his national responsibilities. These were discharged largely through his Chief of Staff, Vice Admiral David Hallifax, who acted on his behalf during his frequent absences. They had got to know each other quite well during John's FOF 2 days; when David had been CO of HMS *Fife*. More recently, Hallifax had flown his Flag at sea as FOF1; so was fully up to speed with operational practices. There were several other subordinate Flag officers. FOFs 1, 2 and 3 had their shore headquarters at Portsmouth, Devonport and near Portsmouth respectively. As has already been seen in an earlier chapter, these admirals directed the affairs of the surface fleet of frigate size and above; taking sea-going opportunities during group deployments or whenever a task group might be formed for a particularly purpose, such as a NATO exercise or a JMC. Minor war vessels, such as the Minehunting/Minesweeping force and the Fishery Protection Squadron were also part of the Fleet; but were separately administered through local shore based area flag officers. The employment and movement of all fleet units, from HMS *Hermes* to the Carlingford Lough anti-IRA patrol vessel, were programmed by the operations staff at Northwood.

At that time, 3 Commando Brigade, Royal Marines, was not under direct Fleet command, except when individual RM commandos were embarked as a prelude to amphibious warfare training. Whilst afloat, they reported to Commodore Amphibious Warfare who, in his turn, was subordinate to FOF3, the Flag officer responsible for aircraft carriers and for the assault ships *Fearless* and *Intrepid*. These two latter ships were fitted with docks, landing craft and the command and control facilities necessary to mount an amphibious landing. The carriers *Hermes* and *Invincible* were optimised for a combined ASW role and for operating the new and highly successful vertical take off and landing aircraft, the Sea Harrier; using 'ski-jumps' to assist take off when heavily laden. In a further configuration, they could embark RM commandos and put them ashore by helicopter. Fieldhouse's old command, *Hermes*, had seen service in a variety of roles. Now she was nearing the end of her useful life; to be replaced by *Invincible*'s sister ships *Illustrious* and *Ark Royal*, both of which were still building.

Flag Officer Submarines and Chief Staff Officer Engineering were collocated in the headquarters. FOSM was Vice Admiral Peter Herbert with whom John had undergone the hard slog of nuclear training at Greenwich in the late 1950s. His responsibilities were very much as Fieldhouse's had been a couple of years earlier. CSO(E) was Rear Admiral 'Spam' Hammersley. He and John went back even further together. They had been shipmates in HMS *Tiptoe* and later in HMS *Dreadnought*. Spam's singular contribution to the nuclear submarine programme over many years had been recognised by promotion to Flag rank. Now, he advised on all aspects of engineering fleet wide, although the support facilities were concentrated in the Royal Dockyards and other Base Ports.

As CTF 345, C-in-C was also the Polaris force commander. This task was carried out in great secrecy in an isolated cell in the underground headquarters, which was known to all simply as the 'hole'. This expanded relic of a World War II Coastal Command HQ, with its metal staircases, narrow passageways and less than perfect air conditioning and lighting arrangements, housed all the other sensitive elements of command and control. There worked all the operations, intelligence and communications staffs. It was there that the C-in-C and his Flag officers received daily briefings before returning to their more comfortable offices above ground. Because of its association with the nuclear deterrent, the hole was subject to the strictest security, being guarded by two Royal Marine armed sentries at all times. Nearby was a huge building site in which was being constructed a purpose-built, thoroughly modern underground HQ. The lengthy building process was nearing completion; but it would not be fully ready for use until after Fieldhouse's departure. All senior officers and their personal and administrative staffs had above-ground offices in a large, multi-story headquarters building. The rest of the site contained various support facilities such as storerooms, the transport pool and rather featureless messes used mainly for feeding officers, ratings and other ranks at their place of work. Adjoining was a patch of married quarters, but there were very limited accommodation facilities for single men and women at Northwood. Most staff officers had local lodgings and came and went to their distant homes at weekends.

The other senior officers attending the daily briefings were Air Marshal John Curtiss, Air Officer Commanding 18 Group RAF, and his Chief of Staff Air Vice Marshal George Chesworth. Command of the Nimrod force of maritime patrol aircraft was co-located at Northwood. Curtiss reported to his own C-in-C at RAF Strike Command at nearby High Wycombe. In other places, particularly within the MoD, relationships between the RN and the RAF had long been fractious. This was absolutely not so at Northwood. As Curtiss put it:

> It was my good fortune to be appointed AOC 18 Group in 1980, just before the arrival of John Fieldhouse as C-in-C Fleet. We immediately established an excellent rapport which developed into a firm friendship which lasted until his untimely death some years later. It was essential that there was complete cooperation between our two commands and with John as C-in-C this was firmly established and thoroughly understood and acted upon at all levels of our two Services.

Chesworth was similarly impressed by the new arrival.

> My immediate impression – which I never changed – was that here was a people's person, with a ready smile and friendly, but very steady, eyes. It did not take any of us long to recognize that here was a man and leader who fully deserved the respect and affection we soon felt for him.

These sentiments were to serve the nation well when the airmen came under the submariner's command during the Falklands War some months later.

While many of his national responsibilities came as second nature to the new C-in-C, this was not so in respect of his two NATO 'hats'. As Allied Commander-in-Chief Channel (CINCHAN), he became a Major NATO Commander (MNC) in his own right. Although his area of responsibility was small, his status was considerable. There were just three MNCs in all. The other two, the Supreme Allied Commander Atlantic (SACLANT) and the Supreme Allied Commander Europe (SACEUR), were a US admiral and a US general respectively. CINCHAN's wartime responsibility for mine warfare and the protection of shipping in the English Channel and adjacent waters was a relatively minor task. The prime benefit was membership of NATO's prestigious Nuclear Planning Group that gave Fieldhouse a seat at the free world's top military table. Moreover, his presence there was seen by other NATO nations as a valuable European presence in an American dominated sphere. As an MNC, CINCHAN had a point of contact with the Chief of Defence Staff (CDS) of each member nation. At the NATO headquarters in Brussels it was with the Chairman of the Military Committee who was an ex-CDS of one of the member nations, elected by his peers on behalf of their governments. Transcending all those of whatever uniform was the Secretary General of NATO, Dr Joseph Luns. Already known to Fieldhouse, he was a giant of a man, both physically and intellectually; who had done a vast amount to hold the Alliance together as a political entity. Assisting him were the various Ambassadors to NATO, known as the PERMREPS. The practical embodiment of CINCHAN's peacetime activities was his control of the Standing Naval Force Channel (STANAVFORCHAN). Organised along the same lines as the STANAVFORLANT, which he had previously commanded, this was a mixed group of NATO mine warfare vessels that operated and exercised together in European coastal waters.

Fieldhouse's second NATO 'hat' was that of Commander-in-Chief East Atlantic Area (CINCEASTLANT). In this role he was a Major Subordinate Commander (MSC) to SACLANT, with whom he sat on equal terms as a MNC. Operationally, this was a considerably more important command, his area embracing much of the 'hot' water of the Cold War. Certainly the East Atlantic would be the scene of frenzied maritime activity in any period of tension or transition to war. Standard scenarios that were exercised on a regular basis were the reinforcement of Europe, carrier battle group forays into the Norwegian Sea and amphibious group operations in Northern Norway. The continuous peacetime activities of the Standing Naval Force Atlantic came under CINCEASTLANT's command when it was operating in eastern waters – which it did for most of the year.

Nine NATO nations were represented on the entirely separate NATO staff at Northwood, headed by a Dutch rear admiral as Chief of Allied Staff. Like their C-in-C, several officers wore dual CHAN and EASTLANT 'hats'. As a group involved mainly in planning for war, they were also accommodated 'down the hole', but without access to the various national activities that were conducted there. Those familiar with the Northwood experience may have weathered the storm of the repetitive acronyms used in the last few paragraphs. Others may well have been sunk without trace, but should perhaps accept that Fieldhouse had inherited a substantial command by any standards. In their simplest terms, his national tasks were to operate Britain's independent nuclear deterrent and to maintain the Fleet in the highest possible state of training, morale and preparedness for war. His NATO role was to promote international confidence and understanding in order to prepare for the smoothest possible transition from peace to rising tension and conflict – in the unlikely event that it might ever occur. It is interesting to reflect upon the balance of time spent between these two activities. Jonathon Band remembers that Fieldhouse devoted about 90% of his intellectual time to his national responsibilities. His actual diary time stood at about 75%, because of NATO's greater demand on travel and entertainment.

* * * * * * * *

John and Midge lost no time in turning their residence, Admiralty House, into a family home. Situated as it was in London's outer stockbroker belt, it was the sort of house in which one would expect to find a wealthy main board director of a leading commercial company. With plenty of parking space, a large garden and spacious public rooms, it formed an ideal location for the endless stream of guests that passed through its welcoming doors. C-in-C was expected to entertain more frequently and lavishly that any other Flag officer in the navy. Happily, the allowances were generous, particularly from NATO sources. John and Midge lived well, but never managed to save for their retirement. John's predecessor, Jim Eberle, had run Admiralty House as a naval mess because his family home was in Devon and his wife very seldom came to London. As has already been seen, Midge was an essential part of John's lifestyle, either at home or on many of his travels abroad. Whichever way he chose to play it, the C-in-C was provided with the necessary staff to entertain effectively. Those who were invited enjoyed the benefits of an excellent table, with vegetables coming fresh from the garden. High on the list of guests were visiting NATO officials; but Northwood was also a shop window for the Royal Navy itself. Politicians, senior civil servants, captains of industry and senior officers from the other services were all invited home to lunch after their appropriate meetings and briefings in the Headquarters. Also welcome were visiting Flag officers and the commanding officers of ships on completion of their official calls.

One of the many COs to have called was Commander Mike Boyce on relinquishing command of the SSN *Superb*. Now Admiral Lord Boyce and the second submariner to have achieved the ultimate office of Chief of the Defence Staff, he recalls with feeling an apposite comment he received from his Commander-in-Chief that day:

> I hope you enjoyed your drive [period in command]. As your career unfolds you will look back on it as the last time you were in complete control of events going on around you!

When John was at Northwood, there were lunch parties at Admiralty House almost every working day plus less frequent evening dinner parties. Jonathon Band reflects on Midge's amazing contribution.

> Midge had very clear views on how the domestic staff should be organised to best advantage. Very occasionally they did not exactly coincide with John's, but she was usually right and invariably got her way. She was a larger than life character – as she still is today – and a hugely welcoming hostess. With her gift for languages, she was able to greet a Belgian with a few words of French or Flemish. She also knew a bit of German and Russian and had a rare ability to embrace people and put them at their ease. Many of those invited were strangers both to their hosts and to each other. I have never known a couple who were so good at 'working a room'. Everyone, regardless of rank or status, was made to feel very much at home.

A photograph of the personal staff shows a total of twenty people and two dogs; but this also includes those in the Admiral's private office. Seated, flanking John and Midge, are Secretary Captain John Shillingford, Jonathon Band, Assistant Secretary Third Officer Judy Payne, the Chief Cook and the Chief Steward. Standing behind are thirteen assorted men and women. These included cooks and stewards, the Royal Marine driver and the boat's crew. The latter were employed on cleaning, gardening and other duties as there was no suitable expanse of water in the Northwood area on which to moor the C-in-C's barge! All were gathered into a loyal and devoted team with one single purpose – to support their Admiral. As John used to say, 'If anyone is grumpy, including me, it reflects upon the performance of the whole team.' The incomparable Chief Cook Palmer was in his third Fieldhouse retinue appointment. Others were serving for the first time and would remain with the family for the remainder of John's active career.

A particular favourite was Sharon Davies (nee Kirkham) who, as a teenager, joined the household as the only Wren Steward. As well as her general duties, she was to work personally for Midge for the next seven years. Because she was always there, she came to be treated almost like a third daughter. Some of her memories deserve to be shared.

> John Fieldhouse was an extraordinary man. He treated the staff as part of the family. He was genuinely interested in our lives. For such a busy man, his memory of names and circumstances within our families was most endearing … I absolutely adored working their parties. Late into the night Midge would get on the piano and we would all sing. It was great fun … I used to go shopping with Midge sometimes. It was her favourite pastime. I often had to tell the boss white lies. 'Yes, Sir, Lady Fieldhouse has had that dress for ages!' He always smiled and looked at me over the top of his glasses … When I was married in 1984, the Boss and Lady Fieldhouse drove all the way to Liverpool for my wedding. I felt so humbled that such a busy man had taken time out to attend. They brought us beautiful gifts … I left in 1986 when I became pregnant. The Boss told me that he might later be going to Brussels. Would I consider joining his staff with my husband? As you can imagine, I would have walked there with my son on my back! … There is not one of us whose life he did not touch in one way or another. As a tribute to Lord Fieldhouse we have held a reunion with Midge and the family every year since his death. After the Navy I felt that life had ended, but he became my inspiration; giving me the encouragement and optimism I needed to face the future. I think he made a great difference to my life. I am now a director of two companies which are doing extremely well. There will never be another quite like him and not a day goes by when I don't think of him.

Jonathon hosted the 2004 reunion in the familiar surroundings of Admiralty House at Northwood. He has a few more words about his illustrious predecessor.

> He was an absolutely straightforward person, always quite clear where his priorities lay. He also made sure we knew what was in his mind so that we could support him effectively. He was demanding to work for

> because he was always busy, both professionally and socially; but no one ever minded because he swept us all up into the magical atmosphere his presence created. I saw him weary at airports and disappointed when things went wrong, but I very seldom saw him irritable. He was a very good-natured man, but there was this hard edge to him – seldom seen, but once seen, never forgotten. What annoyed him most was professional incompetence; someone who had let him or herself down, or their ship, their service or the nation.

* * * * * * * *

As 1981 progressed, Fieldhouse was able to settle in and enjoy all the many different facets of his fascinating job. One of his first moves was to make himself as well known as possible to his commanding officers. It was customary for them to call on C-in-C at Northwood when taking up or relinquishing their appointments. What concerned Fieldhouse was the long period in between. Early in his time, he hoisted his Flag afloat in a big ship at Portsmouth, Devonport and Rosyth in succession. During a day or two in each port he received his COs' calls and entertained them at a series of lunch and dinner parties. Band was always with him for his national commitments.

His regular NATO duties took him to Brussels, to Norfolk Virginia, to change of command ceremonies of the standing naval forces and elsewhere. For the more important meetings, he was usually accompanied by his Secretary. Captain Graham Meredith had worked for Admiral Eberle, but stayed on for several months before being relieved by John Shillingford towards the end of the year. Meredith recalls an October meeting of the prestigious Nuclear Planning Group at the Gleneagles Hotel in Scotland, before moving on to a Trafalgar Night dinner in the wardroom of the Clyde Submarine Base HMS *Neptune*.

Meanwhile, in the MoD, the First Sea Lord Sir Henry Leach was having a less enjoyable experience. In his autobiography *Endure No Makeshifts*, Leach outlines the problem that was to have alarming consequences for the Royal Navy.

> January 1981, saw the start of increasing unease and uncertainty within the Ministry. [John] Nott assumed office [as Defence Secretary] with preconceived ideas that the Navy needed to be cut back, the Air Force needed to be built up and the Army was about right. The origin of these preconceptions was never discovered but they persisted throughout the usual round of initial briefings – in which many questions were asked but scant heed paid to the answers – and beyond. Soon afterwards the new Defence Secretary wisely paid a lightning visit to Washington to meet his United States opposite number. It was while returning from that trip, on a wet Sunday afternoon in Bermuda, that the main milestones of what was to become the notorious 1981 Defence Review were sketched out.

The effect of the proposed cuts on the Fleet promised to be nothing short of catastrophic. Not only was the RN to be saddled with the whole costs of introducing Trident as a replacement for Polaris; in the shorter term, the new aircraft carrier *Invincible* was to be sold to Australia; the two assault ships, *Fearless* and *Intrepid* were to be paid off, as was the ice patrol ship *Endurance*. Within a few years the number of destroyers and frigates – the backbone of the Fleet – would be reduced from the middle sixties to the mid forties. There was to be a corresponding cut in manpower, training, dockyards and other support facilities. Leach and his team entered the fray to try and salvage what they could. The assault ships were given a temporary reprieve, but all efforts to keep *Invincible* for any length of time were unavailing. She and *Hermes* were to be replaced by *Ark Royal* and *Illustrious*, reducing Britain to 'a two small carrier Navy'.

This unfolding drama was followed at Fleet Headquarters with astonishment bordering upon incomprehension. The daily intelligence briefings highlighted the need for the strongest possible Navy with which to confront the growing Soviet maritime threat. The Cold War enemy's order of battle had assumed alarming proportions, both in numbers of ships, submarines and aircraft, and in their size, complexity and missile armaments. While the political battle over defence budgets and inter-service rivalry continued to rage in Whitehall, Fieldhouse concentrated on maintaining the morale and preparedness of the many men under his command. He often quoted the dictum 'We can with confidence only expect the unexpected.' As C-in-C Naval Home Command, and responsible for all those serving in training establishments and elsewhere ashore, Eberle was engaged in a similar exercise.

In his *Here Today Gone Tomorrow*, John Nott tells a rather different story. He writes in some detail of the financial and politico/military debate in Whitehall and on his lack of confidence in the Admiralty Board.

> There were apart from the outstanding Admiral Lewin, several other admirals whom I respected. Admirals Fieldhouse and Eberle were both excellent men, the latter something of a politician, but both had the high intelligence and wide experience which rightly brought them to the top. Neither of them, however, was on the Admiralty Board at the time.

There is little doubt that Nott also respected Leach, but he refers to him as his 'antagonist'. He also asserts that his decision to cut back the navy 'was based on a range of tri-service advice which I received from the central military staffs and from senior civil servants'.

As Leach fought the navy's corner with great tenacity and single-mindedness, supported by Navy Minister Keith Speed, who was forced to resign, one might be forgiven for asking where the Chief of Defence Staff stood on this issue. There is much of interest on this subject, both in Leach's book and in Richard Hill's biography *Lewin of Greenwich*. Hill summarises:

> There were three principal concerns for Admiral of the Fleet Sir Terence Lewin, as he now was, during his time as Chief of the Defence Staff. They were the replacement of Britain's strategic nuclear deterrent; the review of Britain's defence structure in the light of heavy and conflicting demands for expenditure and of financial stringency, particularly during the tenure of John Nott as Defence Secretary; and the higher organisation of the Ministry of Defence. They ran to an extent in that sequence, although, as generally happens, they overlapped and interlaced.

Certainly Leach would have been justified in feeling that he might have received more support from this quarter; but he would also have been fully aware that a naval CDS needed to bend over backwards for it to be seen that he was viewing things from a balanced tri-service perspective. In any event, it seemed that some totally unplanned circumstance would be needed if the navy was to be preserved from even some of the massive cuts that were intended. When this occurred soon afterwards, it was fortunate for the nation that the higher direction of its affairs was in the hands of Lewin, Leach and Fieldhouse, with their cumulative total of 128 years in a navy blue suit.

* * * * * * * *

These weighty events in the MoD were coincident with some of the political manoeuvrings leading up to conflict in the South Atlantic in 1982. The book *The Falklands War* by the *Sunday Times* Insight Team gives a balanced contemporary view of developments. The Argentine's long-standing claim to what they called Las Malvinas had been simmering and bubbling for many years. Following the return to power of the Conservative Government under Margaret Thatcher in 1979, an effort was made to resolve the continuing crisis. Foreign Office Minister Nicholas Ridley's proposals for a 'leaseback' scheme, along the lines of Hong Kong's New Territories, promised to be the most likely way of resolving the dispute by peaceful means. However, this led to problems both in Parliament and with the Islanders, who, though small in numbers, had voices that needed to be heard. The Foreign Office studied an intelligence assessment of possible Argentine intentions at a meeting in June 1981. This contained a range of eight escalating options; from United Nations denouncement, through economic sanctions, isolated landings in the Falklands or South Georgia, to a full-scale invasion. The Insight Team summarised the conclusions of the meeting:

> Britain should try and persuade the islanders to accept a settlement in the form of a leaseback. But too much pressure would create the customary political storm; only 'gentle pressure' therefore should be applied. As usual the Argentinians should be kept 'in play' for as long

as possible. How long did Britain have? Argentina would surely act before the 150th anniversary of British occupation, and that fell due in January 1983.

The 1981 Defence Review's decision to withdraw HMS *Endurance* from the South Atlantic gave a clear signal of the UK's lack of resolve to protect the Islands. But the really crucial factor was General Galtieri's assumption of the Argentine Presidency in December, with the hawkish Admiral Anaya at his side. He was looking for a major public relations success to establish the popularity of the new regime, and it is now known that the decision to prepare for an invasion was taken in secrecy that month. Meanwhile, diplomacy continued.

Ridley's successor, Richard Luce, headed the British delegation at a bilateral round of talks in New York in February 1882. To put it crudely, his brief was to continue to stall. Galtieri and his military junta were fast running out of patience. As the talks broke up, final preparations were made to go ahead with an invasion of the Falklands.

* * * * * * * *

In 1956, George Hayhoe had been First Lieutenant of John's first command HMS *Acheron*. Twenty-five years on he was serving as a Commodore as Director of Plans for the UK Commander-in-Chiefs' Committee. This organisation structured periodic meetings of the C-in-Cs of the three services, and provided a useful background for them to get to know and understand each other better. In December 1981, Hayhoe organised the annual intelligence briefing. This took place in the MoD, and was attended by representatives of the Foreign Office, MI5 and MI6. At this meeting, John drew attention to recent reports from the CO of HMS *Endurance* of disturbing attitudes and actions in Argentina. A Foreign Office official stated 'it wasn't unusual for the 'Argies' to be jumping up and down.' Fieldhouse was not entirely happy with this answer and insisted that his fears should be included in the minutes, but no particular action was taken as he continued to show concern.

By way of a diversion, George Hayhoe's wife Carenza was – and remains – a potter of distinction. In conversation with John, she was able to solve a completely different problem that had been exercising his mind for some time. He had been looking for a modest personal gift that he could carry around with him to present to people. Thus was born the famous 'Fieldmouse' ceramic box. Circular in shape and about three inches across, it had a small mouse on its lid, together with some roses to mark his Yorkshire origins. Several dozens of these were ordered. With their interesting provenance, anyone who has one now may be in possession of a valued collector's item!

Fieldhouse was determined to improve his education by visiting a Royal Marine Commando. This was fitted into his programme on a visit to Plymouth just before Christmas. The CO of 40 Commando at that time was Lieutenant Colonel Malcolm Hunt (later Major General). He remembers his team feeling that it was something of a bore to have been singled out to entertain this rather distant VIP who was unlikely ever again to enter their well-ordered lives. How wrong they were! After John had spent the day walking around, talking to the troops, taking drinks in the Sergeant's Mess and lunching with the officers, he had hundreds of new fans.

In February 1982 Fieldhouse set off for a short visit to the Caribbean. After visiting the deep-water tracking range in the Bahamas, he flew on to join HMS *Fearless*. Captain Jeremy Larken takes up the story.

> *Fearless* was lately out of refit, having completed work-up just before Christmas. We were in the West Indies for the seasonal Dartmouth Training Squadron deployment. We had assembled two frigates and the RFAs *Tidespring* and *Stromness*. It was arranged that John should join us, accompanied only by Jonathon Band, at Curacoa in the Netherlands Antilles and be with us for three days, visiting all ships on passage to Aruba – the neighbouring Dutch island possession ... We took the opportunity to hold a Royal Marine band concert on the vehicle deck – which could be readily converted to a forward-looking amphitheatre to hold virtually all of the ship's company not on watch. This proved a boisterous occasion. With the whole audience on its feet for the third rendering of 'Heart of Oak', 'Rule Britannia' and 'Land of Hope and Glory', John turned to me (surely without a shadow of pre-meditation) and said 'Now, just suppose we were to have to go to war tomorrow!' ... A modest exercise with the Dutch Marines had been organised, and *Fearless*'s Assault Squadron was to conduct a landing through a reef on an Aruban beach. *Fearless* carried both large and small landing craft. The latter were elderly and their plywood hulls decidedly frail. John, with Jonathon, was to be carried in one of these in the first wave of the landing at first light. The Corporal Coxswain, a natural enthusiast, failed to identify the gap in the reef. Not to be deflected from the precise achievement of H-Hour, he crossed the coral, ripping gashes in the bottom of the hull. There remained a passage of clear water to the beach, and the craft had half-foundered before reaching it. Secure on the bottom but with water pouring in, a hefty marine picked John up bodily and expressed enormous satisfaction in delivering him to the beach dry-shod. On returning briefly to the ship, once again John had the bon mot. 'Only the Marines', he said, 'could have perpetuated such a bone-headed enterprise!'

Bone-headed or not, both they and 40 Commando would be on their way to war six weeks later, with their C-in-C knowing rather more about them than before. There can be no doubt of the pivotal role played by the *Fearless* and

Intrepid assault craft, or of the skill of all those involved in the amphibious landing in San Carlos Water. It is interesting that one of the reasons why John decided to make this long journey was to familiarise himself with the nuts and bolts of amphibious warfare.

In an intensely busy programme involving rather too much travel, Fieldhouse decided to visit the most far-flung outpost of his command, in Hong Kong. This consisted of the naval base, HMS *Tamar*, some outlying stations and its squadron of local patrol craft. John had already twice circled the globe from west to east and now resolved to reverse the process. With time always at a premium, the visit was planned as a sequel to a NATO commitment in Canada. Jonathon Band organised the Hong Kong end of the programme and flew there direct with Midge and with his wife Sarah, to be in attendance on the C-in-C's arrival. In 1950, as a newly promoted Lieutenant in the submarine HMS *Astute*, John had perpetuated an embarrassing time zone gaff of a single hour. Now it was the turn of his Flag Lieutenant to commit an absolute howler to the extent of a whole day! Midge, Jonathon and the Captain-in-Charge Hong Kong drove out to Kai Tak airport to meet the incoming flight. As the aircraft disgorged its passengers, there was a growing realisation that the Admiral was not on board. The local RN Captain was far from pleased, having arranged an evening out with a party of guests in a box at Happy Valley races. Although a rest day had been planned and the naval arrangements were unaffected, what John had to say to Jonathon on his eventual arrival, having crossed the international date line twenty-four hours later, is best left unrecorded!

Various interesting things happened in the middle of March, as seen from a Northwood perspective. In accordance with long-standing arrangements, Rear Admiral 'Sandy' Woodward (FOF1) set sail from Portsmouth for the Fleet's major annual training period, exercise 'Springtrain'. He had some twenty assorted ships under command. The well-tried procedure was to carry out a series of weapon training exercises on passage, after which the force would enter Gibraltar for a week of sporting and social activity. On completion of this, a more advanced series of exercises was planned before the majority of ships and submarines returned to home waters. John Fieldhouse had followed this precise programme as FOF2 five years earlier and, as his C-in-C had done then, he intended to join the Fleet after its arrival in harbour.

On 19th March, while the ships were at sea, the spark was ignited which was to lead to the conflagration of the Falklands War. In what turned out to be cover for more sinister intentions, a party of Argentine scrap metal dealers were discovered to have landed at Leith in South Georgia, and had hoisted their national flag from an abandoned tower. In Whitehall, this was seen initially as a minor incident that could be resolved by local resources. Diplomatic protests were made and C-in-C Fleet was ordered to sail *Endurance* from Port Stanley with some extra Royal Marines from the

Islands' eighty strong Garrison; double its usual size because of the annual handover period.

Meanwhile, some of the higher echelons of Britain's military structure had important NATO business to attend to. Accompanied by his Secretary, John Shillingford, Fieldhouse set off for Colorado Springs, USA, for a routine six-monthly meeting of the Nuclear Planning Group. Also present were Secretary of State for Defence John Nott, Chief of Defence Staff Terry Lewin, and their attendants. While they were there, messages were received at Northwood that, despite initial calmness following *Endurance*'s arrival at South Georgia, there were reports of Argentine naval activity in the area and evidence of growing political unrest. Using paraphrased words for security purposes, this update was telephoned to Shillingford in the early hours of the morning, US time. Fieldhouse heard the phone ringing in the adjacent hotel bedroom and, still in his pyjamas, summoned his Secretary to brief him. By breakfast, he himself had spoken to Nott and Lewin. The former suggested that the British delegation should pack up and return home forthwith; but Lewin's attitude was more sanguine. Nothing could be gained, he felt, by alarming or offending the Americans in mid-conference. On reflection, Nott accepted his CDS's advice to continue with the current programme. Nott and Fieldhouse returned to the UK a day later, while Lewin continued with a long-standing commitment to visit to New Zealand.

After a brief update at Northwood, Fieldhouse continued with his planned visit to the Fleet at Gibraltar. He flew out with Midge, a number of staff officers and members of his retinue, knowing that, if needed, he could be recalled very quickly. He was met by his old friend Rear Admiral John Mackenzie, Flag Officer Gibraltar, and escorted to the Convent, the Governor's residence, where, initially, Midge and he were to be guests of General Sir William and Lady Jackson. On arrival there, the C-in-C invited Mackenzie in for a private word. He briefed him on the serious problems in the South Atlantic, and on the need to deliver any incoming messages to him personally; wherever he might be. This was the first Mackenzie knew of the impending crisis.

Fieldhouse hoisted his Flag in HMS *Glamorgan* and the Fleet's shore programme continued as planned. When Woodward waited upon his C-in-C, he too was informed of the latest developments. Contrary to popular belief, they were not personal friends. Indeed, they had had a spat in 1977 when Sandy had turned down John's invitation to become his Chief of Staff. As perhaps the two most distinguished submariners of the early nuclear generation, their relationship was based more on respect of each other's capabilities and reputations. Even as they met then, John would have been sizing Sandy up as a possible war-fighting battle group commander.

The Mackenzies, to whose residence John and Midge had moved as house guests, hosted a party for Woodward, the COs of all ships in company, and any wives who happened to be present in the port. After supper, Midge slipped off her shoes and tinkled away on the piano. It was a relaxed and happy occasion; very much a part of the calm before the storm. On Sunday 28th March there was a naval service in the cathedral; beautifully organised to the accompaniment of the C-in-C's band. As he sat in his pew, Mackenzie was handed an envelope that he passed on to the C-in-C as soon as their devotions were over. The narrative continues with short excerpts from Sandy Woodward's *One Hundred Days*:

> Our last night on the Rock, a Sunday, was quite magical. There in the Upper Caves the pageant scarlet, blue and gold colours of the uniforms, the topical and patriotic music, all combined to produce a traditional and vivid reminder of the old days when Britannia really did rule the waves ... Monday morning dawned bleakly. The Levanter, that nasty, gusty, easterly wind with its sweeping grey rain, was upon us and we sailed out into short choppy seas to begin the exercises to the east and west of the Rock ... We had a busy time that morning getting all the 'Springtrain' ships away to their appointed tasks in good order, and I received a short blast from my Commander-in-Chief for allowing 'dangerous manoeuvring in the Straits' ... At seven o'clock that evening I flew over to *Glamorgan* for discussions with my C-in-C. He briefed me on the deteriorating situation in the South Atlantic and we agreed on the best way forward for the present exercise. He touched on the possibility of placing a more experienced 'Three Star' vice admiral in command of any task force which might be ordered south. I have since been told that Fieldhouse was quite determined that I should stay in command and his words were merely to keep me on my toes ... At 0630 the following morning, shortly before first light, Admiral Fieldhouse was landed at Gibraltar and flown immediately back to the UK.

This chapter closes with some further reflections on the Gibraltar scene. Almost unnoticed, the RFA *Fort Austin* had been sailed south on 26th March, her task being to replenish *Endurance* and any other ships that might be sent to counter Argentine moves against South Georgia. On 29th March, the SSN *Spartan* and SSK *Oracle* were withdrawn from the exercise so that the former could be topped up with the latter's war outfit of torpedoes and prepared to sail. That night Woodward issued orders to all 'Springtrain' ships to make full reports on their readiness for war. It was fortunate that a good number of destroyers and frigates had been involved in this invaluable period of training and human bonding. As Fieldhouse returned to his Headquarters on 30th March, Woodward was firmly established in his mind as the sea-going admiral most immediately in touch with the Fleet; whose eyes were already focused on the perils of distant horizons.

CHAPTER FIFTEEN

Tri-Service Commander-in-Chief

1982

BACK IN THE UK, events had started to move with disturbing speed. A second SSN had been prepared for despatch to the South Atlantic; a third allocated on completion of its important Cold War task. Intelligence sources revealed that much of the Argentine fleet was at sea; both in the vicinity of South Georgia and posing a direct threat to the Falklands Islands themselves. On 31st March it became clear that a full invasion seemed likely to occur in the early hours of 2nd April. In these alarming circumstances, Foreign Secretary Lord Carrington, and CDS Sir Terence Lewin, were abroad. The Chief of the Air Staff, Air Chief Marshal Sir Michael Beetham, was Acting CDS in Lewin's absence. But the crisis was very much a maritime problem, and it was First Sea Lord Sir Henry Leach who stepped into the breach to take the initiative.

In his autobiography, Leach has described with great clarity his meeting with the Prime Minister and the Defence Secretary that evening; from which he departed with an instruction to prepare a task force for the purpose of recapturing the Islands in the almost certain eventuality of their loss. In hindsight, his confident professional intervention seems to have been crucial to everything that occurred thereafter. Nobody doubted for a single moment Margaret Thatcher's courage or political will, but others around her were advising on a less decisive course of action. She captures the moment with these words from her *The Downing Street Years*:

> Before this, I had been outraged and determined. Now my outrage and determination were matched by a sense of relief and confidence. Henry Leach had shown me that if it came to a fight the courage and professionalism of Britain's armed forces would win through. It was my job as Prime Minister to see that they got the political support they needed.

In her foreword to Woodward's *One Hundred Days*, she continues:

> Once again, the hour had produced the man [Admiral Leach]. It was to produce many more throughout the campaign – Admiral Fieldhouse, whose warm humanity and sureness of touch never failed him or us; Admiral Lewin, Chief of Defence Staff, a tower of wisdom and strength: Admiral Woodward himself…

As frantic diplomatic activity continued on both sides of the Atlantic, Fieldhouse set the wheels in motion to prepare an appropriate task force. The absolute essentials were the carriers *Hermes* and *Invincible*; together with the assault ship *Fearless*. Sister ship *Intrepid* had been paid off into reserve; but a quick check confirmed that she could be brought forward within a few weeks, and this was put in hand immediately. The main escorting force was already at sea off Gibraltar, but many more destroyers and frigates would be needed. Because of the enormous distances involved, the resources of the Royal Fleet Auxiliary would have to be supplemented. It also would be necessary to commandeer further shipping from the Merchant Navy to transport the necessary troops, helicopters, weapons, ammunition and stores, and to provide a hospital ship. 3 Commando Brigade Royal Marines would need to be brought to instant readiness, plus any additional army units needed for the landing force. The list of requirements was seemingly endless. Some of the necessary actions fell directly onto the MoD. Others were either taken at Northwood or delegated to dockyards, naval bases or subordinate commands. A typical example was the need to fly folios of South Atlantic charts to the ships exercising off Gibraltar.

After further thought and discussion with David Hallifax, Fieldhouse confirmed his decision to appoint Woodward as the Battle Group Commander. The logical choice would have been FOF3, Rear Admiral Derek Reffell. The four major surface ships were part of his command, and he had previously served as CO of *Hermes* and as Commodore Amphibious Warfare (COMAW). The current COMAW, Michael Clapp, reported directly to him. What weighed against Reffell was that he had recently taken over from Vice Admiral John Cox, and had not yet had an opportunity to command a task group at sea as an admiral. Cox himself was on leave between appointments. He was the only admiral experienced in the use of the new Sea Harrier jump jet aircraft in operational conditions, but it was decided not to recall him to a post he had already vacated. The only other sea-going admiral, FOF2, was ashore in Devonport and not considered. Those who have suggested that Woodward was chosen as an act of favouritism to a fellow submariner fall wide of the mark. His selection was principally a matter of timing. If the crisis had broken either before or after the 'Springtrain' deployment, there is little doubt that the FOF3 of the day would have led the battle group. After the conflict both Cox and Reffell were generous in their praise of Woodward's achievements.

As the Prime Minister's will hardened towards taking a positive move to repossess the Islands, Leach left a meeting at No 10 Downing Street in the early hours of 2nd April with authority to sail the Task Force. He returned to the MoD. Let him take up the story.

> 'Signal C-in-C Fleet to prepare to sail the Task Force' I instructed. I then telephoned Admiral Fieldhouse personally. I knew John Fieldhouse very well indeed. Over recent years we had been Flotilla commanders together; he had been an excellent and far-sighted Flag Officer Submarines when I commanded the Fleet, and an outstanding Controller of the Navy during my early time as First Sea Lord. I could not wish for a better C-in-C Fleet in a crisis nor one whose thinking so completely matched my own. We were 'in each other's minds'. Behind his unruffled calm and almost urbane manner lay a keen mind, resolute determination and a fund of good sense.
> 'The Carrier Task Force must sail on Monday' I said.
> 'Could we not have a little more time, First Sea Lord', the Commander-in-Chief reacted. 'We could then improve the preparation so much.'
> 'No,' I replied. 'I'm sorry but they <u>must</u> sail on Monday.'
> 'Understood,' said the C-in-C. And they did.

At dawn on 2nd April the Argentine invasion force landed and by 8.30am the Governor of the Falkland Islands had surrendered. On the following day Argentine forces landed at Grytviken in South Georgia. Operation 'Corporate' was ordered; the codeword to embrace all South Atlantic operations. At home, *Hermes*, *Invincible*, *Fearless* and the frigates *Alacrity* and *Antelope* were brought to immediate notice. Off Gibraltar, three frigates without guns or anti-ship missiles were denuded of stores and sent home. Rear Admiral Woodward, with *Glamorgan, Antrim, Brilliant, Coventry, Glasgow, Sheffield, Plymouth* and *Arrow*, with RFA support, was ordered to make a covert passage southwards towards Ascension Island. Over the next few days and weeks many more warships were despatched to join the Task Force. Sailing with them would be all available RFAs and numerous merchant ships that had been 'taken up from trade' using special powers invoked by Order in Council.

* * * * * * * *

Admiral of the Fleet Sir Terence Lewin returned from New Zealand on 5th April and became immediately involved with the setting up of a war-fighting command structure. Only two months earlier he had masterminded the introduction of important changes in the MoD that gave increased authority to whoever held his post as Chief of Defence Staff. Effectively, these made him the principal military adviser to the Government in his own right, and no longer the chairman of a committee with collective responsibility. This was a much cleaner arrangement, achieved without serious prejudice to the authority of the individual Chiefs of Staff, who continued to represent their single service views through the Chief's committee. At the first meeting later that day of the so-called War Cabinet, he presented the Prime Minister and her political colleagues with his personally drafted proposal for an objective. It was approved without amendment there and then:

> The overall aim of Her Majesty's Government is to bring about the withdrawal of Argentine forces from the Falkland Islands and dependencies, and the re-establishment of British administration there, as quickly as possible. Military deployments and operations are directed in support of this aim.

In his biography of Lewin, Richard Hill continues:

> 'War Cabinet' was media shorthand for the South Atlantic subgroup of the Cabinet's Defence and Overseas Policy Committee, short title OD(SA). That was a more accurate title because, although there was a quite strong presumption that Britain might have to go to war, it was considered possible for the first few weeks after the Argentine invasion that some means might be found of restoring the *status quo ante* without fighting. That was one of the virtues of Lewin's draft objective; it did not preclude negotiation while the task force moved south.

Under the chairmanship of the Prime Minister, the OD(SA) consisted of William Whitelaw (Home Secretary), Francis Pym (Foreign and Commonwealth Secretary on the resignation of Lord Carrington), John Nott (Defence Secretary), Cecil Parkinson (to represent the Conservative Party) and Terence Lewin. Michael Havers (Attorney General) also joined the group whenever legal advice was needed. Selected senior civil servants additionally attended in support of ministers. In a war situation, the Prime Minister *ipso facto* assumes the role of Defence Secretary. In this situation Nott deferred to Lewin as principal MoD adviser; assuming a more supporting 'devil's advocate's' role.

It is certainly not the purpose of this narrative to follow the workings of this group in any detail; nor the various negotiations that continued in the United Nations, London, Buenos Aires, Washington and elsewhere. What is of concern is Lewin's directive to Fieldhouse, establishing the arrangements for command and control. In pursuance of the OD(SA)'s aim, Fieldhouse was to assume overall command of operations in the South Atlantic as Commander Task Force 317 (all surface ships, land and air forces) and Commander Task Force 324 (submarine forces). Tri-service command was to be exercised from the Fleet Headquarters at Northwood, with responsibility direct to CDS. His command team was to consist of Flag and Air officers already serving within the Headquarters, together with Major General Jeremy Moore (the Major General Royal Marines Commando Forces) as the initial Land Forces Deputy. Air Marshal Curtiss, as Air Commander, was to come under full command. The 'home team' consisted of Vice Admiral David Hallifax (Chief of Staff), Vice Admiral Peter Herbert

(FOSM) and Rear Admiral 'Spam' Hammersley (Chief Staff Officer Engineering), who became Force Logistic Coordinator.

Because of the new command structure, the First Sea Lord, Sir Henry Leach, was no longer within the direct chain of command. However, he continued to exert a major influence by his presence on the Chiefs of Staff Committee, which met daily throughout the crisis and which often attended War Cabinet meetings, and by his drive in galvanizing the whole structure of the Royal Navy into providing the maximum possible support. A significant part of this effort came from the Naval Staff in the MoD, which took the lead on merchant ship procurement, Rules of Engagement, media liaison and other activities with political overtones. Urgency of a proportionately lesser degree was applied by the Chiefs of the other Services. Around the country, where civilians were involved in Royal Dockyards, stores and ammunition depots, and aircraft maintenance and repair facilities, normal working practices were abandoned in the common cause. Defence contracting companies for such obscure products as radar confusing 'chaff' worked around the clock to meet crisis demands.

Although some of the lines of demarcation between Whitehall and Northwood remained blurred, Fieldhouse's role as Commander-in-Chief was indisputable. While the more senior officers in the MoD reported directly to Ministers and were part of the political process, his single-minded task was to concentrate on commanding all the forces likely to be committed to action. He would be responsible for the planning and execution of military operations. Although the nature of his task meant the he would never be in the front line himself; subordinate commanders would look to him for leadership and inspiration. Ultimate military responsibility for the success or failure of what was always going to be a hazardous undertaking rested squarely on his shoulders. He accepted his heavy burden with characteristic equanimity.

It is interesting to draw a comparison between the Falklands War and the D-Day Normandy landings. The C-in-C was required to deliver an initial assault of over 7,000 troops onto hostile shores at a range of about 8,000 miles with minimal air cover. By a simple process of multiplication, the logistical requirement equates to 56,000,000 man miles. Using 100 miles as the Channel benchmark, it could be said that an equivalent effort would have deposited over half a million men on the Normandy beaches within easy range of shore based air cover. Of course this comparison is beset with faulty logic, but it serves to illustrate the scale and complexity of the task. The only forward base available was Wideawake airfield on Ascension Island, over 3,000 miles from the Falklands. The only fixed-wing aircraft capable of offering direct support of landing operations were the handful of Sea Harriers embarked in *Hermes* and *Invincible*. The Argentines could deploy an air force of far greater strength from safe shore bases on the mainland.

Estimates of enemy troops in the islands varied from 7,000 to 10,000. It was standard doctrine that opposed amphibious landings should not be attempted without a very considerable preponderance of force. The only guarantee of recapture of the islands lay in landing at a place where it was certain that the enemy were not present.

Although Leach was well aware of the dangers and was confident of a successful military outcome, there was a marked degree of scepticism amongst his fellow Chiefs of Staff. These doubts were conveyed to Lewin who maintained an open mind. In the early days all hoped for, and many expected, some sort of political solution. Would the prompt despatch of a task force to the South Atlantic cause the 'Argies' to back down? Fieldhouse and his Staff could only continue to prepare for conflict in a few weeks time. He is quoted as having said that 'this is going to be a sad and bloody business.' In his loneliness as the Commander-in-Chief, there is no doubt that he was fortified by his strong relationship with Lewin; going back fifteen years since they had served together in *Hermes*. Hill comments on the equally important relationship between Margaret Thatcher and the CDS.

> Fortunately, trust between the Prime Minister and her principal military adviser was established early and remained secure. It was founded upon common purpose, goodwill and honesty…

A similar enduring bond was to be established between the Prime Minister and John Fieldhouse, even though he was one place further down the chain of command. Air Marshal Curtiss put it like this:

> It was John's intelligence, determination and charm which enabled him to establish a great rapport with Prime Minister Margaret Thatcher and she trusted him completely over the conduct of the campaign. The PM was very interested in every aspect of the war but, having agreed to the outline plan, never interfered with the way it was conducted.

Historian Stephen Prince makes this observation in his paper on *British Command and Control in the Falklands Campaign*:

> The command structure was distinct, compact and dedicated, with a clear chain of command. In particular, the relationships between Prime Minister Margaret Thatcher, Admiral Lewin and Admiral Fieldhouse were both well defined and pursued with mutual sympathy for each other's requirements, something partly generated by frequent contact.

Fieldhouse developed a *modus operandi* to fit in with the routines of his distinguished superiors. From nearby Admiralty House, he would be driven to his office between 6.30 and 7.00am to read his signals and review the overnight situation with Chief of Staff David Hallifax. From 8.00am he would be tied up with intelligence and operations briefings, which could take anything up to an hour. After CDS's regular OD(SA) meeting at 0930, he and Fieldhouse would have a long private chat together. Meanwhile, Hallifax would have briefed Rear Admiral Tony Whetstone, Assistant Chief of Operations on the Naval Staff. He, in turn, would ensure that Leach was fully prepared for the Chief's meeting that Lewin chaired later. C-in-C had a separate meeting with the command team of three and two star officers. The central part of the day was taken up with one-to-one discussions and inviting any visitors back to Admiralty House for a working lunch. There would be a second operations and intelligence briefing at 5.00pm. Later, Hallifax would have a regular call on a secure line with Woodward at sea, reporting to Fieldhouse on completion. The C-in-C limited his personal conversations with subordinate commanders to occasions when he had something of particular importance to say to them.

As early as 4th April, Fieldhouse had recommended that a Maritime Exclusion Zone (MEZ) be established around the Falkland Islands in order to inhibit the Argentine ability to reinforce the garrison. This was established with effect from 12th April and enforced initially by nuclear submarines deployed on patrol off Port Stanley and the entrance to Falkland Sound.

On 7th April, CDS ordered Fieldhouse to plan for the repossession of South Georgia and to deploy the necessary forces – codenamed 'Operation Paraquat'. *Antrim* (CTG 317.9), *Plymouth*, *Brilliant*, *Endurance* and RFA *Tidespring*, together with a company of Royal Marines and SAS/SBS reconnaissance parties were allocated for this task. SSN *Conqueror* also patrolled offshore, on the lookout for reinforcements. This was seen as an early opportunity to achieve moral dominance over the enemy that could be put to good effect later. In hindsight, it was something of a costly diversion of precious resources. Two helicopters were lost in an ill-conceived plan to land the SAS on a glacier. The situation was redeemed by the superb airmanship of *Antrim*'s helicopter pilot. The old Argentine submarine *Santa Fe* was disabled and the Island retaken on 26th April without sustaining casualties.

Meanwhile various elements of the Task Force had been converging on Ascension Island; providing an essential opportunity to fly out additional personnel, equipment and stores, and to redistribute what had been hastily loaded in the UK into more suitable ships for onward passage. At the outset, Northwood had provided the MoD with a list of essential support required from the United States, not least the facilities at Wideawake airfield. Other priority items were the latest Sidewinder air-to-air missiles for the Sea Harriers and enhanced satellite communications. It was fortunate that the strong pro-Argentine lobby in the USA was largely offset by the staunch support of Defense Secretary Casper Weinberger. The exceptionally close links that existed between the USN and the RN staff in Washington also helped to make light of any difficulties. Although Ascension was a British Dependency, the US had obtained a lease for its own national purposes. Without its unrestricted use by British forces engaged in Operation 'Corporate', it would have been impossible to repossess the Islands. This is fully acknowledged in Fieldhouse's *South Atlantic Despatch*:

> By the fall of Stanley, a total of 535 air movements from the UK had taken place. These included RAF Hercules and VC10s and some chartered Belfast and Boeing 707 aircraft. They had brought in 23 helicopters, 5,907 tons of freight and 5,242 passengers ... Nimrods mounted 111 sorties from the Island; the Hercules made 44 airdrops of essential equipment, weapons, personnel and mail to the Fleet and the Victor tankers flew 375 sorties in support of 67 missions involving long range operations by probe fitted aircraft.

Wing Commander David Emmerson was the CO of the Nimrod squadron deployed to Ascension Island. A few months earlier he had taken Fieldhouse for a flight in a brand new Mark II aircraft in the course of which his distinguished passenger had succumbed to airsickness. Now, his Nimrods flew intelligence sorties over the Falklands and along the Argentine mainland. Many Victor tanker sorties were required to keep them airborne for 21 hours.

The fact that Air Marshal Curtiss was already located at Northwood was a major bonus. For months he and his staff had worked closely with Fleet and submarine staffs on routine maritime issues and on operations concerned with the prosecution of the Cold War. At first the Air Staff in the MoD seemed lukewarm about the possibility of success in the South Atlantic but, once the bandwagon began to roll, it did so with increasing momentum. When Curtiss was appointed Air Commander, the full resources of HQ Strike Command at High Wycombe were put at his disposal and his staff was supplemented accordingly. The rapid fitting of in-flight refuelling to so many aircraft was a major achievement. Vulcan bombers were prepared to strike the runway at Port Stanley. At short notice, No 1 (F) Squadron of Harriers GR3, the RAF's ground attack variant of the Navy's air defence Sea Harrier, was deployed to join *Hermes* in the South Atlantic. Never having operated from a sea platform before, these resourceful pilots were soon in action against targets ashore. The whole air effort in support of the Task Force remained at a uniformly high level throughout the war.

Many Army units had already been committed; not least the 2nd and 3rd Battalions, the Parachute Regiment, which were to be in the initial landing force. Later, the 5th Infantry Brigade would be landed to play a lesser but prominent part. Of more immediate concern, however, was the deployment of Special Forces. Fieldhouse was quick to learn that the brave body of men that formed the Special Air Service had its own private way of operating.

The Director SAS at that time was Brigadier Peter de la Billiere, who was himself later to become the British tri-service commander in the First Gulf War. In his autobiography *Looking for Trouble* he writes of his first visit to Northwood, where he found Fieldhouse

> a marvellously straightforward Yorkshireman whose razor-sharp mind was masked to some extent by his benign exterior, and who had the valuable gift of remaining calm even under intense pressure.

Responsible for SAS operations worldwide, the Brigadier reported to the Director of Military Operations in the MoD, but tasks were so sensitive that approval was always needed at the highest level of Government. Two squadrons, about half the regiment, were already on their way to the South Atlantic. Control and information flow would be made possible by the use of recently acquired American lightweight satellite communications terminals. Although de la Billiere played a loner's game and was not under Task Force command, he and Fieldhouse hit it off well together and a SAS cell was established at Northwood to ensure close cooperation. The smaller Special Boat Squadron of Royal Marines, trained to be put ashore by submarine, was also on its way south. Despite two abortive operations, one in South Georgia and another in mainland South America, both of which involved the loss of valuable helicopters, Special Forces made an enormous contribution to the ultimate success of the campaign.

* * * * * * * *

On 17th April, Fieldhouse arrived at Ascension Island accompanied by General Moore, Air Marshal Curtiss, Admiral Hammersley, Brigadier de la Billiere and over a dozen staff officers. This would be his only opportunity to confer face to face with his Task Group commanders before they headed further south towards the war zone. It was an occasion of much importance for a number of reasons. Unfortunately, at a meeting the previous day, a bad atmosphere had developed between, on the one hand, Rear Admiral Sandy Woodward (CTG 317.8), the Battle Group Commander, and, on the other, Commodore Mike Clapp (CTG 317.0), the Amphibious Group Commander and Brigadier Julian Thompson (CTG 317.1), the Landing Force Commander. Together with Major General Jeremy Moore, who did not assume 'in area' command of land forces until nine days after the landings, these were to be the leaders who delivered the victory. When one considers the magnitude of their achievements, it is sad that, in their writings and attendance at seminars, they continue to spar with each other until this day. By his own admission, tact was not the sharpest arrow in Woodward's quiver. At a preparatory meeting in *Fearless*, it seems that he dominated proceedings; embarrassing Clapp and infuriating Thompson with a number of 'red herring' ideas that wasted valuable staff time, having little relevance to the task in hand. Woodward in turn complained that 'a detailed description on the topography of the Falklands' was emphatically not what he needed at that particular moment in time. He wanted to address more general problems of inter-group interest on the passage south during the immediate days ahead. This apparent pulling of rank put the one-star officers on the defensive and, as Clapp put it, 'trust was broken which would take a long time to repair.'

Clapp and Thompson have made no secret of the fact that they would have preferred to have had Derek Reffell as the overall in-theatre commander. As FOF3, he was their line commander for amphibious operations, was more familiar with their problems and would have kept Woodward 'off their backs.' In his 2002 assessment of command and control issues, Stephen Prince wrote:

> As a result of Fieldhouse's structures, there were, however, a number of tensions between Clapp/Thompson and Woodward, as their various biographies confirm. For example, at their meeting near Ascension Island on 16th April, Clapp and Thompson had significant problems with Woodward's approach and assertion of authority, although he remained unaware of this.

In these somewhat ruffled circumstances, the Commander-in-Chief presided over what amounted to a Council of War in HMS *Hermes*, flanked by his land and air deputies. The forenoon consisted of a number of briefings, followed by four seminars, dealing with Command and Control, Intelligence, Logistics and Communications. While at Northwood, he had become very much involved in the inevitable juggling act between military needs and political expediency. At Ascension Island, he was able to give his full attention to the requirements and attitudes of his senior fighting men. From notes taken at the time, Clapp recorded the C-in-C's five objectives:

> Establish the MEZ as soon as possible
> Establish sea and air control as soon as possible
> Repossess South Georgia as soon as possible
> Plan to land with a view to repossessing the Falklands
> Get as far south as swiftly as possible with a significant group

As they deliberated, the 'Paraquat' force was three days short of South Georgia; a group of escorts was 1,000 miles south of Ascension on its way to establish an overt presence closer to the Falklands; and two SSNs were already in the Maritime Exclusion Zone (MEZ) with another approaching South Georgia. Unsurprisingly, discussion concentrated on the significant elements of timing needed to accomplish the objectives.

Woodward recalls that after lunch 'the senior members met in the Admiral's harbour quarters right down aft to mull things over.'

> I still remember standing there ... with some cardboard and a pair of scissors, cutting out different coloured strips, representing different lengths of time ... Basically, it was necessary to work the campaign out backwards, starting from the chilling thought that the Task Group would be falling apart by middle or late June without proper maintenance and the winter setting in ... So we were obliged to make a crucial assumption then and there – that the land battle would have to be over by at least the end of June, and preferably a good two weeks before that ... On that basis, therefore, if the land forces were to be given reasonable time to do their stuff, we had to put them on the beaches by 25th May.

As this planning theme developed, it became clear that the critical path lay with the assault ship *Intrepid.* She was an essential requirement, not only because of her landing craft and troop carrying capacity, but also as an alternative amphibious headquarters ship in the event of the loss of *Fearless.* The earliest that she could reach the South Atlantic fully prepared was 16th May. Thus a 'landing window' extended from 16th to 25th May. Once this had been established, various other dates slotted neatly into place. If the Battle Group left Ascension immediately, it could enter the MEZ by 1st May in order to insert Special Forces and give them enough time to provide the reconnaissance prerequisite for a safe and timely landing. The Amphibious Group could follow later, having used Ascension Island as a forward base for limited training and for optimising the loading of personnel, equipment, ammunition and stores. The C-in-C was also able to reassure Thompson that the Army's 5th Infantry Brigade had been alerted. Subject to MoD approval, this should provide the preponderance of force necessary to complete repossession of the Falklands after the initial landing. Despite many incidents in the intervening period, there was to be no deviation from the battle plan drawn up that day. In the event, the landing took place in the middle of the 'window', on 21st May.

During the flurry of activity in Ascension, Fieldhouse had been quietly sizing up his operational commanders, all of whom were under considerable strain. Although he had been pressed at home to appoint someone more senior, he needed no further convincing that he had a tough and resolute battle group commander. Woodward might not be easy to manage, but he was an accomplished tactician and possessed the essential elements of clear thinking and decisiveness that would be needed in the anxious weeks that lay ahead. Clapp and Thompson had an equally arduous but less lonely road to travel, being collocated in the same ship with clearly defined but overlapping responsibilities. They were still unhappy about the command arrangements, and by an apparent lack of understanding of amphibious matters amongst the Fleet staff. However, they were more than satisfied on two important counts. First, the scale of the initial landing operation had grown in size to well above the brigade strength for which they were staffed, and both had been apprehensive that they might be superseded by more senior officers. Secondly, if they were not to have their choice of Reffell as an overall in theatre commander, they wanted their independence as CTGs preserved. With characteristic consistency and loyalty, Fieldhouse told them that there would be no changes. As the nation's current 'in post' amphibious commanders, he was confident that they would deliver the 'goods' – as indeed they did. As CTGs, they would be reporting directly to him at Northwood. Despite these assurances, there remained a degree of Clapp/Thompson distrust of Woodward. This was unfortunate because with his elevated rank, and until Moore's eventual arrival on scene, the Rear Admiral remained very much the first amongst equals: the coordinating CTG in the South Atlantic. It would be his responsibility to get the whole force to the Islands safely and to provide air and surface resources in the Amphibious Objective Area (AOA) while the troops established themselves ashore.

Having rallied his men, Fieldhouse returned to the UK that evening. Although it had been an important and productive visit, various problems still hung uncertainly in the air. One was the choice of the landing area; in the infancy of planning and largely dependent on Special Forces reconnaissance. Another was the achievement of air control – assumed to be a mandatory requirement before attempting such a landing. A third, of which the C-in-C personally may not have been fully aware, was the groundswell of indifferent feeling between the *Hermes* and *Fearless* camps. This was not particularly unusual, as the history of warfare is punctuated by minor irritants of this sort. It seems certain that Fieldhouse was content to accept the occasional misunderstanding in the interests of maintaining a loose style of leadership based on decentralisation within the simplest possible chain of command. Stephen Prince puts it this way.

> The main problem within Fieldhouse's system was lack of lateral understanding between commanders, something exacerbated by their ambiguous inter-relationship and limited communications. It must be stressed, though, that better understanding and more formalised inter-relationships would have toned down, but not fully resolved, the problematic issues that were essentially resource based. It is unlikely that a revised structure would have altered any of the major restrictions or orders within the campaign.

* * * * * * * *

Five days after John's return from Ascension Island, the Prime Minister made her first visit to Northwood. At 10.00am the telephone rang in the Admiral's outer office. Shillingford took the call. The PM and a number of advisers would be arriving in the headquarters at 11.30 for a special briefing and would like to stay for lunch. The Secretary interrupted immediate business to pass the message on. As was to be expected, the Boss took the news very calmly. 'I will make arrangements for the briefing', he instructed, 'but I would like you to contact Midge and tell her there will be fourteen for lunch.' After a short pause, he added knowingly; 'I don't know which of us has the easier task!' Everything swung into top gear, both 'down the hole' and at Admiralty House. The PM recalls the visit factually in *The Downing Street Years*.

> Later that day I went to Northwood from where military operations and all the logistics were being directed. It was fascinating to see how the decisions were put into effect. I had lunch at the home of Admiral Fieldhouse and his wife, Midge, before returning to No 10.

When the party arrived at Admiralty House, Midge greeted the PM, and the ladies withdrew upstairs before moving down to join the men on the terrace. Shillingford was well placed to overhear their conversation.

> *Midge* 'I am sorry not to be able to give you the sort of lunch I would like to give to a visiting Prime Minister. With more notice we could have done better.'
> *Maggie* 'I am sure it will be better than I could manage at Number 10 because, you see, I have no staff.'
> *Midge* – with feeling – 'That's disgraceful!'
> *Maggie* 'I know. That's why I am having things changed.'
> *Midge* – with arms akimbo – 'Prime Minister, I like your style!'

So it was that two strong relationships were established on that day. In a letter to Peter Kimm after John had died less than ten years later, Margaret Thatcher coined the phrase 'the indestructible partnership' which appears elsewhere in this book. A further exchange of words between the PM and her C-in-C has already been quoted in the introduction.

In order to allow free discussion at what was, in effect, a working lunch, Midge did not join the others at the table. She need not have worried about the food, as Chief Cook Palmer produced his usual wonders. When asked recently to recall his most difficult moment as the Fieldhouse retinue chef, Palmer thought for a few moments before replying:

> I can't remember any particular problems, even when we had The Queen, the Prince and Princess of Wales or Mrs Thatcher. The only one that nearly beat me was the King of Tonga, because we didn't know how many people he was bringing with him. They kept coming out to *Glamorgan* by the boat-load. When the Admiral's cabin was full, we had to take over the wardroom. It was a close call; but everyone got fed!

The next day Fieldhouse received a short hand-written note from Lewin.

> Friday 23rd April
> *Dear John:*
> That was 500% and has done more good than anything since this fracas began. Your chaps were super. You have now landed them with a repeat performance on Sunday. PM was most impressed with Midge too! Love and thanks to her for lunch. See you on Sunday.
> *Yours ever Terry*

* * * * * * * *

As the Task Force deployed and prepared for war, the next few days were a crucial period in the peace negotiations, well documented in various books and not the subject of further comment here. South Georgia was repossessed on 26th April. The same day, a Total Exclusion Zone (TEZ) was established within a 200-mile radius of the Falklands with a prime purpose of closing down air reinforcement of the islands through Stanley airport. As the battle group approached the TEZ, Woodward became concerned about his restrictive Rules of Engagement. He was also having a number of problems in handling the embarked members of the media. This was not his strongest suit, and bad PR resulted when some of his comments were taken out of context. Fieldhouse was not amused, finding himself the 'jam in the sandwich' between the concerns of the MoD and a natural desire to support his subordinate commander.

As April ended, so did the political or preparatory phase of the campaign. Argentina had formally rejected the American peace initiative, clearing the way for a sympathetic international response to Britain's military intentions. The battle group was ready for action, empowered by new and favourable Rules of Engagement. Acting on the orders of the War Cabinet, Fieldhouse spoke to Woodward on the satellite link and instructed him to proceed inside the TEZ and commence the process of repossessing the Falkland Islands.

CHAPTER SIXTEEN

Forward To Victory

1982

IN LORD LEWIN'S BIOGRAPHY, Richard Hill has written of Margaret Thatcher's 'firmness of purpose and ready grasp of all the problems involved. They were not, as the Task Force went south, all military by any means. Lewin's well known dictum, that there is no such thing as a purely military operation, that all operations are politico-military, was never truer than in 1982.' But, as April gave way to May, Operation 'Corporate' became a military reality, with the emphasis shifting to the third member of the higher command triumvirate: to Fieldhouse at Northwood. Although Whitehall remained as busy as ever, much of the work there was in reaction to the Commander-in-Chief's needs. These included such matters as requests for changes in rules of engagement, provision of more merchant shipping and assistance with handling the media, especially where casualties were involved.

Fieldhouse, either directly or through his principal staff officers, was constantly in touch with his Task Group commanders; issuing orders or scrutinising, approving and, where necessary, adjusting their plans on a day-to-day basis. The conduct of the six weeks of battle that settled the war has been vividly described in a number of books by those who participated, both in the South Atlantic and in Whitehall. Woodward, Clapp and Thompson and some of their subordinates capture the heat of the action, the loneliness of independent command, the satisfaction of success and the agony of losses. They bring into focus the narrow margins that existed when required to fight, not only an enemy in conditions of acute disadvantage, but also the calendar and the weather. The accounts of Thatcher, Nott, Lewin and Leach deliver a similar breadth of understanding of the political and MoD scenes. There have been other worthy books by journalists and military historians. Although most acknowledge Fieldhouse's pivotal role, nothing has been written about the war from his perspective and one is forced to conclude that his achievement has not received the degree of recognition it richly deserves. The two people who understood him best and appreciated him most were Lewin and Leach, who both knew what it was like to be a Commander-in-Chief. Lewin's opinions of his old shipmate's qualities are well known, but unwritten by his own hand. Quotes from Leach's book of recollections have already been included, but recently he was asked if he had anything to add to his assessment of the man he later chose to succeed him as First Sea Lord.

> He was well endowed with statesmanlike qualities. He would readily listen to widely varying views on any particular subject before deciding upon a course of action. He had a good and cheerful sense of humour which helped with his sense of proportion. He had a quiet but decisive character, and underneath his almost urbane nature lay steel.

Something will be seen of this latter quality as further events unfold.

* * * * * * * *

This narrative continues with another quote from Fieldhouse's *South Atlantic Despatch*.

> Early on 1st May an RAF Vulcan flying from Ascension Island opened the action against the Argentinian forces on the Falklands with a night bombing attack of Port Stanley airfield which cratered the runway. The 16-hour sortie was supported by Victor tankers and Nimrod aircraft and was the first of five Vulcan missions directed against the airfield and adjacent installations. Early the same morning Sea Harriers attacked the runway at Port Stanley and also the airstrip at Goose Green. That night Port Stanley airport was subjected to Naval Gunfire bombardment from HM Ships *Glamorgan*, *Arrow* and *Alacrity*. This was to be the pattern for the next few weeks, with raids on the airfields at Port Stanley and elsewhere by Harriers and night bombardments by units of the Fleet. These attacks were designed to deny the use of the airfields to the Argentinian forces and to erode their readiness, morale and state of alertness. At the beginning of May, the first of many SAS and SBS reconnaissance patrols landed on the Falklands. These, and those that followed, were variously landed by helicopter, small boats from surface ships and the submarine HMS *Onyx*. During the next three weeks, these patrols were able to gather vital intelligence in preparation for the main landing. Throughout the period, in extremely harsh conditions, they remained undetected.

The weekend of 1st/2nd May was one of great significance to the outcome of the Falklands War. There was a clear need for the surface element of the Argentine Navy to be neutralised before any landing on the Islands could be attempted. The carrier *Veinticinco de Mayo* with two escorting destroyers was known to be at sea to the northwest of the TEZ, and her aircraft posed a considerable threat to the Task Group that lacked airborne early warning. On board was a squadron of A4 fighter-bombers and possibly some Exocet-armed Super Etendards. The latter were of the utmost concern; but fortunately it was known that only a strictly limited number of air-launched Exocet missiles had yet been supplied by the French as part of a larger sales package. To the southwest the elderly cruiser *General Belgrano*, also with two escorts, had moved in close to the TEZ. This group, intercepted by the SSN *Conqueror*, was thought to carry ship-borne Exocet missiles. To Woodward in HMS *Hermes*, it seemed that a classic 'pincer' attack was developing against his carriers. What he needed, and fast, was for the SSNs to remove the Argentine surface threat. A request for an amendment of the Rules of Engagement to allow the *25 de Mayo* to be attacked outside the TEZ had already been approved by the War Cabinet; but, due to circumstances outside their control, both *Spartan* and *Splendid* had lost contact as the carrier manoeuvred and turned away.

Hermes was both equipped and manned for taking direct control of SSNs, but, to his chagrin, Woodward's earlier request for this authority had been turned down. Nevertheless, sensing the importance of dealing with the secondary threat, Woodward signalled *Conqueror* to sink *Belgrano*. This was an audacious move, full of hidden innuendo. He knew that Northwood would remove this unauthorised instruction from the submarine broadcast. He also knew that neither Herbert nor Fieldhouse would be left in any doubt about what needed to be done without further delay. Fieldhouse totally supported Woodward's assessment, and left immediately for a War Cabinet meeting to present his case for a further change to the ROEs.

There followed on that Sunday morning at Chequers a prime example of the harmony that existed within the Thatcher/Lewin/Fieldhouse chain of command. By lunch time the ROEs had been amended and instructions signalled from Northwood to *Conqueror* to sink *Belgrano*. Immediately after lunch, William Whitelaw is reputed to have asked John Fieldhouse if the cruiser had yet been sunk. But things didn't happen quite that fast, even in the mysterious world of nuclear submarines! *Conqueror* duly received the message on next coming shallow to read her broadcast and, after manoeuvring into an attacking position, she sank the cruiser with torpedoes just before 8.00pm that evening. Much has been written of the fact that *Belgrano* was steaming away from the TEZ at the time of the attack. The military view is that this was irrelevant. Either group could well have been feinting before reversing course to continue with a pincer attack. The heavy loss of life was regrettable, but this would have been less with better damage control practices on board or if the escorts had moved quicker to pick up survivors. The tactical importance of the sinking was the nipping in the bud of any coordinated attack on the battle group. The long-term strategic benefit was the withdrawal of all Argentine surface warships to their home bases, not to emerge for the duration of the war. This was a major military success, clouded only by the failure to find and sink *25 de Mayo* instead. Her destruction would have removed some dangerous aircraft from the enemy's order of battle. Later, these were to inflict heavy losses operating from bases on the Argentine mainland.

Apart from the overriding importance of their deterrent affect on the enemy's surface fleet and reinforcement shipping, the SSNs carried out other important tasks. Argentina was known to possess at least one fully operational modern diesel-electric submarine. Much effort was spent both by submarines and ship-borne ASW helicopters in 'sweeping' the ocean clear to ensure safe passage of the Task Force from this threat. After the landing, when Argentine shore-based air effort intensified, SSNs patrolled close inshore, giving early warning of the departure of enemy aircraft from their bases. *Valiant* and *Courageous* arrived later as the boats longest at sea were released to go home. SSK *Onyx* provided the flexibility for operations in shallower inshore waters.

Following the sinking of *Belgrano*, retribution was not long in coming from the expected quarter: from the French built Super Etandard aircraft with their Exocet missiles. Those that remember the Falklands War will recall the shock they received on learning of the sinking of HMS *Sheffield* on 4th May. An absorbing and clinical account of this unfortunate incident forms the first chapter of Woodward's book. Both he and Fieldhouse had foreseen significant British losses, but the dramatic news flashed across TV screens was a wake-up call to the nation of the seriousness and high risk of the conflict. Several commanders made vital contributions towards winning the war but, like Jellicoe at Jutland in World War I, Woodward was the only one who could have lost it in an afternoon. His view was 'lose *Invincible* and the operation is severely jeopardised. Lose *Hermes* and the operation is over. One lucky torpedo, bomb or missile hit, even a simple but major accident on board could do it.' Fieldhouse also held this view and explicitly ordered that the carriers' safety should be a top priority. Although criticised by some, Woodward's battle group disposition far out to the east near the limit of shore based air attack was crucial to optimising their chances of survival. After the loss of *Sheffield*, further attacks could be expected. To be well balanced and fully prepared for this rightly dominated Woodward's thinking.

* * * * * * * *

Amanda heard the news of the sinking of *Sheffield* while on a back-packing holiday in Alice Springs. She called home from a coin box in the middle of the night; as usual reversing the charges. John was at an important working lunch, but left the table for a few moments to talk to his elder daughter.

'Daddy: I've just heard that you've lost a ship!'
'Thank you, Amanda, for keeping me informed.'
'Do you want me to come home?'
'I think we can just about manage without you for the moment; but if you're needed I'll let you know. Goodbye Amanda!'

Amanda recalls a sequel to this conversation after her return from Australia.

> What has always amazed me about naval officers is that they are a crowd of absolute softies. Shortly after the Falklands I happened to meet Captain Sam Salt. He told me how grateful he was to my father for having given him another ship after the tragic loss of *Sheffield*. As he said this, I could see that his eyes were full of tears. When I told Daddy about this later, I could see his tears too!

Wren Steward Sharon Davies remembers taking John his breakfast one morning at the height of the conflict. She caught him unawares, slumped at the table, overcome with grief, reading a casualty list. It was only at moments like this in the near-privacy of his home that he could afford to think deeply about those who would not be returning home; of the shattered marriages, fatherless children and grieving parents. Elsewhere, people drew strength and inspiration from the cheerful face he presented to the outside world. A junior staff officer remembers walking down into the 'hole' a few paces behind him at a moment of crisis. A couple of cleaning ladies were busy scrubbing the floor; almost blocking his way. Instead of hurrying on past them, he stopped for a chat. There was banter and laughter, and he left them feeling that their work was as important as anyone else's. It was a wonderful example of simple humanity and certainly not a waste of time. He probably drew strength from them too.

* * * * * * * *

Back at Ascension, preparations continued for the amphibious landing. On 29th April, Major General Jeremy Moore paid a second visit to the Island to confer with Clapp and Thompson. It had already been decided that the landing would have to be on East Falkland, at a place clear of the enemy, with appropriate beach gradients for landing craft. While Special Forces reconnaissance continued, a short list of three had been arrived at: Cow Bay/Volunteer Bay, Berkeley Sound and San Carlos. The first two were in relatively unsheltered water, closer to Port Stanley, but within possible artillery range of the Argentine defences. Moore returned to Northwood bearing the detailed analysis and the preferred option for San Carlos Water. Later, Port Salvador became the first alternative should San Carlos be found to be held in strength or its sea approaches mined.

Once *Intrepid* had arrived at Ascension, the way was clear for the Amphibious Group to carry on south, but Clapp and Thompson continued to be unhappy about certain planning aspects. One of these was that the guidelines in the manual of amphibious operations (ATP8) were not being strictly adhered to. No 'Concept of Operations' had been produced by Northwood. It was not possible to arrange for adequate rehearsals. There was lack of clarity about the landing force's overall objectives. There was little indication that the requisite air superiority was likely to be achieved. Although the 5th Infantry Brigade would soon be on its way in the liner

Queen Elizabeth II, there were doubts about its role on reaching the islands. Above all, there was continuing distrust of the lack of amphibious expertise at headquarters. Although Clapp would be in overall charge until after the landing, signals were being sent to Thompson for action. As their C-in-C, Fieldhouse must be held partly responsible for this unfavourable mindset; but so much was happening in so many different places, including the political arena, that his instinct would have been to let things run; allowing subordinate commanders to find their own solutions to problems; dealing with them as they thought best and shouting for help from him if they felt they needed it. Within the limitations, uncertainties and 'one off' aspects of this highly unusual war, this is precisely what Clapp and Thompson proceeded to do. In close collaboration with Woodward, they made light of any difficulties and achieved remarkable results in very difficult circumstances. This phase is covered by a further excerpt from Fieldhouse's despatch.

> It was important to select a suitable area for an amphibious assault as close to Port Stanley as possible, because cross-country movement is very difficult and weather conditions do not favour helicopter operations. However, the main danger in selecting an assault area too close to the capital was that it might make it too easy for the Argentinians to launch a counter attack against the beachhead before it could be firmly established. I had not the necessary forces to conduct an opposed landing. Although it was not possible to select a site which would be completely immune to air attack, the troop carriers and their escorts had to be afforded protection at least from Exocet missiles. The missile's effectiveness is greatly reduced if its intended targets are protected by land. The amphibious force also required deep water. After assessing all the factors, including the anti-submarine advantage, San Carlos Water was chosen for the amphibious assault. It is surrounded by hills, with a deep, comparatively sheltered anchorage and with the nearest sizeable enemy force being at Darwin/Goose Green more than 15 miles away.
>
> I was very much aware of the risks which a landing in strength involved. Despite the care with which the landing area had been chosen, the loss of a prestigious target such as SS *Canberra* and her embarked troops would have jeopardised the whole amphibious assault plan. My commanders therefore had to plan the assault to reduce the element of risk to the minimum acceptable. This was achieved by a variety of means. The most careful consideration was given to the disposition of embarked troops and equipment. Cross decking, the movement of men and material from one ship to another, had already been an essential feature of the passage south. This procedure was intensified during the week before the landing to ensure that assets were deployed effectively with as little risk as possible. Despite the intensity of these operations, which were often

> carried out in very poor weather, there was only one major loss. Tragically, on 19th May, a Sea King helicopter, while engaged in cross-decking, struck a large sea bird and immediately crashed into the sea. Eighteen SAS and three Royal Marine officers and men were killed.

As well as this tragedy, there were other setbacks. HMS *Glasgow* was hit by a bomb that passed in one side of the ship and out the other. Due to the great resourcefulness of her company, she was patched up and ready for action very quickly. Meanwhile, Woodward had been successfully 'softening up' the opposition in advance of the landing. There had been multiple shore bombardments. The Sea Harriers, with their American Sidewinders missiles, had had several successes in aerial combat, and various ground targets had been attacked. On 15th May, the SAS had carried out a brilliant raid on the air base at Pebble Island, uncomfortably close to San Carlos Water. Eleven aircraft were destroyed.

On 20th May, the day before the landing, there was a necessary change in the command structure. Major General Jeremy Moore left Northwood to fly to Ascension Island in order to embark in *QE II* for passage to the Falklands to assume command of the landing force when it assumed divisional status. Lieutenant General Richard Trant, then serving as GOC South-East District at Aldershot, became the C-in-C's new Land Deputy. There was a fleeting meeting between the two generals, but virtually no handover. Indeed, until a few days earlier, Trant had not even heard of Northwood! He brought a small support team with him, including Colonel Christopher Dunphie as his Chief of Staff. This left the Headquarters heavy in Army rank, but even shorter than before on amphibious warfare experience. The senior Royal Marine officer remaining was Lieutenant Colonel Tim Donkin.

On 18th May, the Amphibious Group joined up with the Battle Group outside the TEZ. On this day a special meeting of the War Cabinet was called, attended by the Chiefs of Staff. The risks of proceeding without full air superiority were carefully weighed before finally approving the landing. Consequently Lewin informed Fieldhouse that he was authorised to execute the landing on 21st May, subject to final confirmation. 8,000 miles away in the South Atlantic, Mike Clapp takes up the story on 20th.

> In anticipation of the final command I decided finally (with Julian) that H Hour would be 0230 local (0630 GMT) on the morning of 21st May, and so made another signal to Northwood, copying it to Sandy in *Hermes*. As a result, CTF [Fieldhouse] asked to speak to me direct on the secure radio circuit before making his final decision and discussing it with the Prime Minister. The conversation was brief and encouraging:
> 'Are you ready to go?'
> 'Yes, sir!'

> The rest was an excellent conversation with the Admiral very calm and supportive and me trying to match his cool by sounding as cheerful as I could … He then asked me searchingly about the state of the landing force's morale and that of my own people, particularly the civilians. I explained that all morale was, in my view, remarkably high and that neither Julian nor I wished to delay. The weather for the morrow looked ideal with low cloud and we should not miss the chance. He asked me if I had spoken to Sandy and I confirmed that we had had a useful meeting at the end of which we had understood each other's problems better. CTF seemed content with that and told me he would now seek the final confirmation. With that given, he would send a signal releasing us for the assault. He wished Julian and me, and our respective forces well. 'You are,' he ended, 'very much in my thoughts and prayers.'

That night, having left the protective umbrella of the battle group, a considerable armada closed the northern entrance to Falkland Sound. Led by Mike Clapp and Flag Captain Jeremy Larken in *Fearless*, were *Intrepid* and the RFAs *Stromness*, *Fort Austin*, *Sir Galahad*, *Sir Geraint*, *Sir Tristram*, *Sir Lancelot* and *Sir Percivale*; together with *Canberra*, *Norland* and *Europic Ferry*; taken up from trade. In close escort were *Antrim*, *Yarmouth*, *Plymouth*, *Brilliant*, *Broadsword* and *Argonaut*, while *Glamorgan* and *Ardent* created diversions in other parts of the Sound. Conditions were perfect for the final approach; unpleasant but not excessively rough, with low cloud acting as good protection from possible air attack. Everything seemed to be going entirely according to plan. In the early hours of D Day, 21st May, the Royal Marines and Paras started to be ferried ashore. Soon after dawn a Union Flag was flying in the breeze at San Carlos settlement. When a farmer was asked by an officer of the Parachute Regiment if he was surprised to find the Task Force anchored in the bay, he replied, 'No, not a bit. We knew Maggie would come!'

It was a Friday, and the Prime Minister had been busying herself with constituency appointments; visiting a removals company, even riding on a forklift truck!

> Then I rushed back to the constituency office to see if there was any news. Not yet. I never telephoned Northwood on this or any other occasion to find out about operations in progress. I knew that the commanders on the spot had more important things to do than answer unnecessary enquiries from London.

She received a full report from John Nott when she returned to Downing Street that evening.

* * * * * * * *

There were now two distinctive areas of command in the waters around the Falkland Islands. Having committed most of his escorts to supporting the landing, Woodward held back to the east with the battle group; continuing to provide a high level of air cover, ever ready for another, long overdue, air-launched Exocet missile attack. It became known that only five missiles had been available for use, and two of these had already been expended in the 4th May *Sheffield* attack. In company with Flagship *Hermes* were *Invincible*, *Glamorgan*, *Alacrity*, *Arrow*, *Glasgow* and *Coventry*; RFAs *Olmeda*, *Resource*, *Regent*, *Tidepool* and *Pearleaf*; and merchant ships *Elk*, *Fort Toronto* and *Atlantic Conveyor*. This latter ship was of enormous importance. On board were the last remaining fourteen Harriers that had been flown off to the carriers to augment operational squadrons and replace losses. She also carried four large Chinook troop carrying helicopters, considered essential for a quick breakout from the beachhead, and a number of smaller Wessex. Other cargo included material needed to establish a forward runway for use by Harriers and helicopters ashore, and 4,500 winter tents.

Commodore Clapp was in command of operations inside the Amphibious Objective Area (AOA), albeit relying heavily on Battle Group resources. He and Woodward had established a simple method to cope with the possibility of mutual interference. Essentially, this consisted of a 'box' whose base covered the entire area occupied by British troops, landing craft, supporting warships and transports. The height of the box was 10,000 feet, and into this huge volume of sky no Harrier was permitted to fly. Although friendly helicopters would be operating locally, all fixed wing aircraft in the box could be assumed to be hostile. The Harriers would make their interceptions to the westward and in the skies high above the AOA. The ever-authoritative Woodward records:

> It was a strange moment for me, because for the first time I was not effectively in charge of the front line of the battle. Mike Clapp would now take over and my own role would slip into that of a secondary commander, providing the ships and the troops inshore with all of the backup and support that I could. I did not particularly like it. I was used to being the man in charge out there.

Although complete surprise had been achieved for the landing, the expected Argentine air attacks began in earnest that afternoon. About fifteen enemy aircraft were destroyed, either by Harriers directed by warships, or by the protecting ships themselves. Destroyers and frigates in Falkland Sound bore the main brunt of the action. *Antrim* and *Argonaut* were hit and severely battered, *Brilliant* and *Broadsword* damaged. After fierce resistance against insuperable odds, *Ardent* was set on fire and later sank, having sustained heavy casualties. Miraculously, neither of the assault ships nor any of the transports was hit. That night, having discharged her priceless cargo, 'the great white whale', *Canberra*, slipped out of the anchorage to seek safety to the eastward; as did *Europic Ferry* and *Norland*. On the 22nd May (D+1), the enemy air force stayed at home on the mainland, allowing consolidation of the beachhead to continue without interference.

* * * * * * * *

That Saturday afternoon, the Prime Minister decided to call in at Fleet Headquarters on her way to Chequers for the weekend.

> At Northwood I spent some time getting up to date in the Operations Room. I did my best to seem confident, but when I left with Admiral Fieldhouse and we were out of earshot of anyone else, I could not help asking him; 'how long can we go on taking this kind of punishment?' He was no less worried. But he also had the ability of a great commander to see the other side of things. And, terrible as our losses had been and would be in the future, the fact was that we had landed our forces successfully and that serious losses were being inflicted on the Argentine air force.

Tim Donkin was present and adds weight to this account.

> The PM was sitting next to the C-in-C in an armchair specially provided for her. After a briefing officer had given details of casualties, she interjected to convey her absolute horror over the loss of so many lives. Fieldhouse touched her lightly on the shoulder and said calmly and clearly so that all could hear: 'Prime Minister; we shall lose more ships, more aircraft and more men; but we will win.' The C-in-C's easy manner belied his inner steel. This incident was just one of many in which he was able to instil in his staff a feeling of total confidence and loyalty.

* * * * * * * *

On D+3 the Argentine air force renewed its attacks in what had come to be known as 'bomb alley'. It was fortunate that many bombs dropped at low altitude did not have time to fuse before impact. Defence of the anchorage continued by all means available; from the ever reliable Harriers; from the ship-borne Sea Dart and Sea Wolf systems, sometimes too sophisticated to work effectively; from gunfire and point defence systems such as Sea Cat; down to simple small arms fire. Much store had been placed on the early use of the army's Rapier missiles ashore, but this system too was proving troublesome after its long voyage as cargo. HMS *Antelope* was hit and later exploded and sank, this time with minimal casualties. It was still a critical situation; but attrition of enemy air assets continued at a rate that began to suggest that the air battle could be won. Although there had been grievous losses and heavy damage, it was fortunate that the enemy had concentrated on attacking warships rather than going for the larger and much more vulnerable RFAs or transports.

25th May (D+4) was Argentina's National Day and a major effort by her Air Force was expected. Surprisingly, only one unsuccessful raid penetrated the anchorage. But later in the day there were two disasters outside the AOA. HMS *Coventry* was bombed and sunk while operating, with HMS *Broadsword*, as an anti-air warfare 'missile trap' north of Pebble Island. One hour before sunset, the battle group received brief warning of an airborne Exocet attack. Warships took appropriate countermeasures, but SS *Atlantic Conveyor* was hit and set on fire. One of the Chinook helicopters was saved, but the fire spread rapidly. With the rest of her precious cargo, she was abandoned and later sank.

* * * * * * * *

Christopher Dunphie had given a graphic account of the morning briefing at Northwood on 26th May. When C-in-C entered the Operations Room he stood for a few moments, looking round at all those gathered together to deliver and hear the latest news. Instead of moving straight to his chair, he decided to say a few words in the quiet yet determined style that all those who worked for him knew so well.

> 'I can sense an atmosphere of gloom here. I do not like it.' He pointed to one side where General Dick Trant and Dunphie stood out in their distinctive khaki uniforms. 'Since World War II the Army has been used to taking casualties in battle. The Navy has not, and it is something we must all come to terms with. I am quite prepared to lose more ships. I am even prepared to lose one of our carriers; but not both because that would destroy our air effort. What I will <u>not</u> accept is to see my staff with long faces. I want you to straighten your backs and go back to work with smiles on your faces'.

When Trant and Dunphie returned to their office, they agreed that they had witnessed a headmaster's rocket of the highest quality or, when put into its proper context, a truly inspiring act of leadership.

* * * * * * * *

Much interest now centred on the forthcoming land battle. On D-1 General Moore assumed the title, if not the role, of Land Forces Commander and left Northwood to fly to Ascension Island. This turned out to be an untidy arrangement. Before departing, his directive to Thompson had been to 'secure a bridgehead on East Falkland into which reinforcements can be landed, in which an airstrip can be established and from which operations to repossess the Falkland Islands can be achieved.' He went on to say that after his expected arrival on D+7, he intended to assume operational control, land the 5th Infantry Brigade into the bridgehead and develop operations for the complete repossession of the Falkland Islands. Also included in the directive was the need for Thompson to 'push forward and establish moral and physical domination over the enemy.' Once he had got ashore and assessed the situation, Thompson chose to do this by using the 2nd Battalion, the Parachute Regiment, to mount a raid on the Argentine positions at Darwin and Goose Green. At this crucial point in proceedings, he lost communication with his immediate commander. Moore had joined the 3,000 men of the 5th Brigade in the *QE II* off Ascension, only to find that the ship's satellite communications system had broken down, making him incommunicado. The ship pressed on through the South Atlantic, but was considered too politically valuable to risk within the TEZ. Cross-decking to *Canberra* and *Norland* was conducted at South Georgia, delaying Moore's arrival on the scene until D+9. The ten days since he had left Northwood included the amphibious assault and much of the war's bitterest and most costly sea and air fighting in the AOA and elsewhere. Moore had considered being parachuted into the action soon after D Day. In the event, he decided to arrive as planned with the reinforcing brigade. The communications problem was a particular blow because Thompson's existing directive was at odds with new messages arriving from Northwood. In hindsight, it seems that Moore could have done much to relieve the pressure on Thompson had he arrived at San Carlos a few days earlier.

In the days immediately following D Day, as the air battle raged in 'bomb alley', it had been a particularly difficult task to get all 3 Brigade's gear and supporting equipment ashore, into the right places for onward movement. At the forefront of Thompson's mind was his instruction to consolidate the bridgehead so that his troops could move forward to Port Stanley on 5 Brigade's arrival. Following the loss of so many assault helicopters in *Atlantic Conveyor* on D+4, he cancelled 2 Para's raid on Darwin/Goose Green; no longer considering it essential because, being wide on the southern flank, it was off the 'line of march'. It seemed that the final advance across East Falkland would have to be made almost exclusively on foot, and detailed plans for this were immediately put in hand.

* * * * * * * *

In the UK the mood was rather different. Now that our troops were ashore, the media and public were clamouring for early positive action to wind up the war. There were also political overtones, in that it was important to avoid a stalemate that might result in having to make concessions over the Islands' future. Fieldhouse had been kept fully aware of these attitudes in his daily talks with Lewin. It has even been suggested that, on behalf of the War Cabinet, Lewin instructed him to order Thompson to 'press on'. Those who were around the C-in-C at that time are emphatic that this was not so. Fieldhouse was very much his own man. He had the gift of being able to think things through with great clarity and possessed well-tuned political antennae of his own. He knew instinctively what was needed to be done in the national interest. He was also aware that his War Cabinet superiors knew that he knew what was in their minds. He called Julian Thompson to the secure voice terminal and spoke to him in very forthright terms. In the brigadier's own words, 'clear and unequivocal were the orders from Northwood. The Goose Green operation was to be remounted and more action was required all round.'

On the next day, 27th May, 2 Para started its move to the south to prepare for its night attack. Simultaneously, other 3 Brigade units moved out of the beachhead to begin their arduous advance on Port Stanley. The battle for Goose Green was an outstanding success, both militarily and in the eyes of the whole world. At a cost of 20 British dead and 37 wounded, 1,100 of the enemy were taken prisoner, together with two aircraft and much weaponry. This action put fear and dread into the hearts of the largely conscript Argentine army, leaving no doubt that it would be only a matter of time before their final capitulation. In a recent discussion, Thompson reiterated that his only regret was his failure to allocate more resources to 2 Para in order to have reduced their casualties. He added that once a senior commander had made his plan and committed troops to battle, success or failure rested entirely in the hands of individual fighting units. Over the remaining days of the conflict there were many other instances of outstanding gallantry in the field, notably at Mount Longdon, Two Sisters, Mount Harriet, Wireless Ridge and Tumbledown.

The Prime Minister spent the following Whitsun weekend at Chequers and there was no War Cabinet meeting. However, she sent word to Northwood that she would like a personal briefing. Fieldhouse chose to send Captain Freddie Fox (Assistant Chief of Staff Operations) to brief on maritime aspects and Colonel Christopher Dunphie to cover the land battle. When the latter sought some guidance, the C-in-C treated him to one of his disarming smiles:

> What you say, I leave entirely to you. If you get it wrong you can take the blame. If you get it right I shall take the credit. That's why I am sending you.

Everything was very informal at Chequers. There being no suitable table, the three of them got down on the floor together to examine a map. Later, they joined Denis on the terrace and Dunphie was given 'the strongest gin and tonic I have ever had!' Despite this, he remembers the PM's words to them as they departed.

> Now that the battle has started on land there will be an international demand for a cease-fire, including by some of the countries which have hitherto supported us. Tell Admiral Fieldhouse that I can hold the political arena. There will be no meddling in the conduct of the

> war. It is up to him to conduct operations as he thinks best, though I would be grateful if does not delay things longer than is necessary.

Clearly, Mrs Thatcher never sought to influence tactical decisions; nor would Lewin or the Chiefs of Staff have allowed it. As far as the military conduct of the war was concerned, Fieldhouse ran the show in his own way within the War Cabinet's governing directives.

* * * * * * * *

As May ended, the war entered its final decisive phase. The Argentine Air Force had lost many of its best pilots and was close to shooting its bolt. On 30th May, the last air launched Exocet missile was aimed at the battle group, but it passed harmlessly by as countermeasures were taken. In *The Battle for the Falklands*, Max Hastings and Simon Jenkins commented on General Moore's arrival at San Carlos on that day.

> Major General Jeremy Moore proved to be a good front-line commander, constantly visiting his units, encouraging his officers, never allowing his nerve or purpose to be seen to weaken ... The overwhelming burden of the land war fell upon Brigadier Julian Thompson and his brigade staff, whose achievement it is hard to overstate.

Moore's presence certainly eased the tension at Northwood. He reported in with what he called his 'daily waffle' signal – a confidence boosting plain language confirmation that all was proceeding well. Meanwhile, there was plenty of hard fighting yet to do. The decision to carry out a right hook towards Stanley with the relatively untrained 5th Brigade was designed to shorten the war. If fully successful, it would have been hailed as a great coup. Unfortunately, a last throw by the Argentine air force led to the disaster at Bluff Cove, where there were many casualties when landing ships *Sir Galahad* and *Sir Tristam* were attacked. There was a final sting in the tail for the Navy on 12th June when Fieldhouse's old flagship *Glamorgan* was hit by one of the four land-launched Exocet missiles that had been transported to the Islands. The ship was saved, but the thirteen lives lost were the last of many casualties at sea. Meanwhile, land forces had moved quickly forward to invest their final objectives. On 14th June white flags began to appear over Port Stanley. Later that day, General Moore accepted the Argentine surrender.

* * * * * * * *

News of the victory occasioned no triumphalism at Northwood. Thousands of prisoners had to be returned to Argentina. All those who had fought had to be brought home safely; especially the wounded. The Fleet remained widely dispersed, in a poor state of maintenance; with much work to done to restore things to normal. There was also a great sadness about those who would not be returning to their families. After a call from Downing Street, the C-in-C released a simple signal to his subordinate commanders.

> From CTF 317. Personal for CTGs 317.8, 317.1, 317.0. The Prime Minister has asked me to pass to you her personal congratulations on your outstanding victory.

Now that the pressure was off, Her Majesty The Queen paid a visit to Northwood. After touring the Headquarters, a lunch was arranged for a number of senior officers and their wives at Admiralty House. On arrival, Midge with The Queen and the Lady-in-Waiting retired upstairs, while the guests gathered in the hall preparing to be presented. As the Royal party descended, John went forward to greet his Monarch, but lost his footing and tripped at the bottom of the stairs. He took a bit of a tumble, but got up quickly and dusted himself down. In the resulting confusion he turned to present his Chief of Staff, but could not remember his name! 'Never mind,' said Her Majesty, always totally at ease with members of the armed forces. 'Let everyone introduce themselves.' And so they all did.

* * * * * * * *

The inventory of resources committed to Operation 'Corporate' makes very impressive reading. 44 warships of various types operated in the South Atlantic, plus 24 RFAs and 45 assorted merchant ships taken up from trade. 40 Army units or elements of units took part, as did 21 RAF squadrons or detachments. 28,000 men and a number of female nurses and Merchant Navy crew went to the South Atlantic. It had been a magnificent example of logistics and maintenance support in far flung places with stretched resources. 30,000 tons of stores, provisions and ammunition were shipped from Portsmouth and Devonport alone. Not once did men run out of food, ships of fuel or weapons of ammunition.

Casualties were severe, but certainly not excessive in the light of the high risks involved. The cost for the UK was 255 men killed and a further 777 wounded. Argentina's exact losses remain unknown, but Buenos Aires announced a provisional total of 652 men dead and missing in the war. Britain lost 6 ships sunk and 10 others more or less badly damaged. 36 Harriers went to war of which 9 were lost for various reasons, plus double the number of helicopters. Over 100 Argentine aircraft were seized or destroyed.

The total victory, achieved unilaterally amidst daunting difficulties, sent reverberations around the world. The Pentagon assessed that 'the British operation vindicates totally the concept of a professional standing army without conscripts and with an elite officer class. It also vindicates the establishment of specialist corps and highly trained and prepared units ready for instant deployment.' An outstanding performance by all three Services provided another notch in the forthcoming defeat of the Soviets in the Cold War. The recovery of the Islands led to a return of democracy in Argentina. The Royal Navy was allowed to keep the balanced Fleet it has been able to retain until this day, albeit in smaller numbers.

It was not until 8th October that that the *London Gazette* published an extensive list of Honours and Awards. Following citations for the posthumous Victoria Crosses awarded to Lieutenant Colonel H Jones and Sergeant I J McKay of the Parachute Regiment, Lewin headed the list with a Life Peerage. Fieldhouse received a GBE to add to his GCB in the recent Birthday Honours. Task Group Commanders Woodward and Moore received KCBs; Clapp and Thompson CBs.

On the production of this book twenty-three years later, only Jeremy Moore of these principal players has remained silent in terms of biographies or memoirs. He is known to be constant in his praise of Julian Thompson, who he memorably described at the time of the victory as 'the Man of the Match'. In a recent conversation, he expressed the opinion that Mike Clapp was an underrated commander who may not have received the full credit he deserved. He added:

> Everybody seemed to put it all down to Sandy Woodward. But it was John Fieldhouse's war. He was the Task Force Commander. We all did our stuff for John.

The General had this to say about the Commander-in-Chief himself:

> At the beginning of the crisis I didn't know Fieldhouse very well, but I came to have the highest opinion of him as a leader; both as his Land Deputy at Northwood and later as Commander Land Forces in the Falklands.

On 4th July Fieldhouse was at Brize Norton to welcome Sandy Woodward home. He was extremely proud of his Battle Group Commander, and happy for him to enjoy the publicity his achievements so richly deserved. There were many other joyous homecomings. The C-in-C greeted the majestic *Queen Elizabeth II* on her early return to Southampton with the survivors of *Sheffield*, *Ardent* and *Coventry*. He was on board *Canberra* when she made a spectacular entry into the same port, packed with 3 Commando Brigade Royal Marines and surrounded by scores of welcoming boats. The 'Great White Whale' had had an impressive war, with two dangerous runs into San Carlos Water followed by the return of 4,000 prisoners to Argentina. Fieldhouse also went to Portsmouth to meet the badly damaged *Glamorgan*. His Flag had been flying in this ship when the crisis started, and he had fond memories of times shared in earlier years. He was at Plymouth to meet returning frigates, including *Arrow* which was 'beaten up' at such low altitude by the RAF Red Arrows air display team that the crew were forced to hit the deck! At Pompey he was proud to welcome his old command

Hermes. It meant a great deal to him to be amongst so many of the men who had delivered the famous victory all had strived for.

First Sea Lord Sir Henry Leach, whose unswerving steadfastness at the onset of the crisis had been so vital, had his own moment of deep satisfaction. He flew out to join HMS *Invincible* as she neared Portsmouth; being joined for her entry into harbour by The Queen and the Duke of Edinburgh who were there as parents to welcome their helicopter pilot second son, Prince Andrew, back from the war. John and Midge chose to spend part of that day quietly at Northwood, watching the celebrations on TV. To join the family they had invited some of John's earliest naval friends, including Peter Kimm, Gordon Crosbie and John's Dartmouth tutor, Robert Morris, and their wives. Later, when all his senior commanders had finally returned home from the Falklands, a dinner was held in their honour at Admiralty House.

Other events followed in quick succession. These included a large dinner at No 10 Downing Street, a Victory March and all-ranks luncheon at the Guildhall in the City of London, and a Service of Thanksgiving at St Paul's Cathedral. John was content to resume his burdensome peacetime duties, to devote more time to NATO and to concentrate on the important lessons that might be learned from the recent war.

One matter which required his attention was the administrative action following the loss of Her Majesty's ships. It was customary that commanding officers should stand trial by Court Martial in order to clear their names. John would have none of this and, after further discussions in the MoD, his views were accepted. Julian Oswald, a recently promoted rear admiral who himself later became First Sea Lord, felt privileged to have been asked to conduct the Board of Inquiry into the loss of HMS *Sheffield*. He remembers being profoundly impressed by Fieldhouse's concise verbal instructions. He was told to concentrate on establishing those failings that could be remedied. Inevitably he would find that some people had done better than others; but it was not the Royal Navy's way to look for scapegoats. His policy should be to 'accept the bad, praise the good and get on with the job.'

Not long after the war, John prepared to leave Northwood on his appointment to relieve Henry Leach as First Sea Lord. The C-in-C chapters of this story began by quoting his Flag Lieutenant Jonathon Band. As they close, these are the views of his Secretary John Shillingford.

> On receiving my appointment I was slightly overawed by the thought of the responsibility. However I had been fortunate in having worked briefly for John Fieldhouse when he was a Captain in DNW; so I knew him as a thoroughly delightful and supportive person and that I should have nothing to fear from my C-in-C provided I did my job. So it proved. Working for him was the highlight of my career.

But perhaps it is appropriate that the last words from Northwood should come from two senior officers of another Service. Air Vice Marshal George Chesworth found him 'the most inspirational officer it has been my pleasure to serve.' Air Marshal John Curtiss' view was that:

> John's leadership style was unemotive yet firm. He listened to all points of view before deciding on any course of action but, once taken, he threw his full support behind it and gave unswerving support to his subordinates. He had great flexibility of mind and could react quickly to any change of circumstances that demanded a change of plan. Fieldhouse was a great man and I was very fortunate to have served under his Command. I valued his friendship enormously.

Although John was to serve the nation with great distinction for six more years, his outstanding success as Commander-in-Chief in war was his finest achievement. The Prime Minister used these words in a speech at Cheltenham on 3rd July: 'Britain found herself again in the South Atlantic and will not look back from the victory she has won.'

* * * * * * * *

200 years ago, Vice Admiral Collingwood sent his *Trafalgar Dispatch* to the Admiralty, where, after an arduous journey, it was delivered by Lieutenant Lapenotiere on 6th November 1805. Included were these words:

> After such a victory it may appear unnecessary to enter into encomiums on the particular part taken by several Commanders; the conclusion says more on the subject than I have language to express; the spirit which animated all was the same; when all exert themselves in their country's service, all deserve that their high merits should stand recorded; and never was high merit more conspicuous than in the battle I have described.

Fieldhouse's despatch was spelt with an 'e' as opposed to Collingwood's 'i', and his missive took rather longer to deliver; but this didn't matter because much of its contents were already widely known. Unsurprisingly, the concluding paragraph conveyed the sort of message that has altered little down the centuries.

> Operation 'Corporate' became necessary because deterrence failed, but in its execution it represented a triumph of military capability backed by resolute political will. The difficulties of short notice, extreme range and appalling weather under which this operation was mounted were all overcome by a single factor, the quality of our people. The fighting men were magnificent when put to the test and the support they received at every level, at sea from the Merchant Navy, at Ascension Island and in the United Kingdom was superb. I could not have been better served.
> *J.D.E Fieldhouse, Admiral, Commander Task Force 317*

CHAPTER SEVENTEEN

First Sea Lord

1982 – 1985

AFTER LEAVING NORTHWOOD in the autumn of 1982, John and Midge had a memorable holiday in the USA. On an earlier naval visit to St Petersburg on the west coast of Florida, Jonathon Band had made firm friends with local construction company tycoon William H. Mills Jr, whom he then introduced to the Fieldhouses. Bill was deeply fascinated by all things naval and welcomed with open arms the future First Sea Lord and his lady to his homes at St Petersburg and at the prestigious Useppa Island Club. Most generously, he helped John and Midge with the purchase of a spacious apartment on the mainland at nearby Englewood, which became their holiday home for the next six years. There was a fine view over the water, and John used to delight in relaxing on the open deck, glass in hand, watching the boats go by. At sunset he would haul down the white ensign he mischievously chose to fly when in residence. Close at hand was Barnacle Bill's – a rough and ready restaurant ideal for eating out in the evening.

After dinner with the Mills on the first Saturday night of that holiday, John and Midge piled into Bill's 46-foot motor cruiser to call on some other friends, the Wells, at nearby Cabbage Key. It was blowing a gale as they made their approach; with Bill's skipper feeling quite intimidated by the presence of a famous British Admiral, and doing his best 'not to screw up'. At that moment the port engine quit, and they slammed into the dock. Rob Wells and Dockmaster Terry were there to greet them. Terry, a larger than life character of Canadian Indian extraction, was always in the thick of things at Cabbage Key. Bill Mills continues:

> Through the rain I saw Terry and Rob hanging on to a piling, half in the water and dammed near crushed by the boat. They struggled out and we got the boat tied up during a stream of profanities by all involved. We retired to the bar where the drinking began, with Midge playing classical piano to the crowd of mullet fishermen who were sheltering from the storm. That evening started a long friendship between Terry and the Fieldhouses. Many times John would say, 'when I retire, all I want to be is Dockmaster at Cabbage Key.'

As a complete contrast to the burdens of senior military office, John and Midge loved the cheerful and spontaneous informality of their numerous new-found American friends, while their American friends certainly loved them in return. The Fieldhouses sold the apartment after John's serious illness six years later, but Midge still recharges her batteries every winter by returning to the Florida coast they enjoyed so much together. John never achieved his retirement wish, and is still much missed in and around those clear and sparkling waters. His memory is kept alive by a wonderful collection of memorabilia in Bill Mills' homes.

* * * * * * * *

John took over from Henry Leach as First Sea Lord in December 1982. This also made him the Chief of Naval Staff, First and Principal Naval Aide-de-Camp to Her Majesty The Queen, and the professional head of the Royal Navy. For convenience, it has been decided to refer to him as CNS. The immediate years following the Falklands War were a good time for the reputation and standing of the armed forces; something which had been partly of his making. He quickly established a strong team around him. Captain David Allen, who had served him so well as Controller, became his Secretary. Captain John Trinder, who had worked for Henry Leach, stayed on as Naval Assistant to provide continuity.

A priceless asset was June Light who had started work as a shorthand typist in the Admiralty at Bath, moving to the MoD in London during the Mountbatten era. She soon found herself in the First Sea Lord's office and became an immaculate PA to successive CNS over many years. As is to be expected from such a person, she is immensely discreet and loyal about all those she served, never wishing to place one of her masters on a pedestal above any of the others. However, she was prepared to say that she rated John's greatest strength as 'his ability to get on with people – be it the cleaner, Prime Minister or Monarch. All First Sea Lords were good at this, but none as good as he.'

He inherited another prize from an unexpected quarter. Lord Lewin had recently retired as Chief of Defence Staff. During his time as CNS and CDS, Lewin's driver/security guard had been Staff Sergeant Ken Crouch, Royal Marines. Before departing the scene, Lewin mentioned to Fieldhouse that he had been driven everywhere with great finesse and total safety, and suggested to him that he might like to take his man on. Crouch came away from Northwood

> praying that I would be able to continue my service in the Royal Navy and Royal Marines by working for the Fieldhouses. At the interview they played a mother and father act, introducing me to Amanda and Sarah who were both at home. The thing that struck me most was that John Fieldhouse was a people person; a genuine human being with no airs and graces.

Crouch was offered the job and stayed with his new master until his own retirement nearly five years later.

CNS's official residence was the amazingly convenient Mall House Flat; situated high over the western part of Admiralty Arch. On one side lay Trafalgar Square, where Nelson keeps his timeless watch. On the other, was a distant uninterrupted view – at least from the loo – of Buckingham Palace. Within easy walking distance were the MoD, St James' Park, the Royal Academy, clubs, theatres and some of Midge's favourite shops. The key members of the Northwood retinue staff were soon installed, including Chief Cook Mick Palmer and Petty Officer Steward Adrian Hill.

Hill had started his career with six years of Royal Yacht service. That had been a close-knit team, but advancement in the Yacht depended largely on 'dead men's shoes'. Hill's request to transfer to retinue work was accepted, and he joined Admiral Eberle's staff at Northwood as a Leading Steward, staying on at Admiralty House to work for the Fieldhouses. He needed some sea time to qualify for Petty Officer and joined HMS *Amazon* just too late to take part in the Falklands War. When he heard of Fieldhouse's appointment as First Sea Lord, he asked Palmer to put in a good word for him. John and Midge were delighted to have him back and he stayed with them for the next six years. Hill recalls that some improvements were needed to the Mall House Flat to make it into a comfortable family home.

The London scene generated a considerable amount of social activity, and parties continued at a heavy pace. June Light recalls that both John and Midge enjoyed the social whirl; but so many people wanted to meet them that they found it difficult to say 'no'. A later First Sea Lord, Sir Benjamin Bathurst, felt the need to be selective about accepting invitations. 'Once one went to one or two diplomatic receptions, one was rather expected to go to them all'. Bathurst felt that the simple process of doing one's job provided enough excitement and late nights for the tastes of ordinary mortals.

* * * * * * * *

In January 1983, Fieldhouse made his first visit to the Falkland Islands. Sir Robin Butler – then Principal Private Secretary to the Prime Minister and later Lord Butler of Brockwell – has provided two contrasting anecdotes.

> Our visit was very 'cloak and dagger' because the Argentinians had not formally ceased hostilities. We were a very small party, consisting of the Prime Minister and Mr Thatcher, John Coles (the No. 10 Foreign Affairs Private Secretary), Bernard Ingham (the No. 10 Press Secretary), a duty clerk and myself. We travelled to Ascension on a VC 10. The Prime Minister and her husband had beds in the forward compartment and the main fuselage had been stripped of seats so that the other five of us could stretch out on mattresses on the floor. When we had settled down for the overnight flight, John suddenly sat up and, saying that he had not had so much fun since he was a schoolboy,

> suggested that we should have a midnight feast in the dorm. We asked the crew what could be provided and they came up with five delicious slices of Black Forest gateau, which we ate with gusto sitting on our mattresses. We then settled down for the night until we reached Ascension.
>
> We landed in the early hours of the morning, apparently a little too early for the welcoming officer whose turnout was not everything which John thought appropriate. His tone of voice did not rise a decibel but, without making any sort of fuss, a steeliness in his manner must have made it clear to the welcoming officer that he could and should have done better. John Coles and I remarked to each other that John's boyishness and affability did not compromise in any way his insistence on the highest professional standards. We were, needless to say, hugely impressed.

When John accompanied Margaret Thatcher on a later visit to the Falklands, Midge went too. The latter tells how at one stage, while they were out in open country, Mrs T, trying to brush the abundant insect life away from her face, was provoked to say 'Oh, drat these midges!' At which Lady Fieldhouse was heard to mutter, 'In our family we call them margarets.' History has not related how the Prime Minister responded.

* * * * * * * *

The First Sea Lord's diary was constructed around a number of standing commitments. For instance, no Chief of Staff ever missed the early November Armistice Day ceremony at the Cenotaph, nor the previous evening's Royal British Legion Festival of Remembrance in the Royal Albert Hall. Attendance was expected in the Reception Committee for State visits, at the State Opening of Parliament and at the Queen's Birthday Trooping of the Colour on the Horse Guards Parade. A rota system ensured that a least one of the Chiefs attended State Banquets, Royal Garden Parties and the Lord Mayor's Banquet in the City. Whilst at Northwood John had been a senior service commander; in Whitehall he was not allowed to forget that he had become a minor player on a wider political stage. This meant attending a number of Government receptions and social occasions at No. 10.

Within the MoD itself, an endless stream of paper crossed his desk. Chiefs of Staff meetings were arranged on Tuesdays, and more frequent Admiralty Board meetings on Thursdays. Time had to be set aside to brief him on the agendas for these and other important discussions. He received all Flag officers before and after their appointments, and all captains and equivalent Royal Marine officers before they finally left the Navy. There were regular presentations at the various staff colleges, and speeches at dinners, clubs and naval associations. It was also necessary to find the time to take an occasional holiday.

Relaxing in *Hoi Polloi*

At a launching ceremony

JF on the Upper Yangtze River as a guest of the Peoples Republic of China

JF and Midge at the unveiling of the submarine memorial at the RN Submarine Museum

Commissioning of Midge's HMS *Trafalgar*

JF honoured by past and present Flag Officers Submarines at HMS *Dolphin*

CPO Steward Adrian Hill receives his Long Service and Good Conduct Medal

On parade at the Royal Military Academy Sandhurst

In more relaxed mode visiting troops in the jungle

THE WHITE HOUSE

WASHINGTON

December 22, 1988

Dear Admiral Fieldhouse:

On your departure as the Chief of the Defence Staff, I want to extend to you my deep appreciation for your contributions to the special US-UK relationship and to the NATO Alliance.

Over the years, our nations have remained the closest of allies and clearly your service, spanning more than five decades, has directly contributed to that close relationship. Your forthright statesmanship in the NATO Military Committee has been particularly noteworthy as the Alliance continued successfully to deter war and enhance the security of all member states. We in the United States deeply appreciate your selfless dedication and significant contributions to world peace.

Reports of your recent illness sadden us, but rest assured that you have the great appreciation of all Americans for your lifetime of service. Nancy and I pass on a personal hope for a complete recovery followed by a most fulfilling future for both you and Lady Fieldhouse.

Sincerely,

Ronald Reagan

Admiral of the Fleet
Sir John Fieldhouse, GCB, GBE
United Kingdom Ministry of Defence
Main Building, Whitehall
London, SWIH-2HB

JF with his Sea Cadets

With Donald Gosling (hands crossed) at a White Ensign Association Council Meeting in the South of France

JF with sponsors Lords Lewin and Bramall in the House of Lords

Last photograph of JF with his family in the garden at 'Pippins'
From left: Sarah, Mark, Midge and Amanda

Grandchildren at the Fieldhouse Memorial in the Falklands Gardens, Gosport
From left: Tom, Rebecca, Ruby, Jonathan (JJ) and Bethany

Because of the expense involved, a protocol had been established that each Service Chief would be permitted three home and three away official visits per year. This was to enable them to entertain and be entertained by a number of the heads of their respective services abroad. In practice, they travelled more extensively because visits to their own services were accounted for separately. For John, as for all people in high places, it was an extremely busy life with almost every moment of every working day programmed for one purpose or another. For six whole years there was hardly a free evening. Much valued, but often in short supply, were weekend and holiday relaxation at 'Pippins', in *Hoi Polloi* or in Florida.

* * * * * * * *

Around the time that John became First Sea Lord, there were some important changes in the Ministry of Defence. In October 1982, Field Marshal Sir Edwin Bramall had succeeded Lord Lewin as Chief of Defence Staff. In January 1983, John Nott gave up politics to return to his earlier career of merchant banking; being replaced as Secretary of State for Defence by Michael Heseltine. Before departing, Nott produced his Defence White Paper, *The Falklands Campaign: The Lessons*. Following the dramas of the pre-Falklands Defence Review, in which the Navy had received a fearful hammering, he had been persuaded to restore a more equitable balance between the Services. Not only were the losses of ships, aircraft and equipment to be restored. Defence expenditure was to be allowed to rise to the NATO benchmark of 3% growth in real terms until 1986. Nott reached this significant conclusion:

> Following the Falklands Campaign, we shall now be devoting substantially more resources to defence than had previously been planned. In allocating these, we shall be taking measures which will strengthen our general defence capability by increasing the flexibility, mobility and readiness of all three Services for operations in NATO and elsewhere.

The book *The Chiefs*, which Lord Bramall wrote jointly with fellow distinguished soldier and military historian General Sir William Jackson, contains a valuable insight into the six years in which Fieldhouse served on the Chiefs of Staff Committee, initially as CNS and then as Bramall's successor as CDS. With the reputation of the armed forces riding high after the brilliant campaign to recover the Falklands, it had been hoped that the MoD would be entering a period of reequipping and consolidation. However, other matters intervened to keep the Chiefs very much on their toes. The new Secretary of State for Defence was the highly ambitious and mercurial Michael Heseltine. In June 1983, assisted by the euphoria of the 'Falklands Factor', Margaret Thatcher's Conservative Party was elected for its second term. Following his successful showing at the hustings, Heseltine, as the rising star of the Conservative Party, saw his chance to grasp more headlines by developing a defence initiative which he could call entirely his own.

The recent Nott/Lewin reforms, which had worked very well during the Falklands crisis, had give more power to CDS without noticeably eroding the authority of the Chiefs. Heseltine chose to take this process further by functionalising the Defence Central Staff at the expense of the single services. The groundwork was carried out behind closed doors and presented as a *fait accompli* in April 1984. The essence of the scheme was that each service would lose its three-star Vice Chief of Staff to the Centre, where they would become Deputy Chiefs of Defence Staff with responsibility for 'Commitments', 'Systems' and 'Programmes and Personnel'. A fourth three-star post of 'Policy' would be held by a senior civil servant. These four would report to CDS through a four-star Vice Chief of Defence Staff with the status of a full member of the Chiefs of Staff Committee. The Secretary of State proposed further to strengthen his own control by creating a new and largely civilian Office of Management and Budget. Headed by a senior civil servant, this would be responsible for the size and shape of the armed forces.

As can be imagined, the Chiefs did not entirely welcome these proposals and exercised their right to express their concerns to the Prime Minister. Mindful of the Chiefs' contribution to the success of the Falklands War, Mrs Thatcher was sympathetic and some of the less favoured aspects were toned down. Nevertheless, the pruning of single service staffs in Whitehall and the devolution of powers elsewhere inevitably left the Chiefs feeling rather vulnerable. It is to the credit of Bramall, Fieldhouse and others that when the reorganisation was introduced in January 1985 it was made to work effectively. One of the better spin-offs was a marked reduction in inter-service wrangling.

* * * * * * * *

Commodore Terry Thompson, who has been mentioned earlier as Fieldhouse's First Lieutenant in HMS *Walrus*, was by now serving as Director of Defence Operational Requirements on the Central Staff. Before the reorganisation, his team had had a relatively minor role in monitoring and vetting projects coming forward from the single services. Under the new scheme, his department would assume prime responsibility for recommending priorities for defence expenditure within the allocated equipment budget. Thompson called a meeting of the single service Operational Requirements Directors to tell them of the Secretary of State's decision, and that it had to be made to succeed. At the second such meeting, after appropriate consultation, the battle lines were drawn. The Air Staff supported the changes 100%. The Naval Staff expressed complete opposition on all counts and intended to fight them tooth and nail. The Army was content to sit on the fence and await developments.

Thompson thought it odd that Fieldhouse was objecting so strongly, as it was already widely expected that he would become the next Chief of Defence Staff. Because of their long association through having served together as junior officers, John sent for Terry to discuss the matter. He did not express an opinion or try to press the navy's line in any way. He wanted an independent view from the Central Staff on how things were expected to turn out. Terry replied that, as the Secretary of State had already announced what was to take place, it was up to everyone else to make it work. Fieldhouse listened carefully. Eventually a civil service-chaired committee met to resolve these and other differences. The single service staffs never became as closely integrated as Heseltine had envisaged. However, most of his other changes were introduced.

This story provides just one illustration of the sharpness of Fieldhouse's political mind. He must have felt that the strong objections of the Navy, if deftly aired, could lead to compromise and concession on points that really mattered to him.

* * * * * * * *

John Trinder was John's Naval Assistant until August 1984. He recalls his master's skill at fighting the navy's corner in the face of inevitable budgetary constraints.

> Without JF we could have lost a lot of the Navy. He had a wonderful way of manipulating the civil service bureaucracy which no one else could have possibly achieved.

Trinder made the arrangements for all CNS's outside visits and accompanied him on all almost all his overseas tours. The one exception was a trip to Japan, for which David Allen became the happy bag carrier. The first visit, only weeks after taking over, was to Iceland in January 1983. Trinder remembers Fieldhouse delivering one of his most stirring speeches at the US military base at Keflavik – urging a stiffening of resolve in countering the Soviet submarine threat.

Other visits to foreign Chiefs of Naval Staff followed at regular intervals. Greece, Spain, India, Egypt and Brazil were all on the itinerary. For all except Brazil, Midge went too, with Trinder's wife Rosalie included in the party. With the Falklands War a very recent memory, most host CNSs were somewhat in awe of the great Commander-in-Chief – possibly not anxious to expose the inadequacies of their own more humble navies. But John's warm and generous personality soon melted the ice and softened hearts.

The visit to India followed closely after that of the redoubtable Soviet Admiral Sergoi Gorshkov. Trinder recalls that John's party had the same very bright Russian-trained Indian liaison officer as had Gorshkov – who found it much more relaxing to work for Fieldhouse. In Egypt the party was treated to a magnificent VIP tour of the antiquities, a far cry from Midshipman Fieldhouse's camel ride at the Pyramids all those years ago. In Brazil, CNS was presented with a ceremonial pistol that he handed to Trinder as if it was a hot potato. The NA had some anxious moments getting it through customs, but eventually all was well and it ended up in a museum.

Sir Simon Cassels served on the Admiralty Board as Second Sea Lord and Chief of Naval Personnel throughout the whole of Fieldhouse's period as CNS. He found John's relaxed and avuncular style of leadership unusual but extremely effective. He has a delightful memory of the visit of the Chinese Naval delegation.

As an item for the formal session the Chinese had asked to discuss 'mobilisation'. In taking the lead on what was thought to be a personnel issue, the Second Sea Lord had arranged a short presentation on such mundane things as the procedure for the calling up of reserves, issuing of gasmasks, updating of medical records and other documentation. The Chinese seemed totally uninterested and their CNS held up his hand to halt proceedings, saying: 'I think something has miscarried in translation. What we wanted to know was how you mobilised the merchant shipping you needed for the Falklands War.' Where others might easily have been put off balance, John reacted very calmly and quickly. 'As it happens I have come completely prepared for such a question,' he replied, reaching down to his briefcase and removing from it a single sheet of paper which he handed across the table. After a pregnant pause, he said slowly to help with the translation: 'You will see that we started with a blank sheet of paper rather than trying to update a contingency plan, which in fact did not exist.' The Chinese delegation seemed highly delighted to have been privy to one of the MoD's innermost secrets!

A visit to Barrow-in-Furness in May 1983 was a very special family occasion. Thirty-five years had passed since Midge had started her training as a humble Wren radar mechanic. In July 1981 she had launched HMS *Trafalgar*, Britain's latest and most advanced nuclear submarine. Now it was her turn to be the central figure at the commissioning ceremony. A close association was formed which has given her enormous pride and satisfaction until this day.

* * * * * * * *

It was customary for CNSs to change their Naval Assistants half way through their tour in order to provide continuity for their successor. Captain Tom le Marchand took over in August 1984. As a commander, Tom had been CO of HMS *Valiant* during the Falklands War. But he and John went back much further: he and his wife Valerie had first been introduced to John at a summer ball at HMS *Dolphin*. They had married and started a family shortly beforehand, and Tom had been appointed as the Navigating Officer of HMS *Dreadnought*, then refitting in Rosyth. He was keen to meet the great man who had been the CO a few years earlier. In the course of conversation, John had asked if the family would be moving north to Scotland together. 'We would like to but we can't', said Tom. 'I am not quite twenty-five, and until then I am not permitted to put my name down for a married quarter.' Tom thought no more of it, but the next day he discovered that his appointment had been delayed until his birthday, allowing the necessary administrative action to proceed.

All sorts of people who have worked closely with John and Midge have found themselves being treated as one of an extended family. Tom and Valerie were certainly no exception. Now that John had reached the very top of the service, he derived great pleasure from having a young submariner by his side. They had a common bond which enabled them to think alike about many things. Tom soon found his niche as a successful speech writer, but he often found that the end product had been improved as John added embellishments which were entirely his own.

Arriving in CNS's office at the same time was Lieutenant Commander Adrian Munns, one of the Assistant Secretaries. Like Tom, he found it an intensely happy workplace, inspired by Secretary David Allen's humour to offset the long hours and heavy workload. It was the time of the popular TV sitcom *'Allo 'Allo*, in which a French gendarme coined English phrases in an outrageous accent. The dubbing of Juno Light as 'Gin Loot' caused much merriment. Lapsing easily into his Yorkshire vernacular, John got into the habit of calling Tom 'lad'. One day John noticed a small boy standing by Tom's desk as he passed through his outer office. 'Ah', he said knowingly. 'You must be the lad's lad!'

In October 1984 CNS used a personal jet for visits to Yugoslavia and Romania. The latter visit was of particular interest, Romania not having fully emerged from the Soviet sphere of influence. This was Valerie's first trip abroad with the Fieldhouses, and of course Tom was responsible for all the arrangements. After calls at Belgrade, Zagreb, Split and Dubrovnik, there was a final inspection of a Guard of Honour before the short flight to Bucharest where a similar ceremony had been planned. As they got into the aircraft, Tom said to the Admiral 'I've made arrangements for you to do a quick change on board.' 'Why should I change, lad?' was the surprised reaction. 'Look at your trousers, Sir' provided the explanation. John had been wearing a navy blue lounge suit the night before and had started the following day in a uniform top and turn up trousers! After Bucharest the party visited the Black Sea port of Constanta – not far removed from the Soviet Navy's Black Sea bases.

In the following month, November, Fieldhouse set off on an official visit to Pakistan. It consisted of a weeklong tour embracing Islamabad, the North-West Frontier Province, Lahore and Karachi. Tom's father had been CO of the 5th Royal Ghurkha Rifles during World War II, and the party called in at the Fort that had been Tom's birthplace. The le Marchands had been much respected locally, to the extent that John was heard to say to Tom 'I was labouring under the misapprehension that this was my official visit to Pakistan; not yours!' Midge remembers the heavy security everywhere, with hundreds of guards in frilly skirts lining the route to the Khyber Pass. Back in the plains, they were accommodated in a comfortable guesthouse and taken out to dinner on the evening before a day of sightseeing in Lahore. As Tom was getting ready the next morning, a bearer arrived with a note on a silver salver. It was a brief message from Midge. 'Tom, come instantly. I think John's dying.'

In a state of some apprehension he hurried along to the Admiral's quarters, being relieved to discover that John's problem was nothing more serious than a severe and totally disabling tummy upset. This came as no surprise because Valerie was suffering from a similar complaint at the other end of the building. The programme went ahead as planned with Midge as the principal VIP. Valerie le Marchand has never been allowed to forget her *faux pas* when she later described the incident. 'Midge and Tom went out sightseeing, leaving John and me in bed!'

It was during this visit that the word 'debriefing' assumed a new and important significance. As a Moslem country, Pakistan was 'dry'. One evening, on reaching their hotel lobby, Tom suggested that he should come to the Admiral's room for a debriefing session. Having questioned the need for debriefing, John glanced down at the bottle of duty free scotch in Tom's plastic bag and quickly cottoned on. As a sequel to this, Tom recalls a conversation at Euston station when he knocked at the door of John's sleeper compartment after an overnight journey from Scotland.

> 'Good morning, Sir.'
> 'Why should I say good morning to you?'
> 'Why on earth not, Sir?'
> 'You came here last night for debriefing and I couldn't get rid of you until we had drunk all the debriefing material. Now I have got flu!'

Early in 1985, John and Tom flew to Bodo to visit Royal Marine winter warfare training inside the Arctic Circle. For some of the time John was accompanied by the Norwegian Chief of Naval Staff, a good friend who escorted him on an informal call on the King of Norway.

In May, there was a long looked forward to official visit to China. This was four years before the Tiananmen Square massacre and twelve years before the expiry of the Hong Kong New Territories lease, the dominant issue in British/Sino relations. The party flew to Hong Kong where

Fieldhouse opened the new China Fleet Club before taking an onward flight to Peking. After the usual formalities and tourist outings in and around the capital, Fieldhouse was taken to the coast to for an interesting look at a Chinese nuclear submarine; made possible as a *quid pro quo* for an earlier visit by the Chinese CNS to a British SSN at Faslane. He also visited surface units near Shanghai. Official naval business was followed by a grand tour of the Xian Terracotta Army and of the Three Gorges on the Upper Yangstse River. The party returned to Hong Kong by train by way of Canton and the New Territories. On all these official trips Midge was an integral part of the party, often carrying out her own programme. Wherever public transport was used, as for the air flights, Valerie le Marchand had to pay her own way. Tom remembers that this put a considerable strain on their financial resources, but they were once in a lifetime experiences that could not be missed.

* * * * * * * *

The Mall House Flat was always a hive of hospitality, and many people passing through London were invited to come and stay. Sarah had her 21st birthday party there in 1983 and, once she had graduated from St Andrew's University the following year, it became a very convenient home for her while she was job hunting. Mark was often around, and Amanda was a regular visitor from Australia where she had chosen to work and make her home.

One of the highlights of this period, which John's younger brother Richard and his wife attended as guests, was a dinner party in honour of the Prince and Princess of Wales. Midge had done a deal with the children. There wouldn't be room for them to eat at table but, provided they were suitably dressed in a black tie or equivalent, they were welcome to join the party in the drawing room after dinner. In due course Prince Charles settled into a comfortable upright chair, chatting to the three young Fieldhouses who were sitting on the floor in a semi-circle around him. After a suitable interval, Midge arrived on the scene to shuffle people around. The girls got up and moved away, at which point Prince Charles interjected: 'Could I have another five minutes, please? Mark and I are talking motorbikes.' The Prince was genuinely interested to learn more about Mark's experiences in the courier business. Meanwhile the Princess had asked to visit the kitchen. She was at the height of her popularity and youthful beauty having already ensured the longer-term succession to the Throne. The Staff was delighted for a chance to meet her.

* * * * * * * *

In this personal memoir, no serious attempt has been made to go into any detail of the many important issues that crossed John's desk. Apart from his total focus on protecting and advancing the interests of the Royal Navy, he remained close to the fringes of exciting times in international affairs. In the United States, the Reagan Administration's huge increase in defence spending had set alarm bells ringing in the Soviet Union. In December 1983 the Intermediate-range Nuclear Forces (INF) talks had started in Geneva, closely followed by deployment of US cruise missiles to the UK. Arms control negotiations continued against a background of increasing American-led NATO military strength. Fieldhouse remained doggedly determined to preserve the Navy's equipment programme, but it has been suggested that this was achieved at the expense of some much-needed personnel reforms. The Navy had begun to have a retention problem with many of its best men leaving early, attracted by better-paid civilian jobs. However, John is sure to have examined these priorities carefully. There was no point in pandering to people unless they were given the right tools to do their jobs. Anyone who worked with him at this time saw him as an immensely shrewd and effective leader; a good listener who weighed all the options; a man who was very much in touch with the nuances of the changing world around him.

Until this point, the appointment of Chief of Defence Staff had always been made by a process known as 'Buggins' Turn'. By this means, each of the three Services felt able to select and groom a suitable candidate in the certain knowledge of having to produce one every nine years. Some had expected that Bramall, who had succeeded Lewin, would be relieved by Chief of the Air Staff, Sir Michael Beetham. But the matter was settled when Margaret Thatcher let it be known that she wanted Fieldhouse for this post. As Air Marshal Curtiss put it:

> Strictly speaking it was not the Royal Navy's turn, but a sensible break from 'Buggins' allowed the best man to get the appointment. It was very much welcomed by all but some military diehards.

Thus it was that Fieldhouse was about to break the cycle, and to this day CDS remains a Government appointment irrespective of Service.

One morning John asked June Light to step into his office, not to take dictation but to sit down for a private chat. 'I've been to see the Secretary of State', he said. 'He offered the job of CDS and I have accepted on the condition that you will come with me.'

Faced with little alternative, June was delighted to accept. After many years looking after First Sea Lords, she became the first civilian to serve in the private office of a CDS.

* * * * * * * *

In June 1985, as he neared the end of his period of office, Fieldhouse visited naval units in the Falkland Islands. Because of the need to maintain a strong deterrent posture following the war, contingency funds had been provided to maintain a substantial garrison and to build a runway capable of operating large aircraft at Mount Pleasant, to the southwest of Port Stanley. At that time there were about 5,000 servicemen in and around the Falklands, outnumbering the Islanders by nearly three to one. Together with Midge and Tom le Marchand, John arrived at the new airport in one of the first flights of a RAF Tri-Star jet. Until the month before, all flights from Ascension had taken thirteen bone-shaking hours in the belly of a Hercules transport with two in-flight refuellings. John and Midge stayed at Government House with the Civil Commissioner, Sir Rex Hunt, and there were good opportunities for both of them to look around the Islands. Until the end of his life Fieldhouse maintained the keenest possible interest in the Falklands, and a deep sense of responsibility for the many lives that had been lost preserving freedom of choice for the islanders.

The Military Commissioner and Commander British Forces Falklands was Major General Peter de la Billiere of former SAS distinction. While complaining about the increase in the number of VIP visitors since the opening of Mount Pleasant airfield, he wrote these words in his autobiography:

> None were less trouble than the First Sea Lord, Admiral Sir John Fieldhouse, and his wife Midge – one of the least pompous people on earth who, when I addressed her as 'Lady Fieldhouse', immediately announced that her name was Midge ... She once brought the house down with her definition of an expert – 'Ex', she said, meaning a has-been, and 'spurt' something under pressure.

During the visit, a memorial was unveiled to those lost in the tragic incident at Bluff Cove. The General recalls that Midge wanted to free her hands while taking a photograph and gave him her handbag to hold for a few moments. To his embarrassment, this gave the press an unusual photo opportunity to the amusement of all concerned.

On completing his term, John let it be known that, as he was only going to be moving a few doors up the corridor, he would prefer to have a quiet and orderly departure. Tom le Marchand took note of this but was determined that the private office should lay on something special. It happened that CNS was due to pay a farewell visit to Gibraltar, and Tom, who had earlier served as Military Assistant to the Governor, had some good contacts on the Rock. Retired Admiral Sir Raymond Lygo, who was Chairman of British Aerospace, had let it be known that if ever CNS was at a loss for transport, he would be happy to loan his company jet. With Lygo's full connivance, it was used for a highly unusual purpose.

Tom and Valerie le Marchand had accompanied John and Midge to Gibraltar where they were staying as house guests of the Governor, Admiral Sir David Williams, who was fully aware of Tom's plan. On Saturday, the executive jet left Southampton airport with the remainder of John's private staff on board, including David and Margaret Allen, June Light and Adrian Munns. This had been arranged as a complete surprise for David Allen, whose wife had not only persuaded him to buy a respectable lightweight suit, but who had also enticed him to the airport on the pretext of going out to lunch with friends. At the Convent, the Governor's residence, there were no advertised plans for the evening and the Williams and the Fieldhouses gathered in the drawing room for an informal drink. At that moment, to John and Midge's total surprise, the entire staff emerged from behind the curtains. After a celebration with champagne, the party continued with a farewell dinner at the Rock Hotel, kindly arranged by the owner Joe Gaggero. The jet returned to Southampton on Sunday, so no working time was lost in the office. There was an anxious moment later when, in mock seriousness, Lygo threatened to send le Marchand the bill for the use of the aircraft.

Tom would be the first to admit that the strength and cohesion of the office depended primarily on the experience and skills of David Allen. With his enormous fund of common sense and good humour, he had steadied the ship through John's two wearying Admiralty Board appointments. His boss certainly felt that he had been most admirably served, David being a complete master of the over-complicated Whitehall scene. In due course he was promoted Rear Admiral and was knighted for his work as the Defence Services Secretary. Like John, he died before he had a chance to enjoy the full benefits of a well earned retirement – from a heart attack while he was out shooting with his dog near his home in Somerset. In a recent conversation Margaret Allen said of John that 'whoever he spoke to was made to feel that nobody else mattered to him at that particular moment.' She is but one of many to have expressed this sentiment.

* * * * * * * *

This chapter started with some recollections on the warm bond of friendship that existed between the Fieldhouses and their friends in Florida. Ten years later the local community was devastated by John's premature death. These words appeared in an article titled *We just called him John* in the *Useppa Island Times* by Don Truss:

> VIPs are not uncommon on Useppa Island but John was a special person. He had a clear view of problems that beset today's world and a firm grasp of the action required to effect solutions. We listened with interest and rapt attention to his anecdotes, many of which gave added dimension to the day's headlines. Through it all, though, we just called him 'John', whose wonderfully witty and dry comments elicited many laughs.

CHAPTER EIGHTEEN

Defence Supremo

1985 – 1988

ON 1st SEPTEMBER 1985, there appeared a 'Profile' in the *Sunday Times* by journalist James Adams. Under the title 'Smooth touch of the topmost brass', it was a skilful piece of racy journalism; extremely well informed and making a number of thrusts which were either bang on target or very close to the mark. The article is important here because it provides a serious contemporary assessment of John at the peak of his service to the nation. Accompanied by a saucy cartoon, it would have been read with interest in countless well-informed households twenty years ago. The sub-title reads 'Admiral Sir John Fieldhouse takes over as Chief of the Defence Staff, head of Britain's armed forces, this autumn – his reward for masterminding the Falklands victory', and quotations from Adams' article provide an appropriate way to add emphasis to John's story as his career entered its final stages.

> The head of the armed forces requires a unique blend of political awareness and military skill. He has to bob and weave between the incessant demands of the three services and the politicians, who have to keep the voters, industry and Britain's NATO Allies sweet ... By first impressions, Fieldhouse, who is 57, seems an unlikely man for his new job. His figure betrays his love of good food and wine. He is a congenial conversationalist, with a disarming habit of winking alternate eyes at odd moments. He also deploys a ready laugh to undermine tricky questions.
>
> He lists his recreations in *Who's Who* as 'home, family and friends'. Such trite sentiments seem genuine enough, and friends say that his wife, Midge, has been crucial to his career. Fieldhouse and Midge perform an extraordinary double act in a service noted for characters. Midge was described by one friend as 'formidable – like a galleon under full sail.' With her red hair and dominating personality, she had hardly been overshadowed by her husband. She speaks Russian, French and Spanish, and many formal dinner parties have been enlivened by Midge kicking off her shoes at the piano and launching into an impromptu recital. She also has an aversion to the pomposity that is a hallmark of the Navy ... Such domesticity is deceptive, however. It is Fieldhouse who will decide, on our behalf, how we will fight a war – and, in consultation with the politicians, at

what stage the nuclear button is pressed. For that task, his toughness is not in doubt.

'He's the sort of chap who will listen to your problems' says one naval officer. 'When he leaves, you feel pleased, as if you have a friend and ally. It's only when your head falls off that you realise your throat has been cut. Even then you don't mind, because somehow you feel it was necessary and not his fault.' Others dismiss the devious executioner image, and talk of the consummate professional with a refined political instinct. This may be nearer the mark because, almost uniquely in the Navy, he does not have a nickname. It suggests he has more friends than enemies.

* * * * * * * *

In the services, most changes of job involve considerable upheaval. John's last move created fewer problems than most. However, he would require a change of uniform. A gold ring was added to each sleeve for the final time on his promotion to the ultimate naval rank of Admiral of the Fleet. The office move was very simple: to similar quarters just a few doors along the MoD sixth floor corridor. When he got there, the ever-dependable June Light would be available to arrange his programme and take his letters. The change of residence involved a rather longer journey; from Admiralty Arch to the Royal Naval College at Greenwich.

On learning of his appointment, John was reluctant to move into the Kensington apartment his predecessor had vacated, for which there was already another potential occupant. Lord Lewin had lived at Greenwich as CDS, and Fieldhouse felt that he would be more comfortable there, in an atmosphere created by his own people. The residence Lewin had used was not available, but suitable premises were found in the Queen Anne Quarter, in the eastern college block overlooking the River Thames. A degree of renovation was needed, and the family moved to 'Pippins' until their new home was ready for them.

The Fieldhouses took their loyal retinue staff from Mall House Flat with them. Adrian Hill, now advanced to Chief Petty Officer Steward, was supported by Leading Stewards John Woodley and Sharon Davies. Chief Petty Officer Cook Mick Palmer, who had been chased out of John's office with his pile of recipe books ten years earlier, stayed on for the beginning of the Greenwich period. His assistant was Cook Buckland, whose name came to light very recently. On being asked whose photograph it was on the mantelpiece at 'Pippins' of a young man in a mortar board and gown at a university graduation ceremony, Midge replied 'Oh: that's Paul Buckland.' Written on the back, dated four years after John's death, was this message: 'You and the boss made a great difference to my life. Thanks for the seven years and for setting me up for the future.'

As always, the Staff was kept busy with house guests and with various entertainments. By far the biggest project was Sarah's joyous wedding to Chris le Maitre on 6th June 1987. 200 guests were entertained in the College's historic surroundings. Hill recalls making all the catering arrangements including employing and paying members of the College domestic staff. Some time earlier, John and Midge had driven to Leicester for Hill's own wedding, where John delighted family and guests – which included all the staff – by appearing in his naval uniform.

The new CDS found the longer drive to the office very useful. It gave him some valuable moments in the car to study his daily programme and any briefs that had been prepared for him. Once having stayed the night at Greenwich, Peter Kimm asked to see John's programme for the day ahead. He remembers being profoundly impressed by the sheer number of appointments and meetings, in all of which John was required to play a dominant central role. As his driver, Ken Crouch had a good idea of his boss' heavy workload. 'Let's take the easy route home and take our time' John used to say: 'I've got a stack of papers I have to read before we go out this evening.'

Crouch also remembers several interesting conversations. On one occasion, having read an article in a newspaper, he asked the Admiral if he was happy to let more self-seeking colleagues take all the credit for what was happening on the Defence scene. 'When you say a lot,' came the reply, 'people don't always listen to you. If on the other hand you say very little, people tend to sit up and take notice. That's me!' Ken often found himself being used as a sounding board for what the lower deck might be thinking about a particular course of action. He also tells of many acts of kindness, both to himself and to his wife Anne. They were delighted when both the Lewins and the Fieldhouses attended their wedding. At a Buckingham Palace Garden Party, John left the VIP enclosure to seek them out and meet their friends. On another occasion, when John arrived at the Royal Tournament to take the salute in his full ceremonial uniform, he stepped out of the car, spotted Anne in the crowd, veered away from the reception committee for a moment and stepped over to give her a kiss. 'I saw him in all his moods' notes Crouch:

> with tears after a tragedy; laughing happily when he was enjoying himself. I know I cried at his funeral and will always remember him as a father figure. I was so lucky to have worked for and been a friend of such a marvellous man.

* * * * * * * *

As Chief of Defence Staff, John thought of himself as having temporarily left the navy; on secondment, as it were, to a totally unbiased Joint Services role. His private office mirrored this image, being staffed by officers of all uniforms. His Principal Staff Officer was Brigadier Jeremy Blacker (later General), whose main task was to put himself in his master's mind and to prevent him from becoming overwhelmed by the sheer volume of papers and correspondence. It was also his role to 'secure the home base' on the many occasions when CDS was out of the office. There was a Group Captain RAF deputy, a Commander Military Assistant (MA) and a Junior Flag Lieutenant. June Light recalls that there was an excellent spirit in the office, if rather different to what she had been used to. The only slight tremor she remembers was when the Brigadier felt it was inappropriate for soldiers to be invited to sell lifeboat flags. Blacker, who had served John's predecessor for six months, has his own perceptive comment.

> After the flamboyance of Dwin Bramall, John Fieldhouse was a very different sort of leader. He always put a great deal of effort into establishing his case and preparing the ground. Only then, in his quiet way, did he start to move things forward like a massive steamroller. Unless there were compelling new reasons, he never changed his mind, and when he got there he delivered. He possessed great human qualities, and anyone who worked closely for him ended up being entranced by him.

Fieldhouse did not have to serve very long under Defence Minister Michael Heseltine. For some months prior to his arrival there had been a political 'storm in a tea cup' over the future of the ailing Westland helicopter company. This consisted of Westland favouring an American as opposed to Heseltine's preferred European initiative. In *The Downing Street Years* Margaret Thatcher wrote:

> The basic issue at stake in Westland was clear enough. It was whether the directors and shareholders of a private sector firm, heavily but not exclusively dependent on government orders, should be free to decide its future, or whether government should do so. In this sense an important issue was indeed at stake at Westland. If government manipulates its purchasing power, if it arbitrarily changes the rules under which a particular company's financial decisions have to be made, and if it then goes on to lobby for a particular commercial option – these things are abuses of power.

In January 1986, matters came to a head when Heseltine gathered his papers together and walked out of a cabinet meeting at which his colleagues had been united against him. Returning to the MoD, he informed a surprised Fieldhouse of his resignation. The same day, George Younger was appointed to succeed him. He was a steadier and much less excitable person with whom John developed an excellent working relationship over the next few years. Despite the circumstances of his exit, Michael Heseltine could look back on some positive achievements during his three years in office. His political flair had enabled him to rally public opinion in the nuclear debate, triumphing over a Labour Party beset with unilateralist leanings. Any British wavering over the decision to proceed with the new Trident submarines to replace Polaris was laid to rest. Fieldhouse himself was a staunch supporter of Trident, referring to it as 'an unrepeatable best buy'. The public outcry over the deployment of American intermediate range nuclear cruise missiles in Europe had also been allayed. Since the bombing of the Grand Hotel at Brighton in October 1984, which might well have wiped out half the cabinet, there had been an increasingly heavy defence commitment against the IRA in Northern Ireland – one of the first places Fieldhouse visited as CDS. Following his resignation, Heseltine continued to exert political influence from the backbenches. The 1987 election, in which Thatcher achieved her third term, was again largely fought on defence issues.

Of equal importance to his accord with Ministers was John's need to develop and preserve harmonious relationships with top civil servants serving in the Ministry. Fortunately, in his two Admiralty Board appointments he had already learnt how much was owed to their deep knowledge, experience and continuity. His native instinct as the son of Sir Harold, himself a great civil servant, must also have been extremely useful. Sir Clive Whitmore, as Permanent Under Secretary of State at the MoD, was John's principal civil service colleague. Whitmore agreed with the Prime Minister and with Heseltine that John was the best man to succeed Bramall as Chief of Defence Staff. However he felt that:

> The breaking of Buggins' turn made for a tense situation in the Chiefs of Staff Committee when John first moved up from First Sea Lord to CDS. But he handled the Committee very skilfully: he was tactful and sensitive, though without making concessions and compromises which would have diminished his authority. More generally, he chaired the Chiefs of Staff Committee admirably. While not one of the more intellectual CDSs he was clear-sighted in his objectives and pragmatic in achieving them and gave the Committee a great sense of coherence and shared endeavour.
>
> As PUS I of course saw a lot of John, and my relations with him were always good. I trusted him and, I hope, he me; we used to talk frequently and privately; and we worked well together. He was a tenacious and astute defender of the Services' corner but he understood clearly the political and financial realities and he never dug himself into an untenable corner. John was absolutely unstuffy. More often than not there was a twinkle in his eye. But he had that clarity of vision, firmness of purpose and authority of manner that made him a natural leader and an outstanding one at that.

Under Field Marshal Bramall's tenure as CDS, during which Fieldhouse had sat on the Chief's Committee as CNS, defence policy had been edging forward towards strengthening the capability of our forces outside the NATO area. This had been partially obscured by the activity surrounding the implementation of the Heseltine reforms but, on assuming office in November 1985, Fieldhouse moved to restore momentum. In *The Chiefs* Jackson/Bramall commented:

> Fieldhouse with the experience of being C-in-C during the Falklands Campaign behind him and with his deeply held conviction that greater emphasis on a maritime out-of-area strategy was good for the Navy and *ipso facto* good for the country, needed no prompting. He saw that the Soviet threat, although the most dangerous, was at the same time least likely to lead to war. He [Fieldhouse] went on to say:
>
> 'We will not be able to devote substantially greater resources directly to our out-of-area capability than we do today. We must, therefore, ensure that what we do is best tailored to our needs, and that we engineer flexibility and mobility into our NATO forces whenever possible so that double earmarking makes sense.'
>
> His expression 'engineering flexibility and mobility into our NATO forces' reflected the prescient and growing conviction amongst the Chiefs that the 'heavy army' on the Continent rather than the Fleet was the albatross around their necks long before there was any overt sign of the collapse of Communism in Eastern Europe. Fieldhouse and his team were well ahead of the rest of Whitehall where his grumbles about 'sea-blindness' in the bureaucracy were met with scepticism by the majority of policy-makers, who still believed, despite the Falklands, that Britain's growing links with Europe were turning British sea-power into an anachronism.

As one looks back over the last twenty years, it is interesting to reflect on the important part Fieldhouse played in maintaining the wide range of capabilities our forces enjoy today, albeit in smaller numbers.

* * * * * * * *

As was to be expected, travelling again formed a significant part of John's schedule. Before assuming office, he had undergone a process of induction, arranged by the Chiefs of the other two Services. Once installed, he made it his business to visit the armed forces in many of the places where they were assembled to carry out operational commitments or training. These included West Germany, Berlin, the Falkland Islands, Cyprus, Belize, Kenya, Zimbabwe, Hong Kong and Brunei. Visits around the UK were also important, particularly those to Northern Ireland.

One early commitment that gave John the greatest of pleasure was arranged by the Flag Officer Submarines of the day, Rear Admiral Dick Heaslip. In honour of the first-ever submariner to become CDS and to be promoted to the exalted rank of Admiral of the Fleet, a luncheon was held at HMS *Dolphin*, attended by all living holders of the office of Flag Officer

Submarines. Those present included several officers whose World War II exploits had made them role models during the early part of John's career. He certainly found it a deeply moving and thoroughly enjoyable occasion. After lunch, smaller groups broke off to continue celebrating in the wardrooms of alongside submarines.

There is an amusing story of John's visit to Zimbabwe where a British army team was assisting with local military training. In the course of entertaining John and Midge, the Head of the Zimbabwe Defence Force suddenly lost the plot and started ranting and raging about all things British. John took it all very calmly and philosophically, but Midge drew her host's attention to the error of his ways in no uncertain terms and forced him to calm down. Later, there was positive feedback from Harare that the man had been much easier to deal with since Lady Fieldhouse's timely intervention!

As CDS, John had once again become a major player on the NATO stage. He attended the regular Nuclear Planning Group meetings, including one at Gleneagles in November 1986 when Britain was the host nation. The Military Committee of NATO, including CDSs of all member nations, met regularly in Brussels. Each autumn, in rotation, countries hosted a Military Committee Tour. All member nation CDSs and their wives attended in appropriate military settings. Because of his previous international commands and experience, John had become one the most respected elder statesmen on the NATO scene. At one time or another, he and Midge had visited virtually all its capital cities. Although English remained the chosen official language, Midge's linguistic skills were often very useful on the fringes.

Equally demanding were CDS' unilateral visits. As for the Chiefs of Staffs, three home and three away visits a year were allowed for – to include visits outside the NATO area. In the latter category were visits to Sweden, Finland, Jordan, India, Australia, New Zealand, the Bahamas and the United States of America; with Fieldhouse's tour to the USA in April/May 1987 being a particular highlight.

As the complicated INF arms control negotiations continued, Reagan had met Gorbachev for the first time in Geneva in November 1985. The Reykjavik Summit had followed in October 1986, and Margaret Thatcher had played a significant role in reading the Soviet position correctly and in helping to keep Western long-term interests on track. Reagan's proposal to eliminate strategic ballistic missiles within ten years had been abandoned. This had cleared the way for continuing with plans to deploy the improved Trident system from both sides of the Atlantic. Meanwhile the keel of the first British Trident submarine had been laid down in Barrow-in-Furness that September.

Against this background of Britain's primacy as a military ally, the CDS arrived in Washington as the personal guest of Admiral William Crowe,

Chairman of the US Joint Chiefs of Staff. With him were Midge, June Light and Adrian Munns. Since his time in First Sea Lord's office, Adrian had been given a spell in a less rarefied job before being picked out for a return to Fieldhouse service. Anyone who knew Crowe well, as John did, would have been aware of his passion for collecting hats. To this end, Munns had taken personal charge of a rather odd piece of baggage. It consisted of a presentation case containing a hatter's model on which was placed a guardsman's bearskin headdress. Its safe delivery ensured that the visit got off to an excellent start.

In the USA, the Defence and Military Attaché from the British Embassy and a US Air Force escort officer joined the official party. A particularly prestigious programme had been arranged for Fieldhouse over the next eight days. After the formalities in Washington DC, he visited military installations in Maryland, Nebraska, Colorado, Nevada, Washington again and North Carolina, before John and Midge were delivered to St Petersburg, Florida, where they spent a fortnight at their holiday home. They were transported backwards and forwards through several time zones in an exceedingly well-appointed executive jet that had last been used by First Lady Nancy Reagan. The weekend was spent in Caesar's Palace in Las Vegas, whence John and Midge were taken for a sightseeing flight over the Grand Canyon in a light aircraft.

Munns recalls some of the highlights of the programme. Defense Secretary Casper Weinberger held a dinner in Fieldhouse's honour in Washington DC. John attended a meeting of the Joint Chiefs of Staff in the 'Tank' – a specially 'swept' room deep inside the Pentagon. He visited the Headquarters of the Strategic Air Command in Nevada and the North American Aerospace Defense Command in the Rocky Mountains of Colorado. He was given a private viewing of the 'stealth' bomber, the latest breakthrough in military aviation. Everywhere he went he received exceptionally well-prepared presentations of the highest security classification. The word had been passed around that he should be treated as one of the United States' very own. Throughout the period, Midge had her own itinerary during the day, hosted by the wives of various senior commanders. The detailed programme for the USA visit is an indication of the enormous amount of hard work that went into planning such an undertaking. It is also illustrative of the respect in which John was held at the very centre of military power in the Western World. It is a matter of genuine regret that is not been possible to include a personal input to these pages from some of John's distinguished American colleagues. He, himself, had enormous regard for them, their country and everything it stood for. He was never to achieve his dream to become the Dockmaster at Cabbage Key.

* * * * * * * *

All these visits abroad were very important, and had to be fitted in around the regular Chiefs of Staff commitments in which John had already been involved in as First Sea Lord. Some anecdotes serve to illustrate his strength of character and his ability to take what came in his accustomed easy stride. Once he was called out of dinner to take an urgent telephone call, returning to apologise profusely and to continue the evening as if nothing untoward had happened. The next morning, the news broke of the United States bombing of Tripoli by aircraft deployed from UK bases: a controversial act of high military drama in which John had been very much involved.

Captain John Roberts, now Chief Executive of the White Ensign Association, recalls attending a briefing for a junior minister chaired by Fieldhouse. After the initial statement, the minister raised a rather fatuous point which had already been covered in some detail. Roberts was amazed to hear the Admiral take the minister to task. 'Buck up; pay attention and stop wasting the valuable time of my busy Staff Officers!' The room went quiet, the minister turned red and the meeting proceeded efficiently – as if nothing untoward had happened.

In February 1987, Brigadier Malcolm Hunt (ex-CO of 40 Commando, Royal Marines in the Falklands War) joined the Defence Staff as Director of NATO Commitments. Although he was some notches down the chain of command, he used to accompany CDS to NATO meetings. The advanced briefings for these usually occurred in the afternoon, when John would often sit in comfortable chair with his eyes closed, apparently asleep. Hunt soon learnt to carry on talking on these occasions. If he paused for a moment, John became instantly alert and started asking awkward questions.

Every third year, as part of the London Season, the massed bands of the Royal Marines would 'Beat the Retreat' on Horse Guards' Parade. The Duke of Edinburgh, Captain General, took the salute at this inspiring spectacle, and Malcolm Hunt and his wife were asked to host the Fieldhouses on behalf of the Royal Marines. As they awaited the start of the ceremony, a distinguished gentleman in civilian dress approached to take his seat near them in the VIP stand. John greeted him warmly, adding 'Don't be inhibited, Your Excellency, by all these Royal Marines with 'Gibraltar' on their cap badges.' Hunt's reaction was that only Fieldhouse could have got away with directing such a comment to the Spanish Ambassador who smiled and accepted it in good humour.

After the parade, the assembled company headed for a reception in the nearby Foreign Office. There was quite a scrum on arrival and, while Hunt was wondering how to handle his distinguished guests, Fieldhouse took charge of the situation. 'You take the coats and I'll get the drinks', he said decisively. John plunged into the crowd, emerging moments later with four glasses of champagne. Malcolm Hunt was experiencing a common phenomenon. John stood at the very top of the nation's military hierarchy, yet there wasn't an ounce of pomposity in his nature. It was easy to believe that one was having a night out with one of the boys when one was in his presence socially,

In October 1987, Air Commodore David Emmerson relieved Brigadier Jeremy Blacker as John's Principal Staff Officer. It had been David who had taken him flying in a Nimrod while commanding the squadron that later deployed to Ascension during the Falklands War. Emmerson had the considerable advantage of having served as Blacker's deputy for several months before taking over. Throughout his working life, John had always enjoyed the warm relationship between RAF maritime forces and the Submarine Service; and this bond existed with Emmerson. Like many before him, David and his wife Marie found themselves being swept up into John and Midge's extended family. On one occasion, they remember an official function being cancelled at the last minute. Rather than spend the evening alone, he and Midge invited the private office staff down to Greenwich and a good evening was had by all.

Emmerson recalls another incident when Fieldhouse returned on an overnight flight from the USA. He arrived at Heathrow early and his driver could not find him. When he reported this, there was some concern about where precisely CDS might be. In due course, he turned up at the MoD, quite happy to have caught the tube and carried his own baggage.

As a background for a recent discussion, Emmerson prepared an *aide memoire* on a single sheet of paper. The headings ring true and no apology is made for quoting them verbatim.

- Amazing capability to relate to and gain the confidence of people at all levels from Prime Minister to Private Bloggs
- Remarkable talent allowed him to say 'no' to a request, or to give a rocket, yet the recipient left the office with a smile
- Enormous stamina
- Very caring person who always found time to talk to people
- Burnt the candle at both ends and in the middle
- Took responsibilities personally

This last comment requires some further explanation. Emmerson accompanied John and Midge on John's fourth and final visit to the Falklands in the autumn of 1988. In his words:

> In Port Stanley I particularly remember standing alone with JF looking at the memorial to those who died and suddenly realising that there were tears pouring down his face. 'David' he said: 'that's all down to me.' I could only reply 'Absolutely not so, Boss. If it is down to anyone, it is the politicians.'

Apart from the personal factor, Emmerson much admired Fieldhouse's professional judgement in handling the major strategic issues of the day. As cracks began to appear in the Soviet military structure, John strongly advocated the maintenance of an aggressive Western posture. He was wary about making arms control concessions. He was a strong advocate of the Eurofighter – an ambitious project upon which the RAF had set its heart for the future. For years he had fought hard for a new ultra-quiet class of diesel-electric submarine. He showed toughness in his approach to the increasing threat of international terrorism. Most importantly, he had an excellent relationship with the Defence Secretary and in all these and other issues he continued to have the ear of the Prime Minister.

During his last year in office, John enjoyed the loyal support of the incoming Vice Chief of Defence Staff, General Sir Richard Vincent, who held the post for four years before himself becoming CDS and who, later, became Chairman of the Military Committee of NATO. Vincent was already an accomplished Whitehall player, having served as Master General of the Ordnance, the Army's equivalent to Controller of the Navy. Fieldhouse, always a shrewd picker of men and de-centraliser, had recommended to the Secretary of State that the General should take over as VCDS and, once there, should take the lead on arms control issues and on the rapidly changing Cold War scene. On assuming office, Vincent was rapidly indoctrinated into the nuclear deterrent firing chain and despatched at short notice to attend the test firing of a Polaris missile by HMS *Repulse* at Port Canaveral. He recalls that, after launching the missile, the submarine surfaced on a clear starlit night. A message by flashing light was received from a nearby Soviet spy ship 'Congratulations on a successful missile firing', to which the reply went out 'Thank you. That is what deterrence is all about.'

Vincent recognised Fieldhouse as 'keeping a very steady and enlightened hand on the tiller, with a remarkable insight into what needed to be done.'

Jackson/Bramall's *The Chiefs* has been an invaluable source in assessing Fieldhouse's legacy as his career drew towards its close. They concluded:

> The Younger/Fieldhouse team were remarkably successful in arguing the Defence case in successive Public Expenditure Reviews … [they] not only managed to justify some real growth, albeit from a lower baseline, but also secured agreement that their financial targets over those three years would only be reviewed if there was a significant change in the world situation or in the country's economic situation or in the country's economic prospects, which would necessitate a major change in defence policy.

* * * * * * * *

As 1988 progressed, with John nearing the end of his tour as CDS, two conflicting pressures hit him more or less simultaneously. One was the debate about his future employment. The other was the simple fact that, after six years of unsparing effort in the corridors of power, he was nearing physical exhaustion.

For some time John had been under medication for high blood pressure. He was also carrying more weight than was wise, and his lifestyle precluded any useful form of exercise. He was a social as opposed to a heavy drinker and he certainly enjoyed his food. This wasn't a sudden deterioration: it was just that his enormous reserves of energy and stamina were beginning to run down. During those last few months Sarah noticed how tired he was, but then she only saw him when he got home to Greenwich in the evening after a hard day's work. It was then that he liked to collapse in a comfortable chair with his eyes shut, conserving his strength for whatever was arranged for the evening – which he always thoroughly enjoyed.

Midge was also very concerned and did everything she possibly could to support him. For instance it was she, on his behalf, who had continued to pay weekly visits to John's ageing parents at their flat in Harrow and later at their Sunningdale retirement home. When she discussed the immediate future with John, he took the view that there was nothing wrong with him that a long holiday, fresh air, Florida sunshine, some exercise and a sensible diet would not cure. He felt that following a good break he would feel revived and ready to accept the next challenge.

An outgoing Chief of Defence Staff would normally be expected to opt for an easier life after the pressures of high office in Whitehall; but John was only sixty when the moment arrived, and still at the peak of his mental powers. Somehow it seemed to him out of the question that his expertise should no longer be available in the wide military circles in which he had so long moved. The possibility of a Life Peerage was on the cards, which would give him opportunities to express his views in Parliament. There would also be occasions to offer advice should it be sought or needed elsewhere. Non-executive directorships of companies seeking a useful name were not quite his scene at this still active stage of his life. Although they had not managed to save anything, he and Midge were financially secure, so there was no driving incentive to seek further work for income's sake. But none of these temporary activities seemed to offer a satisfactory substitute to continuing in full time service if that was what the nation wanted. If there was a particular important job that he could fill better than anyone else, then John's honest self-awareness and sense of duty would cause him to think very seriously about it.

It so happened that such a post was about to become available: Chairman of the NATO Military Committee. This was a three-year appointment, held by a distinguished officer of the Alliance who had served his term as his nation's Chief of Defence Staff. The last UK holder of the post had been Admiral of the Fleet Lord Hill-Norton in the mid-1970s. Sufficient time had elapsed for the election of another British officer to be deemed acceptable. The election itself was due to take place in December 1988, just as John was due to complete his tour as CDS.

No one could match Fieldhouse's unparalleled record with NATO. As Commander of the Standing Naval Force Atlantic, he had welded multinational groups of destroyers and frigates into efficient fighting units, instantly ready to react and, if necessary, to go to war. As the Submarine Commander East Atlantic Area, his plans and deployments were essential to some of the most secret and sensitive operations undertaken in the Cold War. In both these posts he had been subordinate to NATO's Eastern Atlantic Commander-in-Chief which responsibility he had later held himself. In his other 'hat', as Allied C-in-C Channel, he had been a Major NATO Commander. On the NATO circuit as CDS, he was accepted by North Americans and Europeans alike as having perhaps the soundest military mind of the day, combined with the safest pair of hands. He also had the unique experience of having served as Commander-in-Chief during Britain's short unilateral war to recover the Falkland Islands. It is hardly surprising that politicians and senior servicemen alliance-wide had started to lobby hard for his election that would be on the basis of one vote for each member country.

Tom le Marchand remembers a dinner party at Greenwich after which Midge sought him out for a private conversation. 'They want him to be Chairman of the Military Committee', she said. 'He's too tired, Tom. What can we do?' They discussed the obvious alternatives. Either he would decide to call it a day or he would consider it his duty to allow his name to go forward. John would make his own decision, but was he physically fit enough to endure three more years of public office – even after a good rest? Tom felt a sense of foreboding about the future; a sense of gloom that John would feel in honour bound to take the job if offered; but that if he did so it might prove to be beyond his physical powers.

* * * * * * * *

On 24th November, in a most unusual act of recognition, the Prime Minister gave a dinner party in John's and Midge's honour at No 10 Downing Street. There were twenty-four other guests, including ministers, officers from the armed forces, senior civil servants and their ladies. The party included Curtiss, Moore and Woodward from the victorious Falklands team. Denis Thatcher was unavoidably prevented from attending, but used these words in a very charming letter:

> This evening marks the culmination of one of, if not <u>the</u> greatest of Service careers since the War. You leave not only with great honour but with the admiration and affection of all who have known you and served with you.

The Chiefs of Staff and their ladies dined out John and Midge in style at Hampton Court, where an admirer arranged for them to be entertained by professional singers. Invitations went out for John's own farewell reception in the Ministry of Defence, but this never took place because it had been planned for a date following his return from the NATO meeting in Brussels at which he was taken so gravely ill.

Among the few papers which remain in John's archive is a letter which he received from the President of the United States – who is, of course, *ex-officio*, Commander-in-Chief of all American forces. It was written shortly after he had heard the sad news from Brussels, and is reproduced here in its entirety. On 22nd December 1988, President Reagan wrote:

> *Dear Admiral Fieldhouse*:
> On your departure as the Chief of the Defence Staff, I want to extend to you my deep appreciation for your contributions to the special US-UK relationship and to the NATO Alliance.
> Over the years, our nations have remained the closest of allies and clearly your service, spanning more than five decades, has directly contributed to that close relationship. Your forthright statesmanship in the NATO Military Committee has been particularly noteworthy as the Alliance continued successfully to deter war and enhance the security of all member states. We in the United States deeply appreciate your selfless dedication and significant contributions to world peace.
> Reports of your recent illness sadden us, but rest assured that you have the appreciation of all Americans for your lifetime of service. Nancy and I pass on a personal hope for a complete recovery followed by a most fulfilling future for you and Lady Fieldhouse.
> *Sincerely, Ronald Reagan*

Forty-seven years had passed since forty-seven boys had landed at the town quay and prepared to march up the hill to join the Royal Naval College Dartmouth. It would not have been apparent at the time, but one them was destined to have one of the most distinguished careers of any to have passed through the college gates.

CHAPTER NINETEEN

Twilight Years

1988 – 1992

BY A CRUEL STROKE OF FATE, an immensely tragic drama was about to be enacted in Brussels where, as CDS, John was attending his last formal meeting of the NATO Defence Planning Committee. As had happened so often in the past, he was accompanied by his Military Assistant, Adrian Munns. On that fateful morning they had just left a bi-lateral meeting with Admiral William Crowe, Chairman of the United States Joint Chiefs of Staff. As was usual on those occasions, a formal agenda was discussed with note takers present. After this Adrian and his American counterpart withdrew, leaving the admirals to have a short private chat together.

The two most important military leaders in NATO were personal friends and had built up a very close working relationship. There is no record of what was said but this is likely to have been a somewhat troubled discussion. It had been assumed that the United States would be casting its vote for John in the imminent election for Chairman of the Military Committee, the only other nominee being an Italian officer of considerably inferior credentials. However in Washington political wheels had been turning. Other non-military issues had intervened, resulting in a late instruction to the United States delegation to cast its vote for Rome. This had led to the usual lobbying to persuade other nations to support the latest American position. There was absolutely no personal conflict between the two Admirals. With NATO needing the strongest possible leadership at that particular time, Admiral Crowe is certain to have wanted Fieldhouse at the helm. He may have used the occasion to inform his friend of his disappointment over his government's apparent *volte-face*. Despite this wholly unwelcome political activity, John would almost certainly have been elected, but by a smaller majority than he would have expected or desired. These developments were likely to have been very much in John's mind as he took his leave of Crowe.

John and Adrian started to walk back through the building to the UK Military Representative's office. After ascending a flight of stairs John suddenly became very breathless. They had reached the German corridor and it was decided to rest for a moment in a nearby room. The situation appeared to Adrian to be deteriorating rapidly. He dialled the NATO emergency services and ordered a first aid party and ambulance, having already seen one parked nearby. He then ran to the UK office to collect John's high blood pressure medication from his brief case, feeling that it would be relevant to any subsequent medical examination. Minutes later they were on their way to the Accident and Emergency facility at St Luke's hospital, with John slipping in and out of consciousness.

Once there, Adrian's immediate work was far from done. He handed over the tablets and, as best he could, described exactly what had happened. Distinguished cardiac surgeon Professor Robert Dion was sent for. He was bilingual, so there were no further language problems. Midge, who with John had been staying at the home of the UK Military Representative, was out in Brussels and could not immediately be contacted. On her behalf Adrian gave permission for Dion to operate. He then remained in close attendance, handling all outside calls. Once Midge returned to the residence for lunch she was notified and was driven immediately to the hospital. There is no doubt whatsoever that the extreme promptness of Adrian's actions had been crucial to his master's chances of survival. An absolute tower of strength at a time of greatest need, he stayed on in Brussels for ten days as the link with the outside world and to support the stricken family.

John had suffered a dissecting aneurysm of the ascending aorta and was very close indeed to death. Fortunately a full surgical team was scrubbed and just about to start work on another patient whose surgery it was possible to delay. In Professor Dion's very capable hands an aorta graft was completed in an operation lasting ten hours. Afterwards John lay unconscious for three days with his life in the balance. At this stage Midge became fed up and decided to take matters into her own hands.

'Come on John Fieldhouse,' she chided. 'Say something, if it's only goodbye.' John opened his eyes and replied. 'Hello! What are you doing here?' While being intubated as part of the initial life-saving process, one of his vocal chords had been damaged, changing the easy modulation of his voice delivery to a somewhat hoarser tone. At least he had started to speak again. From that moment Midge knew that he was going to pull through.

The children were totally devastated by what had occurred. Like the others, Sarah hadn't even known that her parents were in Brussels. She arrived by air the next day and Mark soon followed. Highly qualified intensive care nurse Amanda dropped everything and flew in from Australia two days later, arriving at the airport not knowing whether her father was alive or dead. John remained on life support for several more days before anyone other than close family were permitted to see him.

When Richard first saw his brother in St. Luke's he found him comatose and scarcely able to react. Later visits were more rewarding, but he was left in no doubt that it would be a long time before it would be possible for the patient to lead any sort of normal life. John's situation had shocked him profoundly, but in retrospect he was not entirely surprised. As a younger man his elder brother had smoked heavily for many years and had always seemed more interested 'in avoiding rather than taking' physical exercise. While staying at Dolphin House in Gosport a few years earlier, he had suggested to John that he should try walking to his office at Fort Blockhouse a mile or so away. The idea had been dismissed as derisory. Admirals were accustomed to being driven everywhere, and anyway it would have been difficult to have found the time.

Richard has one of the last photographs taken of John before his collapse at Brussels. It is taken from an unflattering camera angle; showing him seated and relaxed at a party with what looks very much like a considerable protruding paunch. 'There is little doubt that he was seriously overweight: the inevitable result of four big dinners a week and virtually no exercise for some years' was his opinion. Yet to Richard 'it was pitiful to find him so frail and weak: a shadow of his former self.' Sadly, these last six words were to be repeated by others all too often.

Richard's sentiments were shared by long standing friend and sailing partner David Black, although he himself would not have used the word 'seriously'. In some of the other photographs taken of John as CDS he looks fit and well if rather portly. It is interesting that before Brussels he had mentioned to David that he was concerned about being overweight and was 'determined to do something about it' on leaving his appointment. Sarah felt that he seemed more tired than usual at this time, but then she only saw him when he was relaxing. Like many sailors, he had become adept at conserving his energy and was an inveterate catnapper. It is possible, however, that the accumulative pressure of professional and social activity had reached a level above which the dam was likely to burst. In addition John had suffered from high blood pressure for some years and was known to have been concerned about the outcome of the NATO election.

Of one thing there was total agreement. He was in wonderful hands at St Luke's. There was widespread praise for every aspect of his care. Certainly nothing was too much trouble for the operating surgeon Robert Dion who never lost confidence in John's ability to be able to return to something approaching a normal life. He took a continuing interest in John's rehabilitation and later he, his wife and three young children were to be entertained at 'Pippins', becoming firm family friends.

The severity of his operation demanded a long and patient convalescence. During this time Midge was indebted to the kindness of the UK Military Representative Air Chief Marshal Sir Michael Knight and his wife Pat who put their official residence at the family's disposal. It must have been quite inconvenient for them with all the coming and going at irregular hours and having to take late phone calls for Midge in their bedroom from people who had forgotten about the time difference. The Knights took all this in their stride and made their assorted guests very welcome.

After six weeks John was considered fit enough to travel and an aircraft of the Queen's flight was sent to transfer him to Southampton airport for onward transport to the Royal Naval Hospital at Haslar. Being loaded by stretcher into the aircraft was to become the first thing he could remember since before his collapse. For instance the Jordanian ambassador had called at the express wish of King Hussein and Queen Noor, staying for over an hour. The attentions of this and many other visitors at his bedside were to remain a complete blank. Despite his temporary loss of memory, the love and attention of the family were an essential element of his recovery. Robert Dion used these words in a letter to Midge soon after their departure from Brussels.

> I was most impressed by the attitude of you and your children remaining confident through all those days amid foreign people in a foreign country. I think you gave us all an extraordinary lesson of humanity in its broadest sense.

* * * * * * * *

John found his own way to break out of the cocoon of security surrounding his presence at Haslar. Surgeon Lieutenant James Campbell (later Captain) remembers entering a public ward to find the Admiral of the Fleet hobbling around acting as a willing assistant to the tea lady! On his eventual return to 'Pippins' he bore little resemblance to the John Fieldhouse who had been there last. Although his mental powers were virtually unaffected, the muscle wastage caused by losing four stones in weight meant that it was going to be a long time, if ever, before he regained his strength. His good friend Tony Whetstone was quick to notice how much the operation had physically weakened him. Although he felt that John had also lost a certain amount of confidence and self-assurance, he was quick to add that 'the sparkle was still there and he was still the same John.' In describing this time, Tony used words that precisely mirrored what had been a recurring theme throughout his life.

> John was always one who weighed up his thoughts carefully before considering his words. He never rushed in to offer an opinion, which is why it was always so highly regarded. He had an uncanny knack of being able to thrust aside the minutiae and put his finger on the nub of any problem.

The only difference was that now this characteristic process had perceptibly slowed down. Brussels had taken so much out of him that it was hardly surprising that he was no longer the strong and confident man so many had known. He felt no bitterness at about what had happened, just a mild annoyance in his inability to perform certain tasks that had previously been second nature. His thoughts were more about doing the best he possibly could with what life still had to offer. Meanwhile the Navy had certainly not forgotten him. For the first year after his operation a driver was put as his disposal, together with a living in cook/steward to help with the domestic arrangements.

It was now that at last he had time to indulge in his hobbies as listed in *Who's Who*; namely 'Home, Family and Friends'. As well as Midge's constant attention, the children continued to remain intensely loving and supportive, though Amanda, having been irreplaceable to her parents in Brussels, had returned to her job in Australia; temporarily out of sight but never out of mind. Any lack of understanding that existed between John and Mark over the latter's failure to settle down to a regular career and lifestyle evaporated in a new bond of mutual affection. Sarah, who of the three had probably the closest filial link with Midge, came down to 'Pippins' every weekend, usually with husband Chris but sometimes on her own. Her warm and bubbly personality was exactly what both her parents needed. It could be said that not only had the whole family rallied around to support him, but also that he had returned to them in a way that would have been impossible had he continued to lead a fully active public life.

Sir Donald Gosling was one of the first to offer practical assistance. A man who had served on the lower deck in the immediate post-war navy, he became an astute businessman who, with a partner, had built up in Central London and elsewhere the much-needed network of multi-storey National Car Parks. This led to his amazingly generous financial support of naval interests and charities, which has continued until this day. For some years Donald had been a great admirer of John and their relationship blossomed further when he invited John to become Chairman of the White Ensign Association of which he was President. During the first summer after John's operation, he invited the Fieldhouses to his seaside property at Juan-les-Pins on the French Riviera. Here they were most thoughtfully cared for in a private apartment right by the sea. When John first entered the water, he needed Donald's support to keep him afloat; but slowly he built up the strength to swim a few yards, always with his host in close attendance.

The favourite sport of his youth now became an important part of his rehabilitation. Clearly sea bathing was the more relaxing and therapeutic because of the benefit of added buoyancy. Fresh water presented more of a problem. John's first tentative efforts in David and Thelma Black's covered pool were unavailing, but slowly he gained enough strength to make some progress, but he always found it difficult to hold his head up for any length of time. There were no steps in the outdoor pool at Richard's home near Beaconsfield, so brotherly assistance was needed to retrieve John from the water.

In February 1989, Donald Gosling arranged for the Fieldhouses to join him for a holiday in his yacht *Brave Goose* in the Caribbean. He recalls a delightful story when they lay in the spectacular setting of one of Nelson's hideouts, Marigot Bay in St Lucia. With John in informal rig of red sailing trousers, open necked white shirt and blue floppy hat, he and Midge decided to go ashore for a walk. At the bottom of the gangway they were accosted by a rather smarter yachtsman. 'Are you the owner of this yacht?' 'Unfortunately no,' replied John with characteristic economy of words. 'Is the owner of the yacht aware that only an Admiral of the Fleet is permitted to wear a Union Flag at the masthead?' 'He is and I am.' End of conversation!

Later, John and Midge were entertained in Donald's new and larger yacht *Leander* named after the cruiser he had served in as a national service rating and in which a small head and shoulders bust of John is mounted in a prominent place to this day.

As 1989 progressed, a degree of normality began to return. On the recommendation of his good friend Professor Tony Naylor he joined the Aga Khan and others to receive an honorary Doctorate of Science (Engineering) at the University of London; plus becoming a consultant to Vosper Thornycroft (UK) Ltd, the warship design and shipbuilding company. Later, with Tony Whetstone, he became a non-executive director of DESC (Ltd), a wholly national offshoot of ICL, charged with safeguarding British interests in high security defence contracts following the parents company's take over by a Japanese consortium. As part of a more local scene, he took on the local Sea Cadet unit and enjoyed several happy occasions with the children. Another favourite project was the Gosport and Fareham Inshore Rescue Service (GAFIRS) that created opportunities for youngsters to run a life saving organisation in Stokes Bay. In the summer this was a busy recreational area with more than its fair share of incidents afloat. During John's stewardship the first steps were taken towards making this team into the well-equipped supplement to the area's full search and rescue resources that it is today. John had always felt naturally at ease with young people and he found these retirement activities particularly rewarding. From 1990, he became heavily committed to his work as Chairman of the White Ensign Association, enjoying the renewed contact with naval colleagues, needs and ideas.

It was not long before the Fieldhouses were able to return to the water themselves in their 34-foot Moody *Hoi Polloi*. Although John had always loved sailing as a relaxation, he no longer had the strength to manage halyards and sheets with any strain on them, nor was he able to jump onto a pontoon to secure the warps. In the past they and the Blacks had usually cruised separately, but after Brussels a strong crewmember was needed whenever John was embarked. Midge was not a natural sailor and was herself severely inconvenienced by the onset of hip replacement problems. This meant that the co-owning couples often sailed together, further cementing an already close relationship. Although John didn't venture so far as he had before, being out in the Solent remained a favourite relaxation and nothing much had changed from the earlier days. There was still plenty of comment about the boat's absurd name, particularly as John was now such a well-known personality. Also, the yachtsman's code of conduct of never raising one's voice was still being broken from time to time by Midge's stentorian tones. Initially, John was disappointed with his weakness, but eventually came to terms with not being able to play a fully active part. One of his favourite off-season activities was pottering down to the boat where he and David would discuss the inevitable list of jobs requiring attention. With typical generosity after he had died, Midge insisted that the Blacks should continue to think of the boat as theirs for as long as they cared to use it 'because that is what John would have wanted.' Four years later their friends decided to swallow the anchor. *Hoi Polloi* was sold and Midge received her share of the proceeds.

John found plenty of things to keep him busy at home. As well as the paperwork associated with his many retirement interests, he resumed his interest in DIY. This meant periods of activity in the garden shed, but gardening itself was too physical and had never been a favourite occupation. On a visit to the Fieldhouse's familiar haunts in Florida, David remembers proceeding at high speed in a dory fitted with a 180-hp outboard engine. The Admiral of the Fleet was at the helm, but his reaction time was not what it once had been and a serious collision almost resulted.

In November, just a year after the operation, morale was further boosted by the receipt of a letter from Margaret Thatcher informing him that she had it in mind to

> submit your name to the Queen with a recommendation that Her Majesty may be graciously pleased to approve that the dignity of a Barony of the United Kingdom for life be conferred upon you.

This was a cause for celebration following the New Year's honours of 1990. Midge had already been a 'Lady' for some years, but this was something very special with the children now entitled to an 'Hon' before their names. However it was to be some time before he would be in a position to make an impact on the House of Lords. To begin with, certain preliminaries needed to be attended to. In a moment of inspiration he chose to take his title from Gosport on the western side of Portsmouth harbour. This rather characterless borough was the poor relation to one of the world's most historic seaports. From its relatively unprepossessing shores it was possible to look across the water to a skyline graced by some of the greatest remnants of Britain's naval heritage. Gosport's most attractive feature was Fort Blockhouse itself, home of the submarine service for so many years. John had been trained there, had driven his boat in and out of Haslar Creek many times, even managing to run aground on one occasion. He had served there on the staff of Flag Officer Submarines and had been the last FOSM to fly his Flag from its ramparts. More recently the sluicing tidal waters of the harbour entrance had seen high drama with the sailing and return of elements of the Falklands Task Force. It was a title most aptly chosen and one that engendered much local pride and satisfaction.

Suitably robed, Lord Fieldhouse of Gosport was introduced to the House between supporters Lords Lewin and Bramall, both his predecessors as Chief of the Defence Staff; while Mark exercised his privilege as eldest son to witness the ceremony from a seat on the Woolsack.

Thereafter he attended the Lords as a cross bencher on a number of occasions and from time to time enjoyed taking family and friends there socially. It was also the scene of his darling Amanda's marriage to New Zealander Bob Chalmers. Although far from well on that particular day, it was a moment John enjoyed with great pride. Following this happy day Bob and Amanda returned to their jobs and home in Melbourne, Australia. John did not live to witness Mark's marriage to Nikola Hare; nor indeed the birth of his five delightful grandchildren. This book contains a photograph taken by Amanda beside her father's memorial of Mark's Ruby and Bethany, Sarah's Tom and Rebecca and her own Jonathan – known as JJ.

He was able to plan well ahead to deliver his maiden speech during the Defence Policy debate on 12th June 1991. This was to be the first discussion in the Lords on defence issues since the dismantling of the Warsaw Pact, with the future of the Soviet Union and the fate of Gorbachev still in the balance. There had been much recent talk of the 'peace dividend' as a likely consequence of a new world order, together with pointers towards further defence cuts announced in the previous year's government study on *Options for Change*. In his heyday speechmaking had come easily to John, but two and a half years on from Brussels it was still going to be a considerable ordeal. Adrian Munns, who had prepared drafts for John's speeches in the past, was now back in the MoD in a more senior capacity. At John's request, he stepped in again as a willing assistant. In addition Midge had bought him a voice recorder with which he practised hard in order to boost his confidence and polish up his delivery. At least it was a convention that a maiden speech should always be heard without interruption. In the event he gave an immensely impressive and courageous performance; full of well-conceived and pithy comment, a timely reminder that the Fieldhouse of old was still around to be listened to intently. One short extract was particularly prescient in the context of subsequent events. 'The greatest danger to peace now lies, I believe, outside Europe. There is a risk of conflict through political, ethnic, cultural and economic issues.' he correctly forecast. Later he produced a delightful turn of phrase that was entirely original:

> Our armed forces make a very large contribution to that most important of all social services: the maintenance of peace. Without peace the other social services are largely devalued.

He ended by paraphrasing a theme, which, in differing contexts, has obsessed the nation's great military leaders through successive generations.

> We must therefore examine our options with the greatest possible care, remembering always that the high quality of our armed forces can be reduced in a few months, but only regained, if at all, over many years.

When one reads this speech in its entirety it is tragic to think that the 'noble and gallant Lord' had only a few more months to live. As things turned out he was to see very little more of the House of Lords. The quality of his speech and the warmth with which it had been received by his fellow peers had given a tantalising glimpse of what might have been.

There was still plenty of humour evident in John's day-to-day life. On one occasion Tony Whetstone had been doing some family shopping in the local Waitrose supermarket. As he produced a chequebook to pay for his purchases, a familiar voice reminded the store assistant that she was about to accept a cheque from a well-known confidence trickster who was being sought by the police on several continents! Tony turned round to see a broad smile on the face of his old friend.

Donald Gosling remembers a council meeting of the White Ensign Association. On that occasion, the distinguished company from the services and the city had gathered in the head office of Allied Brewery in Great Portland Street. Through a misunderstanding on leaving home, the chauffeur had forgotten his master's jacket, causing Donald to suggest to John that he should not attend. John would have none of that. Before calling the meeting to order, he instructed everyone to remove their jackets to avoid any embarrassment to his President. Donald was a great admirer of John's style of leadership. 'He had a tremendous understanding of people; based, I feel, on his early service in submarines, where everyone was so very dependent upon each other.'

Meanwhile John and Midge continued to live a fairly active social life. Close family friends David and Gill Oddie were now back from Australia and had been present at John's maiden speech in the House of Lords. In their home near Winchester they had an unusually low and long-seated armchair into which John loved to sink and snooze when the spirit moved him. Because of his obvious physical frailty they were both rather surprised at the high level of his social activity. But John and Midge had always loved giving and receiving hospitality. Business as usual seemed to be the order of the day. However it was not surprising that John preferred relaxing in small groups. When there were a lot of people around, such as at a drinks party, he used to like to sit on a sofa and chat one to one with a friend or to someone he had a special message for. This was a habit of long standing, not necessarily the consequence of any disability. Tony Whetstone recalls their last visit together to a DESC board meeting. John was in the best form that he had seen him in since his collapse in Brussels and on the way home they dropped into the House of Lords for tea. It seemed that he might even be turning the corner towards the prospect of a brighter future.

Not long after this John and Midge were out walking their dogs. Suddenly John felt serious pains in his leg muscles. In a state of some premonition Midge left him sitting on a wall and hurried to get the car in which to drive him home. He was also suffering from breathlessness and their GP decided that he should be admitted to nearby Haslar hospital for observation. The lower limb discomfort was due to a lack of blood flow to the arteries. There was, as well, fluid on his lungs, another indicator of the return of cardiac trouble. He was seen several times by consultant surgeon Kim Munroe at Southampton. Robert Dion, who had ensured his lease of life after the first operation, came over from Brussels to monitor John's condition and provide a second opinion. The latest MRI scan was not encouraging and there was much debate about exactly what type of corrective operation should be attempted. Both surgeons had the highest credentials, but Munroe favoured a more risky second graft that, if successful, held out higher hopes for the longer term. Despite the family's implicit confidence in Dion's proposal for a less drastic course of action, John was reluctant to return to Belgium for further treatment and decided to take his chance at home. It was arranged before Christmas 1991 that he would be operated on early in the New Year at Southampton General Hospital. With typical thoughtfulness he had decided to delay informing the children. Chris and Sarah were looking forward to a Christmas holiday with Bob and Amanda in Australia, having cancelled a previous visit because of events in Brussels. This went ahead as planned and they and Amanda returned in time for the girls to be present at what was always going to be a make or break situation.

John and Midge spent a poignant last Christmas together. Whilst trying to keep cheerful in an atmosphere of great uncertainty, they both must have had serious doubts about a successful outcome. Richard remembers their visit to Beaconsfield on Boxing Day, with John saying with great feeling: 'I am enjoying Christmas so much. I just don't want it to end.' On top of their brotherly relationship, John and Richard had always remained the very best of friends down the years.

On the day before he entered Southampton General Hospital he happened to speak to Adrian Munns by telephone, displaying a totally characteristic touch of humour at what must have been a very difficult time for him: 'I'm just going in to have a couple of jubilee clips tightened up', he said.

When the time arrived for him to be wheeled into the operating theatre, Midge and Amanda tramped up and down the corridors for hours awaiting developments. The initial procedure was successful but then it was decided to go ahead with the more risky further graft in the arch of the aorta. At first this too seemed to have gone quite well, but then John developed the dangerous MRSA infection. At this time of great crisis Midge and the children were able to fall back on the strong support of the Oddies who kept open house and provided meals and comfort in their home just ten minutes away from the hospital. As an intensive care nurse herself, Amanda remained at the hospital throughout and seldom left her father's side during the last few days following the operation. For much of the time Midge and the others were also there. It was inevitable that his degraded immune system would be quite unable to cope with the infection and he died peacefully in the early hours of 17th February 1992, five days after his sixty-fourth birthday.

* * * * * * * *

A great tide of sadness surged across the Submarine Service, the wider community of the Royal Navy and to many places beyond where John was known and loved. There was an instinctive wave of sympathy and understanding for Midge and the family in the tragic circumstances of their loss. John had had every right to look forward to a thoroughly well deserved and fully active retirement. Instead of that there had been just over three years of often-precarious health during which he had lived under the shadow and fear of the return of the cardiac problems that finally engulfed him. Having so nearly died in Brussels in 1988, he had spent his twilight years in the knowledge that he was living on borrowed time. He had used it wisely and generously; revelling in the company of family and friends and offering what energy that remained to whatever causes he felt most deserved it.

On 24th February there was a very moving funeral service for John's family and his many friends. The small church of St Ambrose at HMS *Dolphin* had always held a very special place in the hearts of the submarine community. A stranger driving into the old Fort would be surprised to learn that there was a historic church on the starboard side. Rectangular in shape, its abiding charm lay in the plethora of submarine badges that adorned almost every available vertical surface, reminding the world of the ultimate sacrifice that had been made by so many other gallant submariners. On and off, John and Midge had worshiped there for many years; often with the children and memorably when he had been Flag Officer Submarines before transferring the command from Gosport to Northwood. St Ambrose had always been well attended but had seldom been known to overflow. There being no chance whatsoever of being able to accommodate all those arriving, the service was relayed by video to many others nearby.

Amanda, Richard and Tony Whetstone delivered the well-chosen readings and, in a defining moment for the misting over of multiple eyes, Amanda choked slightly over some of her words. Yet the abiding memory was of an address of exceptional merit by close friend and Dartmouth term mate Peter Kimm. Himself a deeply religious man and something of an academic, he spoke with great eloquence about John as a person; in the context of his modesty, kindness, faithfulness, gregariousness and courage; all components of the main theme of the address which was of 'love'. At the end of the service the coffin was lifted and turned around. With a gesture of instinctive charm and deepest affection, Sarah stepped forward to make a tiny adjustment to the position of John's admiral's cap, just to make sure it was exactly squared off fore and aft. Then the cortege passed along the *Dolphin* seafront for the final time.

Two days later, on 26th February, the Royal Navy combined with the family to discharge a very special duty; an intensely moving occasion that no one who was there could possibly ever forget. With all colours in Portsmouth at half-mast, the submarine HMS *Opportune* sailed from the jetty at HMS *Dolphin* with Midge, the children and their beloved John's ashes embarked. It was a very cold day, but calm and clear. After backing out astern abreast Ballast Patch, the boat moved slowly ahead through the harbour entrance that had been the scene of many other historic departures and arrivals over hundreds of years. To starboard lay Fort Blockhouse itself, home of the submarine service from its earliest years: to port the Sally Port and the beach from which Nelson had left British soil to embark in HMS *Victory* for the final time. Meanwhile a handful of closest friends were already gathered in the frigate HMS *Brilliant*, waiting to escort *Opportune* from the Outer Spit Buoy. This ship, which had been fought with great distinction in the Falklands War, was now commanded by Captain Toby Elliott who, as a commander, had taken John and Midge to sea in 'her' HMS *Trafalgar* in 1985.

After a short passage through the Solent both ships came to rest at a spot close to where the mighty *Royal George* had foundered with Admiral Kempenfelt on board. There being little or no surface wind, the frigate was able to lie with the port side of her flight deck quite close to *Opportune*'s port bow. On the fore casing Midge and the others stood proud and erect as with short and simple dignity John's ashes were committed to the deep. After these moments of quiet grief those present were reminded in the most startling manner possible that not only had they lost a husband, father or friend, but that the Royal Navy was paying its final respects to a much revered Admiral of the Fleet. A nineteen gun salute, only two less than the entitlement of the Sovereign herself, thundered out from *Brilliant* and from Fort Blockhouse not far away. In the lives of great men it is sometimes difficult to find an acceptable balance between privacy and the trappings of fame, but on this occasion exactly the right blend had been forthcoming. So with great love and due honour the consummate seaman returned to the wide waters that had been the inspiration of a career of unparalleled achievement in modern times.

After the more immediate obsequies in Hampshire, one final important act remained. On 27th May 1992 the memorial service at Westminster Abbey allowed a much wider group to celebrate John's life; accepting it, as it were, on behalf of the nation in a way reserved for very few highly distinguished servants of the Crown. This was an occasion of the greatest pomp and protocol, embellished by fine organ music, choral and solo singing, orchestral works by musicians of the Royal Marines, and of moving hymns and stirring words.

In the accustomed way of such ceremonies, most of the over two thousand who attended were required to be in their seats in good time; providing them with an opportunity to absorb the atmosphere of that great place and to enjoy seeing a wide range of guests from all walks of life arriving. In advance of the procession of the clergy, the representatives of Her Majesty The Queen, Prince Philip, Duke of Edinburgh, and other Members of the Royal Family were conducted to their places in the Quire by the Dean. Soon afterwards the service came to life with the singing of the four verses of the Naval Hymn. A predominantly naval gathering broke into a crescendo of sound, giving the impression that many lungs were near to bursting with pride. During this hymn a second procession made the long haul from the West End to the Altar. A vice admiral, a rear admiral and a captain, escorted by another captain, bore the Fieldhouse orders and decorations. Tony Whetstone, carrying the British Empire insignia, recalls being almost overwhelmed by the resonance around him; mightily relieved when the party arrived at its destination exactly at the hymn's familiar climax: 'Thus evermore shall rise to thee, Glad hymns of praise from land and sea.'

The readings were by the incumbent First Sea Lord, Admiral Sir Julian Oswald, Chief of the Defence Staff, Field Marshal Sir Richard (later Lord) Vincent, and by Richard Fieldhouse. There was an eerie moment when Richard's intonations sounded very like those of his elder brother. Peter Kimm's daughter Fiona sang a beautiful soft anthem, accompanied by the Abbey choir. Her father yet again excelled himself in the pulpit. Three months after having spoken about John the man, he eulogized about John the leader of men, speaking of his long peacetime service and of his command of UK forces during the Falklands War. Following the Last Post and Reveille there was a final explosion of sound as the assembled multitude burst into two verses of the National Anthem. With so many past and present members of the armed services present, this was a true indication of where their loyalties lay. Like the Admiral of the Fleet before them, their actions had been governed by the will of politicians but their allegiance lay unswervingly to The Queen.

As hundreds of people emerged into Westminster Square, the Abbey bells rang out in a half-muffled peal. Friends and acquaintances stood around in groups, chatting and laughing together as this was a time for thanksgiving and not for tears. Inquisitive members of the public ringed the fringes; admiring the ceremonial uniforms; looking for familiar faces amongst the great and the good; wanting to know the purpose of such splendour at the throbbing heart of the nation. Slowly the crowd dispersed as people went their separate ways. The family and personal friends crossed the street to attend a reception in the House of Lords. Some working men and women returned to their Whitehall offices, it still being early afternoon. Others gathered together in clubs or pubs for a celebratory drink. Many had already spent several hours travelling and were keen to begin their long journeys home. It had been an occasion of many mixed emotions; but the one shared by all was a feeling of pride and privilege over having known a very special person, the like of whom they would never see again.

* * * * * * * *

Midge returned to 'Pippins' to start picking up the pieces. At first it was very difficult for her. However she chose to spend her time, it was always going to be impossible to replace the warmth and companionship of a loving relationship. But it soon became apparent that the other half of what Margaret Thatcher had referred to as an 'indestructible partnership' was determined to do everything within her powers to ensure that the Fieldhouse tradition lived on. Through her own strength of personality and reputation she evolved into a sort of 'fairy godmother' to the submarine service. Because of her strong and forthright personality many submariners already regarded her with a mixture of awe and admiration. Now, as the widow of the most senior officer that service had ever seen, her pluck and courage became more widely recognised and she attracted an even deeper affection than she had previously known. She served in a variety of capacities on the boards, committees or as an ex-officio member of the Submarine Association, the Submarine Officers Life Members Association, The Society of Friends of the Submarine Museum and of the RN Submarine Museum itself. She was invited to maintain the family link with the White Ensign Association and took over the chairmanship of the local Sea Cadet unit. She maintained her close ties with HMS *Trafalgar*, of whose activities commanding officers failed to keep her fully informed at their peril. For many years on the anniversary of John's death until submarine training moved to Plymouth, she was the guest of honour at a Fieldhouse Memorial Dinner in the Senior Rates mess at HMS *Dolphin*. These were elaborate affairs, with a typical menu card showing six courses, a selection of fine wines, a happy photograph of John and the simple inscription 'He spent his life in the service of his country.'

To this day Midge attends other regular annual reunions, not least a gathering of the personal staff who had served them with loyalty and devotion over many years. She also attends the annual wreath laying ceremony at the Submarine Memorial on the Embankment in London. It is unprecedented for the widow of a distinguished naval officer to maintain such close and active ties with so many men and women of every rank and rate. David Oddie tells of an occasion when he invited her to attend a garden party he had arranged for his local branch of the Royal Naval Association. With her mastery of the 'common' touch and in her own inimitable style she had a few words of humour or sympathy for everyone. Later, all spoke very highly of the impact she had made on them. Looking down from a great height with his usual benevolent smile, John cannot be the least bit surprised, but must surely be very proud of her. Generously provided for in widow's pension funds, Midge has held steadfast to her self appointed task. With its wonderful selection of photographs and memorabilia 'Pippins' remains a shrine to John's memory and to that of a great team. No one entering its doors could fail to recall the immensely happy and successful partnership they enjoyed together.

Meanwhile John's name and image have become established in a variety of places, some before his death and some after. There is a Fieldhouse Close in Port Stanley in the Falkland Islands, and another road in Lee-on-the-Solent. The new Warrant Officers and Senior Rates Mess in the Clyde Naval Base, one of the finest of its kind built for any of the services, is 'home from home' for 1,500 people. There is a new Fieldhouse building in HMS *Excellent* and a room at the Joint Services Training College at Shrivenham. His portrait hangs in several places, notably in Gosport Town Hall and in the Senior Gunroom at Dartmouth College where he fed as a hungry boy during the Second World War. Each year the Worshipful Company of Shipwrights, of which he had been a freeman and liveryman since 1981, presents a Fieldhouse Memorial Medal to the best qualifying nuclear submarine engineer officer. A more tangible memorial is a noble one and a half life size head and shoulders bust, mounted on a plinth in Gosport's Falklands Gardens. Sculptor Jill Tweed has deftly caught the jaunty angle at which John often seemed to wear his cap. This image of the town's most famous citizen is strong and comforting as it looks out upon the historic harbour; adding to its rich and timeless heritage. The inscription reads:

Unveiled by HRH The Duke of Edinburgh – 22 Feb 1993
Erected by the Borough of GOSPORT,
The SUBMARINE SERVICE, and his
Friends in appreciation of a
Great and much loved Man

The gardens were rededicated by Baroness Thatcher on the fifteenth anniversary of the Falklands conflict and the many people using the harbour ferry every day pass close to this peaceful scene. A large coloured map on the paving is a constant reminder of the enormous distance it was to the islands, putting into true perspective the magnitude of the Commander-in-Chief's accomplishment.

In 2005 the new John Fieldhouse Building became the central feature of Gosport's Royal Navy Submarine Museum. This had been made possible by a £2,200,000 Heritage Lottery Fund grant matched by a similar sum raised through fundraising and private subscription. In terms of the number of people of future generations who will appreciate its facilities, this is likely to become John's most meaningful and significant memorial.

* * * * * * * *

This is not an official biography and no attempt has been made to carry out a critical analysis of the career of this remarkable man. Readers must draw their own conclusions from whatever has found its way into these pages. They contain the memories of many people and are offered in celebration of his life. Peter Kimm's skilful assessment of John's qualities was moulded for the spoken word and is included as an Appendix. Written at the time of his death, it is a complimentary tribute that has stood the test of time.

Fieldhouse was first and foremost a people's person. After an unspectacular start, he emerged from the pack after a successful early career in command of submarines; some of which was at the extreme cutting edge of the Cold War. His leadership, wisdom and management skills, both afloat and ashore, allowed him to ease through the middle ranks with almost indecent haste, earning him exceptionally early promotion to Flag rank. His wide experience as an admiral led him to be the right person in the right place at the right time to command the complex tri-service operation to recapture the Falkland Islands; undoubtedly his most prestigious single achievement. He rounded off an exceptional career with several years in Whitehall; first as professional head of the Royal Navy, and then as Chief of the Defence Staff. He was the first and only submarine officer to reach the rank of Admiral of the Fleet, now in abeyance and unlikely to be resurrected. He showed great courage and humility in an all too brief retirement, much of which was spent in precarious health. He was revered by those close to him and his admirers ranged far and wide across the nation, not least amongst the lower deck, other ranks and service families. History is likely to place him on the same pedestal as any of his illustrious predecessors who gave unstinting and singular service to Queen and country.

In one of his classic novels of early nineteenth century sea going life, Patrick O'Brian wrote that 'Patriotism, promotion and prize-money have been described as the three masts of the Royal Navy'; and in two out of three instances, this aphorism, so true in Nelson's time, could be applied personally to John Fieldhouse, the renowned Commander-in-Chief and supreme twentieth century Cold War warrior. Patriotism was probably his principal motivator. Promotion came his way in abundance. In place of prize-money, his 'third mast' was of a greater value than any amount of silver or gold. It was the indelible mark he left upon the hearts and minds of those who knew him and on the greater world around him.

Appendix A

JOHN DAVID ELLIOTT FIELDHOUSE

Summary of

Dates, Ranks, Appointments, Honours and Awards

	12.02.28	Born in Leeds, Yorkshire
Cadet	01.09.41	Royal Naval College Dartmouth
	02.05.45	HMS *Frobisher*
Midshipman	01.09.45	HMS *Nigeria*
	04.11.45	HMS *Norfolk*
	01.01.47	HMS *Fame*
	22.03.47	HMS *Easton*
A/Sub Lieutenant	30.04.47	Royal Naval College Greenwich
	05.01.48	HMS *Excellent* for Courses
Sub Lieutenant	10.10.48	
	25.10.48	HMS Dolphin for S/M Training
	14.03.49	HMS *Thule* as 4th Hand
Lieutenant	01.10.49	
	27.11.49	HMS *Astute* as 3rd Hand
	21.07.51	HMS *Aeneas* (1st Lieut from 28.03.52)
	12.11.52	HMS *Totem* as First Lieutenant
	29.03.53	Married Margaret (Midge) Cull
	04.01.55	HMS *Dolphin* as Ratings Training Officer
	28.08.55	HMS *Adamant* for Commanding Officers' Qualifying Course
	28.12.55	HMS *Adamant* as Spare Submarine Commanding Officer
	26.03.56	HMS *Acheron* in Command
	21.01.57	HMS *Sea Eagle* as SM Staff Officer
Lieut. Commander	01.10.57	
	10.01.58	HMS *Tiptoe* in Command
	16.12.58	Staff of Flag Officer Submarines as Flotilla Exercise Plans Officer
	24.09.59	Royal Naval College Greenwich for Nuclear Reactor Course
	29.07.60	HMS *Walrus* in Command
	03.09.62	Staff of Flag Officer Submarines as Flotilla Material Officer
Commander	31.12.62	
	27.07.64	HMS *Dreadnought* in Command
	01.11.65	Temporary Duty in Ministry of Defence
	05.06.66	Joint Services Staff College
	30.03.67	HMS *Hermes* as Executive Officer
Acting Captain	07.12.67	HMS *Hermes* in Command
Captain	31.12.67	
	01.04.68	HMS *Neptune* as Captain SM 10th Submarine Squadron and as Queen's Harbourmaster Clyde

	17.10.70	HMS *Diomede* in Command and as Captain F 3rd Frigate Squadron
Commodore	21.01.72	Commander Standing Naval Force Atlantic
Captain	23.02.73	Ministry of Defence as Deputy Director Naval Warfare
	01.11.73	MoD as Director of Naval Warfare
Act Rear Admiral	10.12.74	Flag Officer Second Flotilla
Rear Admiral	07.01.75	
	22.11.76	Flag Officer Submarines and Commander Submarines Eastern Atlantic Area
Vice Admiral	01.04.78	
	01.04.79	MoD as Controller of the Navy
New Year's Honours	1980	Appointed Knight Commander of The Most Honourable Order of the Bath
Acting Admiral	05.05.81	Commander-in-Chief Fleet, Allied Commander-in-Chief Channel and Commander-in-Chief Eastern Atlantic Area
Admiral	23.07.81	
Birthday Honours	1982	Promoted Knight Grand Cross of The Honourable Order of the Bath
South Atlantic Honours	1982	Appointed Knight Grand Cross of The Most Excellent Order of the British Empire
	01.12.82	MoD as Chief of Naval Staff and First Sea Lord, and as First and Principal Naval Aide-de-Camp to Her Majesty The Queen
Admiral of the Fleet	02.08.85	MoD as Chief of the Defence Staff until December 1988
	12.10.89	Honorary Doctorate of Science (Engineering) at the University of London
New Year's Honours	1990	Created a Life Peer of the United Kingdom. Assumed title and style of Baron Fieldhouse of Gosport
	12.06.91	Maiden Speech in the House of Lords
	17.02.92	Died in Southampton, Hampshire
	26.02 92	Funeral in HMS *Dolphin*
	28.02 92	Committal of ashes at sea from HMS *Opportune*
	27.05.92	Service of Thanksgiving in Westminster Abbey

Appendix B

Milestones of Period in High Office

1982 – 1988

1982	April	Argentina invades Falklands Islands
	June	Surrender at Port Stanley
	October	Bramall succeeds Lewin as CDS
	December	Fieldhouse succeeds Leach as First Sea Lord
1983	January	Hezeltine succeeds Nott as Defence Secretary
	June	Thatcher wins second term
	October	US intervention in Granada
	December	Geneva INF talks begin
1984	January	Cruise Missile deployment in UK begins
	April	Heseltine presents proposals for MoD reform
	July	Chiefs meeting with Prime Minister on the reforms
	October	IRA bombing of Grand Hotel in Brighton
1985	January	Reorganisation of the MoD
	March	Gorbachev becomes Soviet Head of State
	August	Fieldhouse succeeds Bramall as CDS
	November	Reagan/Gorbachev Geneva Summit
1986	January	Heseltine resigns over Westland affair
		Younger becomes Defence Secretary
	April	US bombing of Libya
		NATO 3% annual budget increase ends
	September	Keel laid down for Britain's first Trident submarine
	October	Reagan/Gorbachev Reykjavik Summit
1987	June	Thatcher wins third term
	December	Reagan/Gorbachev Washington Summit
		INF treaty signed
1988	April	US/Soviet agreement on withdrawal from Afghanistan
		Reagan/Gorbachev Moscow Summit
	August	Iran/Iraq Armistice signed
	December	Fieldhouse retires as CDS
		Serious illness precludes election as Chairman of the Military Committee of NATO
1989	June	Solidarity Party wins Polish elections
		Start of the fall of Communism in Eastern Europe and events leading to collapse of the Soviet Union

Appendix C

LORD FIELDHOUSE

His Maiden Speech in the House of Lords delivered during a debate

on

Defence Policy

12th June 1991

My Lords, it is a privilege for me to speak for the first time in this House on this most important subject. I ask indulgence should I stray, quite unintentionally, into contentious areas. Through the tense years of cold war and the uncomfortable period of uncertainty that followed and still exists today, I have learnt one lesson above all others. I make no apology for repeating the point, it is so important. We can with confidence only expect the unexpected.

For most of my time in senior command, the greatest threat has been from the Soviet Union, with its overwhelming military capability. However, there has, thank heavens, been a welcome change. A reduced level of tension and important arms control agreements have been reached. But I suggest that it is often overlooked that that this situation has been achieved only through collective strength within the NATO Alliance. It has withstood the tests of time and the self-interest of its member nations. It will, I believe, still pay us to be cautious over the speed at which we enjoy the so-called peace dividends, for, where capability exists, intentions can change overnight.

The greatest danger to peace now lies, I believe, outside Europe. There is a risk of conflict through political, ethnic, cultural and economic issues and there is absolutely nothing new about that. There have been 80 wars since 1945; over 15 million people killed and for one year only in this whole period have British servicemen or women not been killed in action.

The overriding lesson each time we have become involved has been the necessity to maintain a broad spectrum of forces, realistically structured, well equipped and properly supported. I cannot claim to be a prophet, but I foresee a continued threat to world order and hence the need to protect our vital interests worldwide. We hope that this can be done through the medium of the United Nations, but I do not believe that that organisation can always be relied upon to act in our best interests, as has been the case recently.

All this leaves the question: on what principles should we build our forces from now on? In the past, our forces have largely been structured to meet the greatest threat from the Soviet Union, but it has been apparent to all that they have also had to be capable of meeting sudden, unforeseen dangers arising elsewhere in the world.

My first conclusion is that it is vital that our forces maintain their mobility and flexibility and – that all-important third element – sustainability, so that they can respond effectively and at short notice, if required, to whatever threat turns up.

In recent months, we have heard much – perhaps far too much –- about achieving economies through smaller yet better armed forces. However, in reality that may be difficult to achieve. It is particularly so in some of the special capabilities we have developed and need to maintain. My own business highlights anti-submarine warfare and particularly our submarine force. But, while the Gulf campaign proved beyond doubt that quality holds advantage over quantity, it is always a matter of balance, for there is a level of quantity below which we must not go if quality is to be maintained.

This philosophy applies across the spectrum of maritime, air and land forces. Perhaps I may be allowed to focus briefly on the sea. We are, after all, an island nation and will remain dependent on the sea for the vast majority of the trade which is essential to our continued prosperity. Recent experience in the Gulf has again demonstrated the versatility of our destroyer and frigate force and their helicopters. This is valuable both in blockade operations and combat. The mine counter-measure vessels had, and still have today, a crucial role in clearing the sea lanes. The amphibious capability, while not used in the Gulf, offered a potent threat through its mere presence. Supporting these vessels from afloat was a vital capability. In addition, for the land forces, well over 90 per cent. of all stores, vehicles and equipment and almost all the 100,000 tonnes of ammunition needed had to be moved by sea.

I have a particular concern here and am happy that it became apparent earlier this afternoon that I hold it in common with others of your Lordships. In war, we have to rely upon merchant shipping to undertake dangerous military duties. The number of British-manned ships, sailing under the British flag and available for defence purposes, is now at a crucial level and may already be too few. We ignore this situation at our peril.

Our armed forces make a very large contribution to that most important of all the social services: the maintenance of peace. Without peace the other social services are largely devalued. I conclude by saying that in this uncertain world we must insure that we retain an adequate war fighting capability of a high standard to safeguard our national interests. We must therefore examine our options with the greatest possible care, remembering always that the high quality of our armed forces can be reduced in a few months, but only regained, if at all, over many years.

Hansard Vol. 529 No. 101

Appendix D

ADMIRAL OF THE FLEET THE LORD FIELDHOUSE OF GOSPORT GCB GBE

An Address for his Service of Thanksgiving in Westminster Abbey

on 27th May 1992

by

Captain P R D Kimm OBE Royal Navy

John Fieldhouse was one of the thirteen-year-olds who went to Dartmouth in 1941. I was another. But we didn't get to know each other really well until we were Midshipmen together in the East Indies in '45/46, principally in HMS *Norfolk*.

When, three months ago, I was privileged to speak at John's funeral, I thought it inappropriate to discuss his professional achievements, and confined myself to his personal qualities: to the courage which had illuminated his life to its very end; to his modesty, lack of 'side', immense kindness, loyalty, warmth, gregariousness. All these, I suggested, were only other names for 'love'; and I quoted St Paul on love's abiding properties.

I also spoke of John the family man, and of the wonderful way he and Midge complemented each other. Mrs Thatcher, in a letter, described the address as having been about John and Midge, and referred to the 'wonder and loyalty of this indestructible partnership'.

So I am sure you will all wish to join me in thanking Midge, as well as offering her and the whole family our love and sympathy. Dear Midge, dear Fieldhouses, the emptiness that you feel without him is agonisingly real; but that reality does not quarrel with the realities of our faith. Love is not quenched by death; and the partnership, Midge, is indeed 'indestructible'.

Two days after his funeral, the submariner's ashes were committed to the deep off Spithead from HM Submarine *Opportune*. HMS *Brilliant* was in attendance; and, after the committal, she fired the great 19-gun salute to an Admiral of the Fleet – which was answered by another one from Fort Blockhouse. I personally had not been expecting this, and found it profoundly moving. The funeral had been so 'family' in complexion that one had tended to forget just how big a man John had been on the military stage, nationally and internationally. It is now time to think on this.

At no stage of his journey to the top did he lose the qualities of which I have already spoken. Warmth and humanity shone through his whole career; and though, by the end of it, he was a statesman among statesmen, he was still as comfortable – and as welcome – on the for'ard messdeck and in the sergeants' mess as he was in the highest corridor of power.

There is an element of luck in a naval career: and John was lucky on several occasions. But luck only provides opportunity to shine; and unless one has got what it takes – no dice. John did have what it takes; and to each of the increasingly important jobs he was given, he brought, in addition to those human qualities, a shrewd, analytical mind, immense professionalism and an abundant measure of Yorkshire commonsense. Thus his judgement - both of affairs and of people - was sound. Thus his perspectives were wide, and he thought big. Thus, again and again, he cut through complexity, put his finger on the crux, and tackled the problem with realism and determination. And all this he did quietly, and while exuding a remarkable – and highly infectious – calm.

And so, in 1975, he became a Flag Officer. First he commanded the Second Flotilla. Then, successively, he was Flag Officer Submarines, Controller of the Navy and C-in-C Fleet. In all these appointments, he practiced what he so often preached and 'expected the unexpected' – for, without knowing it, he was making a vital, personal contribution to the Navy's readiness to face its biggest national military challenge since World War II; the Falklands War.

There is a particular poignancy about today in that we are gathered in John's memory precisely ten years after the most critical phase of that war in which he held tri-service command-in-chief. Ten years ago the day before yesterday, *Coventry* and *Atlantic Conveyor* were sunk. Ten years ago today, 2 Para set out for Goose Green, 3 Para and 45 Commando for Teal Inlet; and the SAS landed in strength on Mount Kent. On 14 June, two and a half weeks hence, it will be exactly ten years since the Argentine surrender at Port Stanley. At this service in John's memory, he would wish us to remember too the Falklands' dead, and all who have suffered as a result of that war.

After his time at Fleet, John moved on to the navy's highest appointment. We who were his contemporaries as Midshipmen would not have tipped him as an obvious future First Sea Lord. Perhaps that geniality, quietness and modesty hid the rest of the potential of those early days. But he was the one that got there! And after his time in First Sea Lord's office, he moved up the corridor in the Ministry of Defence and took professional responsibility for all three armed services as Chief of the Defence Staff. And had it not been for his sudden illness, even that would probably not have been the end of his career, as he would almost certainly have become Chairman of the Military

Committee of NATO. Admiral of the Fleet. GCB. GBE. A Peer of the Realm. And all achieved quietly and kindly. Doesn't that say it all?

Well no, actually I don't think it does; for, even though it be a statement of the obvious, I do not think this address in this hallowed place would be complete without explicit mention of the essential rightness of John's work. The profession of arms in a benevolent democracy is intrinsically noble: and the likes of John Fieldhouse may with justice claim to be, first and foremost, servants of peace.

John actually made precisely that claim in his maiden speech in the Lords, as Nelson had made it in his. Nelson, with typical flamboyance, had declaimed that because he 'had seen much of the miseries of war, he was, from his inmost soul, a man of peace'. John in typically dry, low-key, said 'Our armed forces make a very large contribution to that most important of all the social services: the maintenance of peace.'

So here, where the shrine of the Confessor witnesses to the paramount value of peace, but where Henry V's accoutrements of battle hang above his tomb, and the Unknown Warrior lies with the Kings, let us thank God for one of the most distinguished lives of military service since World War II: service to Her Majesty, to His Majesty her father before her, and to their peoples: service to NATO and the Commonwealth: service to the deterrence of war, the frustration of aggression and the maintenance of Christ's peace. And let us also give thanks for a friend beyond price.

List of Abbreviations

ACNS(O)	Assistant Chief of Naval Staff (Operations)
ACNS(OR)	Assistant Chief of Naval Staff (Operational Requirements)
ACNS(P)	Assistant Chief of Naval Staff (Policy)
AOA	Amphibious Objective Area
AOC	Air Officer Commanding
ASW	Anti-Submarine Warfare
BOST	Basic Operational Sea Training
CDS	Chief of the Defence Staff
CINCHAN	NATO's Allied Commander-in-Chief Channel
CINCEASTLANT	NATO's Commander-in-Chief East Atlantic Area
CNS	Chief of Naval Staff and First Sea Lord
COMAW	Commodore Amphibious Warfare
COMSUBEASTLANT	NATO's Commander Submarine Forces East Atlantic
COMSUBLANT	NATO's Commander Submarine Forces Atlantic
COQC	Submarine Commanding Officer's Qualifying Course
CSO(E)	Chief Staff Officer Engineering
CTF 317, 345 etc	Task Force Commander for Specific Operations
CTG	Task Group Commander
CTU	Task Unit Commander
DASO	Demonstration and Shakedown Operation
DDNW	Deputy Director of Naval Warfare
DNOR	Director(ate) of Naval Operational Requirements
DNOT	Director(ate) of Naval Operations and Trade
DN Plans	Director(ate) of Naval Plans
DNW	Director(ate) of Naval Warfare
DR	Dead Reckoning
EP	Estimated Position
F 3, 8 etc	Captains Commanding Frigate Squadrons
FOF 1, 2 and 3	Admirals Commanding Surface Flotillas
FOM	Flotilla Material Officer
FOSM	Flag Officer Submarines
FOST	Flag Officer Sea Training
GOC	General Officer Commanding
ICL	International Computers Ltd
INF	Intermediate-range Nuclear Forces
JMC	Joint Maritime Course
JMOTS	Joint Maritime Operational Training School
JSSC	Joint Services Staff College
MA	Military Assistant

MEO	Marine Engineer Officer
MEZ	Maritime Exclusion Zone
MNC	Major NATO Commander
MoD	Ministry of Defence
MPA	Maritime Patrol Aircraft
MRI	Magnetic Resonance Imaging
MRSA	Methicillin Resistant Staphylococcus Aureus
NATO	North Atlantic Treaty Organisation
OD(SA)	Cabinet Overseas Policy Committee (South Atlantic)
PA	Personal Assistant
PERMREPS	Ambassadors to NATO of Member Countries
PWO	Principal Warfare Officer
RFA	Royal Fleet Auxiliary
RNVR	Royal Naval Voluntary Reserve
ROE	Rules of Engagement
SACEUR	NATO's Supreme Allied Commander Europe
SACLANT	NATO's Supreme Allied Commander Atlantic
SAS	Special Air Service
SBS	Special Boat Squadron
SNFL	Standing Naval Force Atlantic
SOO	Staff Officer Operations
SOSUS	Sound Surveillance System
SM3, 10 etc	Captains Commanding Submarine Squadrons
SSBN	Ballistic Missile Armed Nuclear Submarine
SSK	Diesel Electric Hunter/Killer Submarine
SSN	Nuclear Hunter/Killer Submarine
STANAVFORCHAN	Standing Naval Force Channel
STANAVFORLANT	Standing Naval Force Atlantic
STO	Senior Technical Officer
SWO	Staff Warfare Officer
TAS	Torpedo and Anti-Submarine
TEZ	Total Exclusion Zone
VCDS	Vice-Chief of Defence Staff
VCNS	Vice-Chief of Naval Staff
WEO	Weapons Electrical Officer
XO	Executive Officer
YARD	Yarrow-Admiralty Research Department

Index

2nd Bn, Parachute Regiment 154, 172, 173
3rd Bn, Parachute Regiment 154
3rd Commando Brigade, Royal Marines 133, 148, 172, 176
5th Infantry Brigade 154, 157, 165, 171, 172, 174
18 Group, RAF 134-5
ARA *25 de Mayo* (Argentine aircraft carrier) 162, 163
40 Commando, Royal Marines 143
1981 Defence Review 139, 142, 183
A4 Skyhawks (fighter/bombers) 162

HMS *Acheron* (SSK) 37-8, 116
active sonar 54
HMS *Adamant* (depot ship) 37
Adams, James, `Profile' 193-4
Aden withdrawal 62, 64, 65
Admiralty organization 88-9
HMS *Aeneas* (SSK) 29-31
HMS *Ajax* (frigate) 92, 102, 104, 105, 106, 107, 108, 109, 111-12
HMS *Alacrity* (frigate) 121, 149, 162, 169
Allen, Rear Admiral Sir David 124-5, 180, 185, 187, 191-2
NRP *Almirante Pereira da Silva* (Portuguese frigate) 82
ITS *Alpino* (Italian frigate) 82
HMS *Amazon* (frigate) 181
Amphibious Objective Area (AOA) 169
Anaya, Admiral Jorge 142
Andrew, HRH Prince 177
HMS *Andromeda* (frigate) 92
Anne, HRH Princess Royal 55
HMS *Antelope* (frigate) 149, 170
HMS *Antrim* (GM destroyer) 149, 153, 168, 169
HMS *Ardent* (frigate) 168, 169, 176
HMS *Argonaut* (frigate) 168, 169
HMS *Ark Royal* (aircraft carrier 1950) 58, 120
HMS *Ark Royal* (aircraft carrier 1981) 134, 140
Armstrong, Neil (astronaut) 72
around the world deployment 102-14
HMS *Arrow* (frigate) 149, 162, 169, 176
Ascension Island 63, 72, 151, 153-4, 155, 157, 165, 182
Ashmore, Admiral of the Fleet Sir Edward 60, 61, 62, 64, 65, 72, 85, 89, 91, 105
HMS *Astute* (SSK) 28-9, 144
MV *Atlantic Conveyor* (container ship) 169, 171, 172
HMS *Aurora* (frigate) 80-3

Baker, Captain Charles 96
Bali 19, 107
Band, Admiral Sir Jonathon 132, 136, 137, 138-9, 143, 144, 179
Barents Sea 33, 34, 42
HMS *Barfleur* (destroyer) 39
Bathurst, Admiral of the Fleet Sir Benjamin 84, 181
The Battle and the Breeze, Edward Ashmore 65
The Battle for the Falklands, Hastings and Jenkins 174
Beetham, Marshal of the Royal Air Force Sir Michael 147, 190

Belfast (chartered transport aircraft) 154
HMS *Belfast* (cruiser) 15
Bell Davies, Vice Admiral Sir Lancelot 41, 89
HMS *Berwick* (frigate) 102
Black, Dr David 122-3, 209, 211, 212-13
Blacker, General Sir Jeremy 196, 202
HMS *Blake* (helicopter cruiser) 98, 114
Boeing 707 (chartered aircraft) 154
Bombay 18-19, 106
BOST (Basic Operational Sea Training) 76-7
Boyce, Admiral Lord 137
Bramall, Field Marshal Lord 183, 190, 197, 214
FSG *Braunschweig* (German frigate) 81
MY *Brave Goose* (yacht) 211
HMS *Brilliant* (frigate) 120, 149, 153, 168, 169, 218
HMAS *Brisbane* (destroyer) 107
HMS *Britannia* (royal yacht) 55
HMS *Broadsword* (frigate) 168, 169, 171
Bromage, Commander John 27
Brown, Captain David 99, 110-11, 112
Bryson, Admiral Sir Lindsay 125-6
Buccaneer (strike bomber) 58
Buckland, Cook Paul 194
HMS *Bulwark* (aircraft carrier) 39, 64
Burgess, Rear Admiral John 125, 126-7, 128
Butler, Lord, of Brockwell 181-2

HMS *Caesar* (destroyer) 18
HMS *Cambrian* (destroyer) 18
Campbell, Surgeon Captain James 210
HMS *Camperdown* (destroyer) 39
SS *Canberra* (liner) 166, 168, 170, 172, 176
HMNZS *Canterbury* (frigate) 112
HMS *Caprice* (destroyer) 18
Carrington, Lord 47, 147, 150
HMS *Carron* (destroyer) 18
HMS *Carysfort* (destroyer) 18
Cassels, Admiral Sir Simon 12, 126, 186
HMS *Cavalier* (destroyer) 18
HMS *Ceylon* (cruiser) 39
Chalmers, Bob 214
USS *Charles F Adams* (destroyer) 80, 81
Charles, HRH Prince of Wales 55, 189
Chesworth, Air Vice Marshal George 134, 135, 178
Chinook (troop carrying helicopters) 169, 171
Churchill, Sir Winston 10, 24, 34
CINCEASTLANT 136
CINCHAN 135
Clack, Captain Thomas A C 29
Clapp, Commodore Mike 148, 155-6, 157-8, 165-6, 167-8, 169, 176
Clark-Kerr, Sir Archibald (later Lord Inverchapel) 19
Clayton, Admiral Sir Richard 92, 93, 99, 125, 126
Clayton, Sir Hugh 18
Coats, Midshipman Sandie 14
Cod War (Third) 88
Cold War 24, 41, 42-3, 60, 68, 105, 118, 122, 131, 140, 176, 203
Coles, John 181-2
Collingwood, Vice Admiral Cuthbert 178
Colville, Sir John 18

Commodore Amphibious Warfare 148, 155, 158, 165-6, 169
COMSUBEASTLANT 118
The Conduct of Fleet Submarine Operations 56, 116
HMS *Conqueror* (SSN) 122, 153, 163
Controller's tasks 125-6
Coote, Captain John 31, 32, 33, 34-5, 40
HMS *Cornwall* (frigate) 129
HMS *Courageous* (SSN) 164
Courcy-Ireland, Captain Garth de 93, 96-7, 98-9, 100-1, 104-6, 108-9, 112, 113, 114
Courtier, Greg 33-4
HMS *Coventry* (destroyer) 149, 169, 171, 176
Coward, Vice Admiral Sir John 119-20
Cox, Vice Admiral Sir John 84, 148
Crosbie, Commander Gordon 11, 12, 177
Crouch, Staff Sergeant Ken, RM 180-1, 195
Crowe, Admiral William, USN 199-200, 207
HMS *Cumberland* (cruiser) 18
HMS *Cumberland* (frigate) 129
Curtiss, Air Marshal Sir John 134-5, 150, 152, 154, 155, 178, 190, 205

HMS *Daedalus* (RN Air Station, Lee-on-the-Solent) 31, 32
HMS *Dainty* (destroyer) 39
HMS *Daring* (destroyer) 39
Dartmouth, Royal Naval College: interview board 7; organization 8-9; Royal visits 9-10; Luftwaffe attack 10-11
DASO (Demonstration and Shakedown Operation) 68, 69, 71-3, 203
HMS *Dauntless* (WRNS training school) 30
Davies, Leading Wren Steward Sharon (*née* Kirkham) 138, 165, 194
de la Billiere, General Sir Peter 155, 191; *Looking for Trouble* 155
Defence Central Staff reforms 184
HMS *Delight* (destroyer) 39
deployment programme 103-4
HMS *Devonshire* (cruiser) 9
HMS *Devonshire* (GM destroyer) 92
HMAS *Diamantina* (frigate) 107
Diana, Princess of Wales 189
HMS *Dido* (frigate) 64, 112
HMS *Diomede* (frigate) 75-8
Dion, Professor Robert 208, 209, 210, 216
HMS *Dolphin* (submarine base) 24, 25, 26, 116, 187, 198, 217, 222
Donkin, Brigadier Tim, RM 167, 170
HMS *Dreadnought* (SSN) 39, 44, 50-6, 69, 116, 121, 130, 187
HMS *Dryad* (Navigation school) 23, 75, 100
DTO (Dockside Test Organisation) 130
Duncan, House Cadet Captain Robert 12
Dunphie, Brigadier Christopher 167, 173

HMS *Eagle* (aircraft carrier) 58, 64
HMS *Easton* (destroyer escort) 22
Easton, Sir Robert 75, 129
Eaton Hall 11

Eberle, Admiral Sir James 124, 131, 132, 137, 140
Eckersley-Maslin, Rear Admiral David 114
Edinburgh, HRH Prince Philip, Duke of 201, 221
Electric Boat Company, Groton 128, 130
Elizabeth II, HM The Queen 55, 175, 177
MV *Elk* (freighter) 169
Elliott, Captain Toby 218
Emmerson, Air Vice Marshal David 154, 202
Empson, Admiral Sir Derek 65
HMS *Endurance* (Antarctic patrol) 121, 140, 142, 144, 145, 153
USS *Enterprise* (aircraft carrier) 109, 112
SS *Erna Elizabeth* (tanker) 81
MV *Europic Ferry* (ferry) 168, 170
HNLMS *Evertsen* (Netherlands frigate) 80, 81
HMS *Excellent* (Gunnery school) 23, 221
Exocet missiles 95, 162, 163, 164, 166
Eyden, Rev Montague (Headmaster) 5

Falkland Islands 120, 142, 149, 153, 181-2, 190-1, 202
Falklands Campaign: The Lessons 183
Falklands Task Force 148-9, 150, 151-2
The Falklands War, *Sunday Times* Insight Team 141
HMS *Falmouth* (frigate) 86
HMS *Fame* (destroyer) 22
HMS *Fearless* (assault ship) 133, 140, 143, 148; Task Force 149, 155, 157, 168
Fieldhouse of Gosport, Admiral of the Fleet John David Elliott, Lord: character 4; schooldays 5-6; Dartmouth examination 6; life at Dartmouth 9; life at Eaton Hall 11-12; life in the training cruiser 13-14; visits surrendered U-boats 13; passage to East Indies 14-15; Midshipman's training 15-16; in Landing Party 17; gunroom life in *Norfolk* 19-21; at Greenwich 22-3; experience gained abroad 22; professional training courses 23-4; volunteers for submarines 24; submarine training 25-6; 4th hand in *Thule* 27; to USA in *Astute* 28; as First Lieutenant 29-30, 31-2; meets Midge 30-1; marriage 32; patrols in *Totem* 33-5; passes Perisher 35-6; first command 37-8; SM Staff Officer, Londonderry 38; commands *Tiptoe* 39-43; shares bed 41; buys house 44; commands *Walrus* 46-8; Flotilla Material Officer 49-50; commands *Dreadnought* 51-6, 79; gives up smoking 56; Joint Services Staff Course 56-7; XO of *Hermes* 58-64, 79; selected for promotion 61; commands *Hermes* 64-6; Captain SM 10 67-74; commands *Diomede* 75-8; Commodore STANAVFOR 78-86; Deputy and Director of Naval Warfare 87-91; Flag Officer Second Flotilla 92-101; deployment, UK to Bombay 102-6; deployment, Singapore to Auckland 106-8; deployment, Dunedin to UK 110-4; moves FOSM to Northwood 121-2;

sends *Dreadnought* to South Atlantic 121; buys yacht 122-3; Controller of the Navy 124-31; Fleet Commander 132-46; prepares Task Force 148-9, 150-1; rapport with Prime Minister 152; role at Northwood 152-3; visits Task Force 155-8; sinking of *Belgrano* 163; concern for losses 165, 202; orders landing 166-7; confidence in commanders 170, 171, 172-3, 173-4, 175; greets returning ships 176-7; First Sea Lord 179-92; holidays in Florida 179-80; Chief of Defence Staff 193-206; physical exhaustion 204; suffers aneurysm 207-8; convalescence 209-10; retirement activities 211-13; becomes Baron 213-14; maiden speech 214-15; illness and death 216-17; funeral 217-18; memorial service 219-20
Fieldhouse, Sir Harold (father): with Board of Guardians 2, 3; war service 2-3; marriage 3-4; honours 4; retirement 7, 90, 91, 131, 204; knighted 28, 197
Fieldhouse, James Richard (brother) 3, 5, 10, 32, 189, 208-9, 211, 216, 218, 219
Fieldhouse, The Lady Margaret 'Midge' (*née* Cull) 30-1; moves to Clyde 37; assists at Londonderry 39; scrubs out *Walrus* 47; family life 49; flies to Singapore 61; moves to Scotland 69; with Squadron wives 71; London flat 90; takes over Flotilla House 93; enforced silence 96-7; firm views 97; visits San Diego 112, 113; at Dolphin House 119; scratched by file 128; launches *Trafalgar* 130; at Admiralty House 136-8; visits Gibraltar 145-6; at Mall House flat 181; names insects 182; *Trafalgar* Commissioning 186; defines `expert' 191; maintains the tradition 222-3
Fieldhouse, Hon Mark (son) 35, 37, 69, 90, 189, 208, 211, 214
Fieldhouse memorials 221-2
Fieldhouse, Hon Sarah le Maitre (daughter) 49, 69, 90, 189, 195, 204, 208, 209, 211, 216, 218
Fieldhouse-Chalmers, Hon Amanda (daughter) 44, 69, 90, 164-5, 189, 208, 211, 214, 216, 217, 218
Fieldmouse box 142
Fields, Gracie 14
HMS *Fife* (GM destroyer) 92, 94, 95, 132
Fife, Rear Admiral James, USN 28
HMS *Finwhale* (SSK) 114
Fisher, Captain John, RFA 104-5
Flag Officer Submarines: tasks 116-18
Fleet organization 133
USS *Forrestal* (aircraft carrier) 34
RFA *Fort Austin* (fleet replenishment ship) 146, 168
MV *Fort Toronto* (freighter) 169
HMS *Forth* (depot ship) 26
Fox, Captain Freddie 173
Francis-Jones, Captain Jake 99, 112, 119
USS *Franklin Delano Roosevelt* (aircraft carrier) 34
Fraser, Lieutenant Commander I E, VC RNR 19
Frewer, Commander Ken 70, 71
HMS *Frobisher* (cruiser) 12-14

Gaggero, Joe 192
Galtieri, General Leopoldo 142

Gannets (AEW aircraft) 58
Garson, Captain Bob 61
ARA *General Belgrano* (Argentine cruiser) 122, 163
George VI, HM King 10
USS *Georgia* (SSBN) 128
Gibraltar 51, 94, 144, 145, 191-2
Gieves, Messrs 7
HMS *Glamorgan* (GM destroyer): FOF2 flagship 92, 95-6, 109-14; deployment 102, 104, 105, 106, 107, 108; flagship again 145-6; Task Force 149, 162, 168, 169, 174, 176
HMS *Glasgow* (destroyer) 149, 167, 169
Glindeman, Rear Admiral H P, USN 109
RFA *Gold Rover* (fleet tanker) 102, 104-5, 108, 109
Goose Green 172, 173
Gorbachev, President Mikhail 199, 214
Gorshkov, Admiral Sergei 185-6
Gosling, Sir Donald 211-12, 215
Gosport 213-14
Gosport and Fareham Inshore Rescue Service 212
Graham, Leslie (Star Hotel, Newcastle, NSW) 108
Grove, Rear Admiral John 44, 52

Haakon VII, King of Norway 9
IJNS *Haguro* (Japanese cruiser) 15
Halifax, Nova Scotia 29
Hallifax, Admiral Sir David 94, 95, 132, 148, 150, 152-3
Hammersley, Rear Admiral 'Spam' 39, 44, 51, 52, 134, 150, 155
Harriers GR3 (ground attack aircraft) 154
Hastings, Max (correspondent) 174
Havers, Michael, Attorney General 150
Hay, Commander Donald 35, 36
Hayhoe, Captain George 37, 142
Hayhoe, Carenza 142
Heaslip, Rear Admiral R G 'Dick' 54, 55, 88, 198
Heath, Captain R J P 32, 118
Henry, Captain Mike 70-1, 83
Heptinstall, Captain Roger 77
Hepworth, Rear Admiral David 89-90
Herbert, Admiral Sir Peter 45, 46, 75, 134, 150, 163
Hercules (transport aircraft) 154, 191
HMS *Hermes* (aircraft carrier) 58-66, 133, 140, 148; Task Force 149, 151, 154, 156, 163, 164, 169, 176
Heseltine, Michael, Lord, Defence Secretary 183-4, 185, 196-7
Hezlet, Vice Admiral Sir Arthur 'Baldy' 34, 47
Hill, Chief Petty Officer Steward Adrian 181, 194, 195
Hill, Rear Admiral Richard 114
Hill, Richard, *Lewin of Greenwich* 58, 60, 121, 141, 150, 152, 161
Hill-Norton, Admiral of the Fleet Lord 204
HMAS *Hobart* (destroyer) 107
Hoi Polloi (yacht) 123, 212-13
Hong Kong 61-2, 144
Horlick, Vice Admiral Sir Ted 125
How to Become a Naval Officer, Gieves Ltd 7, 8
Hughes, E A 'Daddy' 11
Hunt, Major General Malcolm, RM 143, 201

Hunt, Sir Rex 191
Husk, Captain R J 47-8, 70
Hutchings, Captain Brian 53

HMS *Illustrious* (aircraft carrier) 134, 140
The Impact of Polaris, ed., Captain J E Moore 70, 71
Ingham, Bernard 181
HMS *Intrepid* (assault ship) 133, 140, 144, 148, 157, 165, 168
HMS *Invincible* (aircraft carrier) 133, 140, 148; Task Force 149, 151, 164, 169, 177
HNLMS *Isaac Sweers* (Netherlands frigate) 86
TCG *Izmir* (Turkish destroyer) 82

Jackson, General Sir William 145, 183
Jackson-Sytner, Commander Peter 28
Jacobsen, Captain John 118-19
HMS *Jamaica* (cruiser) 18
Jenkins, Simon (journalist) 174
USS *John F Kennedy* (aircraft carrier) 105
Joint Maritime Courses 30, 38, 41, 85, 98-9
Joint Services Sailing Centre 123
Jones, Lieutenant Colonel H: VC 176
HMS *Jupiter* 79, 80
Juxon-Smith, Colonel 57

HMS *Kelly* (destroyer) 9
Kennedy, Commander Al 39, 41, 43, 45, 51, 72
Kimm, Captain Peter 6-7, 14, 15, 18, 21, 24, 159, 177, 195, 218, 219, 222
Knight, Air Chief Marshal Sir Michael 209
HMCS *Kootenay* (frigate) 112

Lacher, Commander 'Fred', FGN 82, 85
Lambert, Surgeon Vice Admiral Roger 45
Larken, Rear Admiral Jeremy 51, 95, 96, 143, 168
le Fanu, Admiral of the Fleet Sir Michael 60, 67, 91
le Maitre, Chris 195, 211
le Marchand, Captain Tom 186-7, 188, 189, 191-2, 205
le Marchand, Valerie 186, 187, 188, 189, 191
Leach, Admiral of the Fleet Sir Henry 94, 120, 121, 124, 131, 140; *Endure No Makeshifts* 139; prepares Task Force 147, 148-9, 177, 180; assessment of Fieldhouse 162
MY *Leander* (yacht) 212
Leathes, Captain Bob 102, 103, 106, 107, 112, 113
Leeds 1-2
Leningrad (Soviet helicopter carrier) 82, 105
Lewin, Admiral of the Fleet, Lord 58, 60, 62-3, 91, 94, 121, 124; Chief of Defence Staff 140-1, 145, 147, 150, 167, 176, 180, 214
Liardet, Rear Admiral Guy 80, 81, 82, 83
Light, Miss June 180, 187, 190, 191, 194, 196, 199
HMS *Llandaff* (A/D frigate) 102, 107
HMS *London* (GM destroyer) 114
Luce, Richard, Foreign Minister 142
Lucy, Lieutenant Commander Peter 32, 35
Luns, Dr Joseph 85, 135
Lygo, Admiral Sir Raymond 191, 192

McIntosh, Vice Admiral Sir Ian 29, 64
McKay, Sergeant IJ: VC 176
Mackenzie, Rear Admiral John 102, 104, 105, 106, 109, 111-12, 145, 146
Mackenzie, Vice Admiral Sir Hugh 50, 67
Magennis, Leading Seaman JJ: VC 2, 19
HMS *Maidstone* (depot ship) 26
Major, John, Prime Minister 73
Margaret, HRH Princess 83
Maritime Exclusion Zone 153
Mason, Roy, Defence Secretary 97
Mays, LRO Jeff 97
HMS *Mercury* (Signals school) 23
Meredith, Captain Graham 139
Mew, Dartmouth ferry 8
Mills, Commander Ken 73, 82
Mills, Lady 76
Mills, William H, Jr 179-80
HMS *Minerva* (frigate) 62
HMS *Montclare* (depot ship) 26, 27
SS *Mooltan* (P & O troopship) 14, 16
Moore, Captain John 70
Moore, Major General Sir Jeremy, RM 150, 155, 165, 167, 171-2, 174, 176, 205
Morris, Robert (tutor) 177
Morris, Warrant Officer Communications Yeoman David 100
Morton, Admiral Sir Anthony 124
Mountbatten of Burma, Admiral of the Fleet Earl 9, 19, 33, 43
Mulley, Right Hon Fred, MP 124
Munns, Commodore Adrian 187, 191-2, 200, 207-8, 214, 216
Munroe, Kim 216
NATO 118, 135-6, 199, 205
Naylor, Professor Tony 212
HMS *Neptune* (Faslane base) 68, 139
Newby, LRO Charlie 98
HMS *Nigeria* (cruiser) 14, 15-16
Nimrods (maritime patrol aircraft) 154, 162, 202
HMS *Norfolk* (cruiser) 16-21
HMS *Norfolk* (frigate) 130
HMS *Norfolk* (GM destroyer) 83-5
MV *Norland* (ferry) 168, 170, 172
Northwood 121-2, 134, 136, 137-8
Nott, Sir John, Defence Secretary 139, 140-1, 145, 150, 168, 183; *Here Today Gone Tomorrow* 140
nuclear training 44-6
nuclear-powered submarines 43-4, 51, 54

Oberon class 117
O'Brien, Admiral Sir William 72, 76
Oddie, Captain David 217, 221
Oddie, Gill 49, 90, 215, 217
OD(SA) (Overseas Defence (South Atlantic) Committee 150, 153
USS *Ohio* (SSBN) 128
Olaf, Crown Prince of Norway 9
RFA *Olmeda* (fleet tanker) 169
RFA *Olwen* (fleet tanker) 121
HMS *Onyx* (SSK) 117, 164
Operation `Corporate' 149, 161-76
Operation `Monitor' 64, 65
Operation `Paraquat' 153, 156
HMS *Opportune* (SSK) 218
HMS *Oracle* (SSK) 146
Orontes (Orient Line troopship) 22

Oswald, Admiral of the Fleet Sir Julian 177, 219
Owen, David, Lord, Foreign Secretary 121
HMAS *Oxley* (SSK) 107

Palliser, Vice Admiral Sir Arthur 20
Palmer, Chief Petty Officer Cook Mick 93, 119, 137-8, 159, 181, 194
Parker, Captain Blake 57
Parker, Captain Doug 63, 64, 65
Parkinson, Cecil 150
Patterson, Rear Admiral Wilfred 18, 19
Payne, Third Officer Judy 137
Pearl Harbour 112
RFA *Pearleaf* (support tanker) 169
Perisher (Commanding Officers Qualifying Course) 35-6, 41, 83
Phillips, Commander Rex 63, 64, 66
HMS *Phoebe* (frigate) 64, 121
Pilolevi, Princess, Tonga 111
HMS *Plymouth* (frigate) 102, 109, 149, 153, 168
Polaris Force: deterrent patrols 69, 71, 73-4; manning 69; operating 69-70, 134; workups 71-2, 203
Polaris programme 48, 50, 67-9
Pollock, Admiral of the Fleet Sir Michael 67
Ponsonby, Commander Francis 70
Porpoise class 117
HMS *Porpoise* (SSK) 53
HNLMS *Potvis* (SSK) 114
Power, Admiral Sir Manley 15
Practical Management in Ships 77
Prince, Stephen, *British Command and Control in the Falklands Campaign* 152, 158
HMCS *Protecteur* (fleet replenishment ship) 86
Provest, Captain Tony 95
Purvis, Vice Admiral Sir Ned 51
PWO (Principal Warfare Officer) 89, 103
Pym, Francis, Foreign Secretary 150

Quainton Hall (school) 5-6
RMS *Queen Elizabeth II* (liner) 166, 167, 172, 176
RMS *Queen Mary* 63

Raikes, Vice Admiral Sir Iwan 29, 116
Rapier missiles 170
RAPWI (Repatriated Allied Prisoners of War and Internees) 17
Read, Midshipman John 14
Reagan, President Ronald 199, 206
HMS *Redpole* (frigate) 23
Reffell, Admiral Sir Derek 88, 148, 156
RFA *Regent* (stores ship) 169
RFA *Reliant* (stores ship) 61
HMS *Renown* (SSBN) 68, 71, 72-3, 118
Renshaw, Sir Leonard, Vickers 130
HMS *Repulse* (SSBN) 68, 71, 72, 73, 203
HMS *Resolution* (SSBN) 55, 68, 69, 73-4
RFA *Resource* (stores ship) 169
HMCS *Restigouche* (frigate) 112
RFA *Resurgent* (ammunition stores) 109, 121
HMS *Revenge* (SSBN) 68, 71, 72

Reviews: Coronation (1953) 33; Clyde (1960) 55; Silver Jubilee (1977) 120
Rickover, Admiral Hyman G, USN 43, 128
Ridley, Nicholas, Foreign Office Minister 141
Ring, Jim, *We Come Unseen* 122
Roberts, Captain John 201
Rooney, Joe 27
HMS *Rothesay* (frigate) 102, 107
Royal Naval College Ashley Down 11
The Royal Naval College Dartmouth, E A Hughes 11
Royal Naval College Greenwich 22-3

Salt, Rear Admiral Sam 165
Samborne, Captain Peter 44, 45-6, 51
San Carlos Water 165, 166
ARA *Santa Fe* (Argentine submarine) 153
SAS (Special Air Service) 153, 154-5, 162, 167
HMS *Saumarez* (destroyer) 15
Sayer, Commander Geoffrey 64
SBS (Special Boat Squadron RM) 153, 155, 162
USS *Scorpion* (SSN) 130
Scott's Shipyard, Greenock 46
HMS *Scylla* (frigate) 92, 106
HMS *Sea Eagle* (A/S Warfare school, Londonderry) 30, 31, 38
Sea Harriers (fighter/bomber) 88, 133, 148, 151, 153, 162, 167, 169
Sea King (ASW helicopter) 80-1, 98, 99
Sea Slug missiles 112
Sea Vixens (fighter) 58, 59
HMS *Sealion* (SSK) 77
Semarang, Java 17, 18
Sharp, Lieutenant Commander Richard 47
Sharp, Lieutenant Commander 'Olly' 28
Shearer, Moira 39
HMS *Sheffield* (destroyer) 149, 164, 176, 177
Shillingford, Captain John 137, 139, 145, 158, 177
shipbuilding industry 129
Ships Taken Up From Trade (STUFT) 149
Shrub, Lieutenant Commander 'Bushy' 96-7
Sidewinder missiles 153, 167
RFA *Sir Galahad* (landing ship) 168, 174
RFA *Sir Geraint* (landing ship) 168
RFA *Sir Lancelot* (landing ship) 168
RFA *Sir Percivale* (landing ship) 168
RFA *Sir Tristram* (landing ship) 168, 174
HMCS *Skeena* (frigate) 80, 81, 82
Skipjack class 43
Smalley, Commander Bryan 37-8
Smyth, Midshipman Hugh 14
HMS *Soberton* (coastal minesweeper) 132
SOSUS (Sound Surveillance System) 40, 130
South Georgia 144, 145, 153, 160
HMS *Sovereign* (SSN) 114
HMS *Spartan* (SSN) 130, 146, 163
Speed, Keith, Navy Minister 140
HMS *Splendid* (SSN) 130, 163
Squires, Vice Admiral 'Tubby' 44, 45-6, 51
Stacey, Rear Admiral Mike 98
HMCS *Stadacona* (Canadian base) 29

Standard Operating Procedures 103-4
Standen, George, VSEL 130
Standing Naval Force Atlantic 77, 78-86, 136
Standing Naval Force Channel 135-6
Steinhoff, General J 85
Stinson AT-19 Reliant (training aircraft) 16
RFA *Stromness* (stores ship) 143, 168
Submarine Flotilla 26
Submarine Squadrons 26
Submariner, Captain John Coote 32
Super Etendards (fighters) 162, 164
HMS *Superb* (SSN) 120, 137
HMAS *Supply* (replenishment ship) 107
surveillance patrols 33-5, 42-3, 118
HMS *Sussex* (cruiser) 18
HMAS *Swan* (frigate) 107
Swiftsure class 117

T-conversion class 31-2
Tait, Admiral Sir Gordon 124
IJNS *Takao* (Japanese cruiser) 19
HMS *Tamar* (Hong Kong base) 144
RFA *Tarbatness* (stores ship) 102, 109
Taufa'ahau Tupou IV, King of Tonga 110
HMS *Terror* (barracks, Singapore) 110
Terry, Dockmaster, Cabbage Key 179
Thatcher, Sir Denis 181, 205
Thatcher, Margaret: Baroness: Prime Minister 141, 147, 148, 149, 152, 199, 205, 213, 222; *The Downing Street Years* 147, 158-9, 196; visits Northwood 159, 170; briefings 168, 173-4; visits Falklands 181-2; decisions 184, 190
The Chiefs, Bramall and Jackson 183, 198, 203
HS *Themistocles* (Greek frigate) 82
Thompson, Major General Julian 155-6, 157-8, 165-6, 167, 171-3, 174, 176
Thompson, Captain Terry 48, 184-5
HMS *Thule* (SSK) 27
RFA *Tidepool* (fleet tanker) 169
RFA *Tidespring* (fleet tanker) 102, 143, 153
HMS *Tiger* (helicopter cruiser) 92, 94, 98, 99, 100-1, 114
Tiger Moth (training aircraft) 23
HMS *Tiptoe* (SK) 6, 39-43, 116
HMAS *Torrens* (frigate) 107
Total Exclusion Zone 160
HMS *Totem* (SK) 31-5, 116
Trafalgar class 117
HMS *Trafalgar* (SSN) 130, 186, 218, 220
Trant, General Sir Richard 167, 171
Treacher, Admiral Sir John 112
Tri-Star (RAF transport) 191
Trident ballistic missile system 128-9, 140, 197, 199
Trinder, Captain John 180, 185
HMS *Triumph* (SSK) 28
Trussler, Lieutenant Commander Brian 39
USS *Tulibee* (SSN) 105
Turner, Captain E J D 'Ernie' 26, 27
HMS *Turpin* (SSK) 39-40
Tweed, Jill 221
HMS *Tyne* (depot ship) 39

Type 22 frigates 129, 131
Type 23 frigates 129-30

HMS *Upholder* (SSK) 131, 203
US Seventh Fleet 106
Usher, Commander Peter, RCNC 50, 130

Valiant class 117
HMS *Valiant* (SSN) 46, 50, 51, 53, 55, 69, 118, 119-20, 164, 186
HMAS *Vampire* (destroyer) 107
Van Der Post, Laurens 19
VC10 (RAF transport aircraft) 96, 106, 154, 181
ARA *Veinticinco de Mayo see 25 de Mayo*
HMAS *Vendetta* (destroyer) 107
HMS *Vernon* (TAS school) 23, 24, 94
Vickers, Barrow-in-Furness 44, 68, 130
HMS *Victorious* (aircraft carrier) 60
Victors (tanker aircraft) 154, 162
Vincent, Field Marshal Lord 203, 219
HMS *Virago* (destroyer) 15
Vosper Thornycroft 50, 130, 212
Vulcans (bombers) 154, 162

Wadman, Captain Phil 71
Walker, Lieutenant Commander C G O 'Kipper' 45
Wallace, Captain Barry 51, 55
HMS *Walrus* (SSK) 46-8, 116, 184
HMS *Warspite* (SSN) 55
Wasp (A/S helicopter) 81
Webster, Vice Admiral Sir John 88
Weinberger, Casper, US Defense Secretary 153, 200
Wells, Rear Admiral David, RAN 106
Wells, Rob 179
Wessex (ASW helicopter) 83, 106, 169
Westland affair 196
Wheatley, Rear Admiral Anthony 77
Whetstone, Rear Admiral Tony 27, 31, 71, 153, 210, 212, 215, 216, 218, 219
White Ensign Association 211, 212, 215, 220
Whitelaw, Viscount, Home Secretary 150, 163
Whitmore, Sir Clive 197
Whittall, Admiral Al, USN 128
Williams, Admiral Joe, USN 128
Wlliams, Admiral Sir David 191
Woodley, Chief Petty Officer Steward John 194
Woodward, Admiral Sir John 'Sandy' 53, 87-8, 144, 145, 146, 147, 205; *One Hundred Days* 87, 146, 147, 164; Task Force 149, 153, 155-6, 160, 163, 167, 169, 176

HMS *Yarmouth* (frigate) 168
Yarrow Shipbuilders, Glasgow 75, 129, 130
Yarrow, Sir Eric 76
Younger, George, Lord, Defence Secretary 196, 203

HMS *Zulu* (frigate)